SOCIAL NETWORK ANALYSIS for EGO-NETS

SOCIAL NETWORK ANALYSIS for EGO-NETS

Nick Crossley • Elisa Bellotti • Gemma Edwards
Martin G Everett • Johan Koskinen • Mark Tranmer

Los Angeles | London | New Delhi
Singapore | Washington DC | Boston

Los Angeles | London | New Delhi
Singapore | Washington DC | Boston

SAGE Publications Ltd
1 Oliver's Yard
55 City Road
London EC1Y 1SP

SAGE Publications Inc.
2455 Teller Road
Thousand Oaks, California 91320

SAGE Publications India Pvt Ltd
B 1/I 1 Mohan Cooperative Industrial Area
Mathura Road
New Delhi 110 044

SAGE Publications Asia-Pacific Pte Ltd
3 Church Street
#10-04 Samsung Hub
Singapore 049483

© Nick Crossley, Elisa Bellotti, Gemma Edwards, Martin
G Everett, Johan Koskinen and Mark Tranmer 2015

First published 2015

Editor: Chris Rojek
Assistant editor: Gemma Shields
Production editor: Katherine Haw
Copyeditor: Kate Campbell
Marketing manager: Michael Ainsley
Cover design: Lisa Harper-Wells
Typeset by: C&M Digitals (P) Ltd, Chennai, India
Printed in India at Replika Press Pvt Ltd

Library of Congress Control Number: 2015935668

British Library Cataloguing in Publication data

A catalogue record for this book is available from
the British Library

MIX
Paper from
responsible sources
FSC
www.fsc.org   FSC® C016779

ISBN 978-1-4462-6776-9
ISBN 978-1-4462-6777-6 (pbk)

CONTENTS

LIST OF FIGURES

LIST OF TABLES

ABOUT THE AUTHORS

Nick Crossley is Professor of Sociology at the University of Manchester and co-founder and co-director of the Mitchell Centre for Social Network Analysis. His most recent book is *Networks of Sound, Style and Subversion: The Punk and Post-Punk Worlds of Manchester, London, Liverpool and Sheffield, 1975–1980* (Manchester University Press, 2015).

Elisa Bellotti is lecturer in Sociology at the University of Manchester and a member of the Mitchell Centre for Social Network Analysis. Before arriving in Manchester in 2008, she worked as Research Fellow at the University of Turin and the University of Bozen, Italy. She works on social network analysis and qualitative methods, with an interest in sociology of consumption and sociology of science. She recently published *Qualitative Networks: Mixed Methods in Sociological Research* (Routledge, 2014).

Gemma Edwards is a lecturer in Sociology at the University of Manchester, and a member of movements@manchester, the Morgan Centre, and the Mitchell Centre for Social Network Analysis. She has written on social movements, the role of interpersonal networks in activism, and mixed-method SNA. Her current work includes collaborative projects on covert social networks (Leverhulme), and the relational practices of shared living (ESRC). She is author of the book *Social Movements and Protest* (Cambridge University Press, 2014).

Martin G. Everett is Professor of Social Network Analysis and Co-Director of the Mitchell Centre for Social Network Analysis at the University of Manchester. Martin has over 30 years of experience teaching and researching in social networks. He is a past president of the International Network for Social Network Analysis (INSNA), a Simmel award holder (the highest award given by the organisation) and a Fellow of the Academy of Social Sciences. Martin is also a co-author of the software package UCINET, one of the world's most commonly used tools for analysing social networks. He has consulted extensively on the use of networks with government agencies as well as public and private companies.

Johan Koskinen is a lecturer in Social Statistics at the University of Manchester, where he has been since 2012. He works primarily on statistical modelling and inference for social network data. His most recent book, co-edited with Dean Lusher and Garry Robins, is *Exponential Random Graph Models for Social Networks* (Cambridge University Press, 2013).

Mark Tranmer joined the University of Manchester in 1999, where he is currently a Senior Lecturer in Social Statistics in the School of Social Sciences. He teaches various aspects of quantitative social science at both the undergraduate and the postgraduate level. His main research interests include multilevel modelling, social network analysis, animal social networks, and the analysis of multilevel networks.

ACKNOWLEDGEMENTS

The authors would like to thank Steve Borgatti and Analytic Technologies for permission to use screenshots from UCINET; Bernie Hogan for permission to use screenshots from NameGenWeb; and Marc Smith for permission to use screenshots from NodeXL. They would also like to thank Routledge for permission to reproduce Figures 4.2 (p. 87), 4.3 (p. 88) and 4.7 (p. 91) from Elisa Bellotti's (2014) *Qualitative Networks: Mixed Methods in Sociological Research* (London, Routledge).

1

INTRODUCTION

Learning Outcomes

By the end of this chapter you will:

1. Know how 'network' is defined in social network analysis.

2. Be familiar with three different approaches to social network analysis: ego-net analysis, whole network analysis and two-mode analysis.

3. Know what is distinctive about ego-net analysis.

4. Understand the pros and cons of ego-net analysis, relative to whole network analysis, and where it is most appropriate to use each approach.

5. Understand some of the ways in which network data are stored and represented for purposes of network analysis, and also certain fundamental concepts and measures used by network analysts.

6. Be familiar with the basic plan for the book as a whole.

Introduction

In this book we offer a comprehensive introduction to one of the most widely used forms of social network analysis (SNA): actor-centred or 'ego-net' analysis. An ego-net is the network which forms around a particular social actor, be that a human actor or a corporate actor, such as an economic firm or national government. In theory it involves all other actors (alters) with whom an ego enjoys a specific type or types of tie (e.g. emotional closeness, information sharing, economic exchange, etc.) and all relations (of the same type or types) between those alters. Useful and important work can be conducted without information on ties between alters, however, and this aspect of the definition of an ego-net is therefore sometimes relaxed: an ego-net is then simply a list of alters with whom a target individual (ego) enjoys a particular type of relation.

Thus defined, ego-nets can be visualised, as in Figure 1.1, using coloured shapes ('vertices') to represent an ego and her alters (the nodes of the network) and connecting lines ('edges' or 'arcs') to represent ties between them. The 'ego' is coloured black in Figure 1.1 to distinguish her from her (grey) alters.

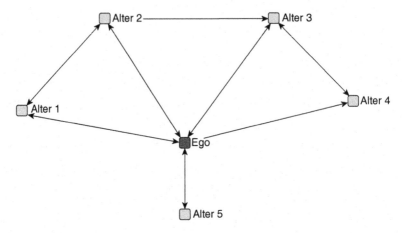

Figure 1.1   Visualising an ego-net

Ego-net analysis is one of several approaches to SNA. Like each of the others and like any other research method, it has strengths and weaknesses and is more appropriate in some circumstances than others. Our decision to focus the book exclusively upon ego-net analysis is not an expression of preference on our part or an argument in favour of it over other forms. We have all used a variety of forms of SNA in the course of our work. Our decision to focus upon ego-net analysis here is based upon the observation that it tends to receive less coverage than other approaches in general texts on SNA, when we, as teachers of the range of SNA methods, find that many newcomers to the approach either wish to use an ego-net approach or probably should use it, given the nature of their research problem, and when a large number of papers published on networks, including many influential papers, use this approach. In short, we have written this book because there is no other book-length introduction to ego-net analysis and there should be.

Ego-net analysis is best understood in the context of a wider appreciation of SNA and of the concept and importance of social networks more generally. We therefore begin this chapter with a brief review of the field and of the two key alternatives to ego-net analysis within SNA: whole network analysis and two-mode analysis. This will allow us to draw out the distinctiveness of ego-net analysis and its strengths and weaknesses, relative to the other approaches. Furthermore, it will allow us to explain when and where ego-net analysis is more (and less) appropriate as an approach compared to the other approaches. The chapter ends with a brief discussion of the plan for the rest of the book.

Networks and Network Analysis

Connection is a constitutive fact of social life. A social world comprises not only a plurality of social actors, both human and corporate (e.g. firms or governments), but also interaction and enduring ties between those actors. Actors influence one another and exchange resources, becoming interdependent. They cooperate, compete, conflict, support and seduce one another. And these interactions and ties make a difference. For example, where ties cluster, generating a dense nexus of mutual influence, we often find greater homogeneity in attitudes, preferences and practices (Coleman 1988). To give another example, pathways of ties through networks provide channels for the diffusion of culture, resources, information and often viruses too. Finally, where specific patterns of ties give rise to trust and norms of cooperation ('social capital') this can facilitate forms of action, both individual and collective, that would not be possible in the absence of that particular configuration of ties – although this is usually at the cost of certain constraints (Coleman 1990). Networks are social structures which, as Durkheim (1964) said of social structures more generally, afford both opportunities and constraints for those entangled within them.

Some of the effects just mentioned can be generalised across a network. Everybody within the network is affected to a similar degree. Some apply to certain sub-groups within a network more than others, however, and some may apply specifically to particular actors, on account of the position they occupy within the network. This might be a matter of who they know, to invoke everyday wisdom, or, more generally, of the types of people they know. However, it may be a matter of network structure; where they fit within a pattern of relations: for example, which parts of a network they uniquely bridge (Burt 1992, 2005) or the pattern of connection in their immediate network neighbourhood.

These observations raise important methodological questions. How do we capture and analyse relational phenomena? With a certain amount of tweaking, which we discuss in Chapter Three, many of the standard methods of data gathering within social science can be used to generate relational, network data. Nodes and their ties must be systematically surveyed but we can do that with a questionnaire, a structured or semi-structured interview, through direct observation (participant or non-participant), by trawling archives and texts, and perhaps by other means too. Furthermore, in the 'information age' and more especially the age of Web 2.0, a great deal of relational data is routinely generated in the course of everyday life, prompting some to ask if social scientists should not be taking more advantage of these sources too (Savage and Burrows 2007). Of course many social scientists are now taking advantage of them.

What we do with relational data when we have them, how we store and analyse them, poses more problems for conventional social scientific approaches, however. Relational data differ from the data usually analysed in social science and require dedicated techniques for their storage, representation and analysis. This is where SNA comes in. SNA is the collective label for a set of interconnected concepts, theories and techniques, developed for the most part within a relatively cohesive, interdisciplinary research 'network', devoted to the gathering and analysis of relational data (for a comprehensive introduction see Borgatti et al. 2013, Scott 2000 or Wasserman and Faust 1994).

SNA has a long history, stretching back to the 1930s (see Freeman 2006, Scott 2000) and its development has involved seminal contributions from sociologists, anthropologists, social psychologists, business analysts and increasingly also political scientists and economists. The distinctiveness of the approach owes at least as much to a wider interdisciplinary reach, into a branch of mathematics known as graph theory, however, and to collaboration between social scientists, mathematicians and increasingly also statisticians. It is not an exclusively quantitative approach and in this book we will stress the gains to be made from adopting a mixed method, qualitative and quantitative, approach to it (see also Bellotti 2014, Crossley 2010, Edwards 2010, Edwards and Crossley 2009). However, it is the interplay between social science and graph theory, in large part, which facilitates relational analysis and marks SNA out as a distinct research methodology.

What Are Networks?

All networks comprise two essential elements:

- A set of nodes.
- A set or sets of ties.

Optionally, they may also include:

- A set of node attributes.

Nodes

What counts as a node will vary between research projects and is at the discretion of the researcher. Anything might be defined as a node for purposes of SNA if it is meaningful to define it thus in the context of a particular study; that is, if a researcher has good reasons to want to regard it as a node, and if it is capable of the type of tie of interest to the researcher. Nodes might be: human individuals, chimpanzees, organisations, cities, nation-states, etc. Network analysis is a formal analytic approach, focused upon patterns of connection. It can be applied to any type of connection between any type of object. However, most analytic routines and algorithms assume that all nodes are, in principle, equally capable of engaging in the type of connection under consideration and this is therefore a constraint upon node choice. Each of the nodes in a friendship network must be capable of forming a friendship with any and every other, for example, at least in principle.

This doesn't mean that every node will be a friend with every other. That wouldn't be a very interesting network to analyse! Nor does it preclude the possibility that certain conditions might make friendship between some nodes more likely than others. Indeed, one of the questions we might be interested in is whether certain properties, either of the network or the nodes (e.g. beliefs or identities), affect the likelihood of connection between them. Such patterns and properties are only of interest, however, where we believe that, in principle, any node could form a tie (e.g. a friendship) with any other. It may be interesting if we find that members of one ethnic group less often form business ties with members of another ethnic group, for example, or if one ethnic group is found to be marginal in the network of a particular business community but only because we believe that, in principle, any member of the node set could form a tie with any of the others.

The relative absence of constraints upon node choice imposed by the theories and procedures of SNA does not mean that anything goes with regard to node selection. To reiterate our above point, nodes and node sets must be defined and selected carefully, with reference to the ideas and theories driving a particular research project. As in statistics, a network analysis is only as good as the data upon which it is based and it is the responsibility of the researcher to ensure that their data are meaningful and of a high quality. SNA packages will generate impressive visualisations and numerical arrays out of any old rubbish but it will still be rubbish. 'Garbage in' leads to 'garbage out' (the GIGO principle) and we must be careful to ensure that the nodes/node set that we select for analysis will allow us to answer the scientific questions that we have set for ourselves.

The question of which nodes to focus upon for a social network analysis is often a matter of where to draw the boundaries around a node set. Some networks are already bounded for us. If we are interested in friendship patterns between children in a school or shop-floor workers in a factory, for example, then the boundaries of the formal organisation itself suggest obvious boundaries for our node set, and there will usually be a register of some sort that we can use, listing all members of that set. Many of the networks that we want to analyse have no neat boundary, however. When Saunders (2007) elected to survey the network of environmental organisations in London, for example, she confronted a range of problems. In particular she had to decide which of the organisations known to her counted as environmental organisations (there are plenty of obvious inclusions and exclusions but inevitably also a high number of more ambiguous cases) and she had to tackle the problem of accessing those which were not, at the start of the project, known to her. Many potential populations of interest have no clear and unequivocal criteria of inclusion and nothing approximating a membership list or register that we can draw upon to define them. To quote a well-known American statesman, they involve both known–unknowns and unknown–unknowns, and we have no option but to try to work around this. Such problems are not unique to SNA. They pose a problem for all types of social science research. But they are no less of a problem either.

Ties

As with nodes, the formalism of SNA means that any type of tie can be focused upon, as long as all potential pairs of nodes are capable of entering into them and they are meaningful and appropriate to both the research questions being asked and the theories and conjectures which are driving them. If we are interested in the spread of sexually transmitted diseases, for example, then we need to know who engages in risky sexual practices (i.e. practices which facilitate disease transmission) with whom. Any other relation between the members of our node set is irrelevant because it does not facilitate transmission of a pathogen. Unless, that is, we want to track the diffusion of safe sex messages too, in which case we might also be interested in who talks to whom about intimate matters. If, by contrast, we want to predict the manner in which an economic crisis may cascade from one country to others then we need to know which countries, within the relevant set of countries, trade heavily with which of the others. And if we are interested in social capital and the potential for certain sorts of collective action within a community we may want to know the pattern and extent of relations of trust (or cooperation) between its various members. There is no type of tie which is correct for all research purposes. It always depends and is in many cases highly specific.

In some cases, of course, we may be interested in multiple types of relationship amongst the same population of nodes. Salient ties in many networks of interest are 'multiplex' (they have many strands, incorporating multiple types of relation). Studying students in a college, for example, we might want to know who studies together, who socialises together between lectures, who socialises together in evenings and at weekends, and who lives together. We might expect some overlap between these relations and SNA affords various ways of exploring such overlaps, but each is a distinct type of relation and it is reasonable to expect that some pairs of nodes may be linked in one of these ways but not the others.

Similarly, ties may have different strengths and we may wish to record and take account of these in our analyses. This might be captured by using a Likert Scale on a questionnaire; for example, by asking respondents how much, on a scale of 1–5 (or whatever), they like each of the people whom they have nominated as friends, how well they know them or how often they see them, etc. Alternatively, it might be captured through observation. Ethnologists observing animal interaction in the wild, for example, will often count how often any two animals interact in a particular way, weighting their ties accordingly. Such detail is not always necessary or even helpful. Often it will suffice to ascertain whether two nodes enjoy a tie or not. But weighting is an option.

Finally, ties can be directed or undirected. We say that a tie is directed when it is meaningful to ask whether or not it is reciprocal. Liking is directed, for example, because knowing that John likes Jane does not tell us whether Jane likes John. She might but she might not. Living with someone, by contrast, is necessarily reciprocal and therefore 'undirected'. If we know that John lives with Jane then we know that Jane lives with John, or rather we know that they live together.

Node Attributes

Node attributes are not necessary to the definition of networks and play no role in many network analytic routines, even when they are known. However, they can be included and may be very important in some cases. We may wish to know whether nodes in a network disproportionately form ties with others who are similar to them in some respect, for example – an effect referred to as 'homophily'. Alternatively, we may wish to know whether particular node attributes are correlated with certain network positions. Are men more central than women within a particular network, for example? Do particular ethnic groups disproportionately find themselves in a particular position? These are categorical node attributes but in other cases nodes might have ordinal or interval level properties. We might wish to determine whether income is correlated with popularity, for example, or whether individuals are disproportionately likely to form ties with others of the same or a similar age as themselves.

Whole Networks

Beyond the choices we make about node and tie sets, SNA offers a range of possibilities about the way in which we capture and analyse networks. This book is focused upon one very specific way: ego-net analysis. Before we narrow down on ego-nets, however, it is important to introduce the two main alternatives within the SNA toolbox: whole network analysis and two-mode analysis.

When we analyse a whole network we identify a relevant population of nodes and, as far as possible, conduct a census survey of all members of that population, seeking to establish the existence or not of a relevant tie between each pair of nodes in that population. In a population of 20, for example, there are potentially 190 undirected ties or 380 directed ties (see Box 1.1 for an explanation of this) and whole net analysis requires that we know about the existence or not of each one of them.

BOX 1.1

Calculating the Potential Number of Ties in a Network:

A Worked Example

- In a population of 20 nodes, assuming it is not meaningful to refer to a node's relationship with itself (it is meaningful in some cases but often not), each has a potential 19 ties (the figure is 20 if nodes can enjoy ties with themselves – 'reflexive ties').

- So the maximum potential number of ties in the network is 20 x 19 = 380.

- This calculation assumes that our network is directed, however. It treats node number 1's tie to node number 2 as distinct from node number 2's tie to node number 1. Each of the 20 nodes potentially 'sends' a tie to each of the 19 others (20 x 19) and each potentially 'receives' a tie from each of the 19 others.

- If our network is undirected this calculation is problematic because it counts each tie twice, giving us double the number of (undirected) ties in the network. We therefore halve our original answer: 380/2 = 190.

This information is stored within an adjacency matrix (see Figure 1.2). This is a matrix whose first column and top row each list all of the nodes in the network, in the same order, with ties between nodes being indicated in the cell where the row of one meets the column of the other. In Figure 1.2, for example, there is a number 1 in the cell where Paul's row intersects with

Ed's column. That indicates that they have a tie. The 0 at the intersection of Ed's row and Jo's column, conversely, suggests that they have no tie. This is a basic, binary network. If our ties were weighted the numbers populating the cells would reflect the weighting. If Paul had rated his relationship with Ed as '5' on a Likert scale or we had observed that he telephoned Ed five times during the period covered by our survey then we would have put a '5' in the cell where his row intersects with Ed's column.

	John	Paul	Ed	Jo	Mick	Keith
John	1	1	0	1	1	0
Paul	1	1	1	1	0	1
Ed	0	1	1	0	0	1
Jo	1	1	0	1	0	0
Mick	1	0	0	0	1	1
Keith	0	1	1	0	1	1

Figure 1.2 An adjacency matrix

Note that the diagonal running from the top left to the bottom right of Figure 1.2 comprises the cells where each node's row coincides with its column, potentially recording the node's relation with itself. As noted above, it is often meaningless to ask if a node has a relation with itself. This is reflected in the main software packages, such as UCINET, whose default setting for many analytic routines is to ignore the diagonal. The ties from an actor to their self ('reflexive ties') may be relevant, however, and can and should be included in computations where this is so. If our network involves ties of 'esteem', for example, then we may wish to measure and record each node's self-esteem, as well as their valuation of others, particularly if we believe that the former influences the latter or is affected by the opinions of others.

Note also that each pair of nodes ('dyad') in the network is represented twice in the matrix, once on either side of the diagonal. There is a cell where John's row meets Keith's column and a cell where Keith's row meets John's column. In the matrix for an undirected network each of the two cells will contain the same information, thereby giving an element of redundancy. The same tie will be recorded twice. For a directed network, however, this doubling up allows us to capture the direction of ties and any asymmetry in a relation. The intersection of John's row and Keith's column records whether John 'sends' a tie to Keith, whilst the intersection of Keith's row and John's column records whether Keith sends a tie to John. If a tie only exists in one direction, we can capture this.

A whole network can be visualised in a graph, in the manner shown in Figure 1.3. Nodes (also referred to as 'vertices' in this context) are represented by small grey squares. Ties are represented by lines which connect them

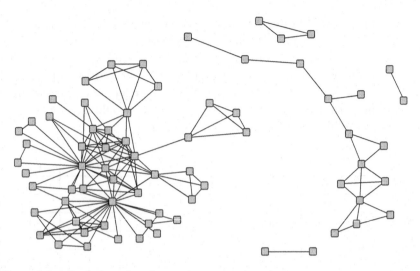

Figure 1.3   A whole network

(also referred to as 'edges'). If this was a directed network then the lines would have arrow-heads indicating direction (connecting lines in graphs of directed ties ('digraphs') are sometimes referred to as 'arcs') and if the ties were weighted their weighting might be represented either by giving edges differing thicknesses or by way of numerical labels at the side of each edge.

Similarly, node attributes might be represented in a graph. Categorical attributes can be represented by giving vertices different colours and shapes, for example, and ordinal or interval level attributes can be represented by varying the size of vertices. If Figure 1.3 was a network of trade relations between countries, for example, then we might indicate the continent to which each country belongs by way of a colour code, their system of government (e.g. democratic or not) by reference to different shapes, and their GDP by way of size – the bigger the GDP, the bigger the node.

Graphs are a great way of representing network data and can be very useful. They can be misleading, however, especially if we try to read them as we might read a scatterplot, imputing vertical and horizontal axes to them and assigning significance to a node's location along these axes. Nodes are often assigned a location in the graph space, by the main software packages, using algorithms which locate them close to others which have a similar profile of ties to them. There are different algorithms, however, based upon different principles. All only ever approximate a layout which operationalises their chosen principle, often with many 'errors'. Analysts routinely change layouts, manually, either for aesthetic reasons or in order to better illustrate an observation that they have made regarding the network.

This is permissible because SNA operates with a different conception of space to the Cartesian conception employed in scatterplots. Network space is defined exclusively by patterns of connection. A node's position in a network refers to its pattern of ties and bears no relation to its location (high or low, left or right) on the graph plot. Similarly, we commonly refer to the centrality of nodes (see below), deeming some more central than others, but again the various definitions of centrality that we work with all refer to patterns of connection rather than location on a graph plot. The least central node in a network may well be positioned towards the middle of a graph plot. Finally, 'distances', in network analysis, are measured in ties (or 'degrees') rather than centimetres or scales represented along graph axes.

BOX 1.2

Paths and Geodesic Distance

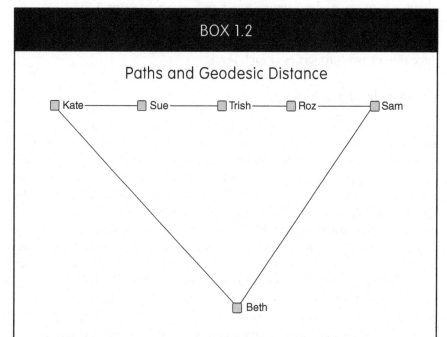

- In the above network there are two paths connecting Kate and Sam.

- One path goes via Sue, Trish and Roz. It has a length of four degrees.

- The other path goes via Beth. It has a length of two degrees.

- The geodesic distance between Kate and Sam is the shortest path length between them; in this case, two degrees.

- Note that although Kate appears closer to Roz than to Sam on the plot she is closer to Sam in network terms because her geodesic distance from Sam is only two degrees, whereas her geodesic distance from Roz is three degrees.

- Note finally that Kate has two paths to Roz (one via Beth and Sam, the other via Sue and Trish). In this case they are both the same length: three degrees.

If two nodes are directly tied then they are at a distance of one degree. If they are not directly tied but each have a tie to a common, third node and are, in this respect, indirectly tied, then they are at a distance of two degrees. If their indirect connection involves two intermediaries, and therefore three ties, then they are connected by three degrees, and so on (see Box 1.2). These chains of connection are referred to as paths. Any two nodes may be connected by multiple paths but it is usually the shortest of these paths that we are interested in. The distance of the shortest path between any two nodes, measured in degrees, is referred to as the geodesic distance between these nodes. Geodesic distance will not usually correspond to the physical distance between nodes as represented on a graph (see Box 1.2).

Whole networks have a large number of properties, which can be defined at various levels. It would be useful to briefly outline these levels and introduce one or two properties at each level.

The Whole Network Level

These are properties which exist at the level of the whole network. There are many of them. Simple examples include: order, which is the number of nodes in the network; and density, which is the number of ties in the network expressed as a proportion of the number of ties there could be, given the number of nodes. There are six nodes in the network in Box 1.2, for example, and six ties. To work out the density of this network we would calculate the number of ties that there could be, using the method explained in Box 1.1. Assuming that ties are undirected and that it makes no sense to ask if a node has a ('reflexive') tie to itself, that gives us $(6 \times 5)/2 = 15$. We then express the six ties that we have found to exist as a proportion of the 15 that could exist: i.e. $6/15 = 0.4$. Our network has a density of 0.4. Note that density always varies between 0 (no ties in the network) and 1 (every possible tie is present).

Another whole network property is number of components. A component is a subset of nodes, each of which has a path connecting it to each of the others. There are five components in Figure 1.3, for example: a big one to the left of the plot, a long stringy one to the right, two dumbbell shaped dyadic nodes and a triangular shaped triadic component. We discuss components further below.

Endogenously Defined Sub-Groups

A network's node set can often be divided into various subsets on the basis of patterns of ties. Components are subsets, for example, each distinguished by the paths connecting their constituent members. And they may be important. We would expect diffusion, contagion and/or cascades to happen within components, for example, depending upon the type of tie we are looking at, but not across components because distinct components are not connected to one another. Similarly, we would not expect all members of a network to become involved in collective action if that network involved distinct components because the lack of connection between components would prevent coordination between them. We would only expect concerted action within components.

Another example of an endogenous sub-group is a clique. This is a subset of three or more nodes, each member of which is connected to every other. The density of a clique is always 1 because all possible ties are actualised. Cliques are important because their membership is highly cohesive, making the diffusion of information within them very quick and the potential for collective action, where triggered by an external event, much greater.

Components and cliques are defined by their cohesion. Members are more connected to one another than to others outside of the group. Not all sub-groups are defined by their cohesion, however. Sub-groups might be defined where their members occupy equivalent positions in a network, irrespective of their cohesion, and SNA offers a number of distinct definitions of equivalence. The most straightforward is structural equivalence. Two nodes are structurally equivalent if they have ties to the same alters, irrespective of whether they are tied to one another. Nodes that have no ties within a network ('isolates') are a special case of this and nicely illustrate the distinction between structurally equivalent sub-groups and cohesive sub-groups. All isolates within a network are structurally equivalent to one another because they have exactly the same pattern of ties (i.e. no ties at all). They are clearly not a cohesive group, however, because they have no ties to one another. A whole branch of SNA, referred to as blockmodelling, is devoted to modelling networks on the basis of such equivalently positioned groups ('blocks').

Finally, a very popular form of sub-group analysis focuses upon the often observed division within networks between 'core' nodes, which are all relatively well-connected to one another and apparently dominant, and more peripheral nodes with a greater density of ties to the core than to one another but only a low density of ties in both cases. Core–periphery analysis might assume a categorical form, in which case we seek to partition our nodes into two categories: core and periphery. Alternatively it may be continuous, in which case we calculate a 'coreness' score for each node. The core–periphery divide is important because the core is often the dominant sub-group within a network.

Exogenously Defined Sub-Groups

Sub-groups may also be defined by factors external to the network, especially node attributes. All of the women in a network involving both men and women constitute an exogenously defined sub-group, for example, as do different ethnic groups in a multi-ethnic network. Analysis of exogenously defined sub-groups typically centres upon the effect (or lack of effect) of node attributes on patterns of connection, or, alternatively, where attributes are potentially changeable (e.g. political identity or musical taste), it centres on the effect of connection upon attributes: e.g. processes of social influence, which persuade actors to change their behaviour or tastes.

Many networks, for example, are characterised by homophily; that is, nodes are disproportionately linked to other nodes with whom they share a salient social status ('status homophily') or an interest, taste or value ('value homophily') (Lazarsfeld and Merton 1964). This suggests either that people like to form ties with others similar to themselves or that they are influenced by others to whom they are connected (or both). Having established the existence of homophily in a network, our analysis might turn to exploring which is the more likely possibility. Alternatively, we might be interested to see whether particular node attributes (e.g. ethnicity) are associated with particular positions in the network: e.g. membership of the core or a given structurally equivalent block.

The Node Level

In addition to their exogenously defined attributes, nodes have properties in virtue of their pattern of connection. In particular they can be more or less central to the network, as defined by one or more of the very different types of centrality identified in SNA. At a very basic level, for example, nodes vary in their number of ties within the network; that is, their 'degree centrality'. Some inevitably have more ties than others; that is, a higher degree or degree centrality. They are more degree central. Degree is only one measure of centrality, however. There are many others, including closeness, betweenness and eigenvector centrality. These other forms are explained in texts devoted to whole network analysis (e.g. Borgatti et al. 2013, Scott 2000 or Wasserman and Faust 1994).

Dyads and Triads

Recent advances in the statistic modelling of networks have focused upon dyads and more especially triads as units of analysis. For example, early statistical approaches focused upon issues of reciprocity. They hypothesised that, in certain types of directed networks, involving certain types of tie, a node was more likely to 'send a tie' to an alter if the alter sent a tie to them. This hypothesis was tested (and usually confirmed) by looking at the number of reciprocated ties in a network and comparing it against the number one would expect by chance, given a particular density of ties.

BOX 1.3

Some Key Concepts

Clique: A subset of nodes all of whose members are directly tied to the others, giving them a maximum density (i.e. 1).

Component: A subset of nodes, all of whose members are linked by a path.

Degree Centrality: There are many ways of comparing nodes' levels of centrality within a network. The most straightforward – degree centrality – is to compare their respective numbers of ties.

Density: The number of ties in a network expressed as a proportion of the total number that are possible.

Path: A chain of connections and intermediaries linking two nodes in a network, such that information, viruses and other such things can pass between them.

Reciprocity: In a directed network any node A might 'send' a tie to a node B without necessarily receiving a tie back (A might like B (a tie of liking) whilst B does not like A or perhaps does not even know who they are). Reciprocity refers to a situation within a pair of nodes where each does send a tie to the other. It was of interest in early statistical approaches to network analysis as it was hypothesised that a tie from A to B is more likely when B sends a tie to A. Obviously certain types of tie are unlikely to be reciprocated. If B bullies A (a tie of bullying) it is unlikely that A will also bully B.

Status Homophily: A tendency within a network for nodes to be disproportionately tied to others who share one or more salient statuses with them (e.g. gender, ethnicity or age).

Structural Equivalence: Any two or more nodes are perfectly structurally equivalent where they have exactly the same pattern of ties: i.e. they are tied to exactly the same alters in exactly the same way.

Transitivity: The idea of transitivity suggests that any two nodes are more likely to enjoy a tie if each is tied to a common, third party. If Paul and Pete each have a tie to Frank, for example, then the idea of transitivity suggests that they are more likely to have a tie to one another compared to a situation in which they have no friends in common.

Value Homophily: A tendency within a network for nodes to be disproportionately tied to others with whom they share particular values and/or tastes.

Turning next to triads, statisticians were keen to test the thesis of transitivity associated with the work of Mark Granovetter (1973, 1982); that is, the claim that two nodes are more likely to have a tie when they each have a tie to a common third party. This can be tested by comparing the actual number of transitive triads in a network against the number expected by chance, controlling for both density and reciprocity. Complex statistical methods of modelling networks (Exponential Random Graph Models or ERGMs) have been devised from these relatively simple beginnings in recent years (Lusher et al. 2013).

We have barely scratched at the surface of whole network analysis here but we have hopefully said enough for scene-setting purposes (for a comprehensive introduction see Borgatti et al. 2013, Scott 2000 or Wasserman and Faust 1994). With this said we will briefly turn to two-mode networks.

Two-Mode Networks

In addition to whole networks, network analysts sometimes analyse two-mode networks. In a two-mode network we have two different types of node and the type of tie that we are interested in exists only across these two types, not within them. A common example is a network of people (first mode) and events (second mode), with 'attendance' as the observed tie. People are tied to events where they attend those events but they are not, at least in the first case, tied to one another by a relation of attendance (people attend events but they do not attend one another) nor are events tied in this way (events do not attend events).

Two-mode networks can be captured in matrices, like single-mode networks, with one mode (e.g. people) represented along the rows and the other (e.g. events) represented down the columns. These matrices are referred to as incidence matrices. Similarly, two-mode networks can be represented as graphs, as in Figure 1.4, where events are represented by grey squares and participants by black circles.

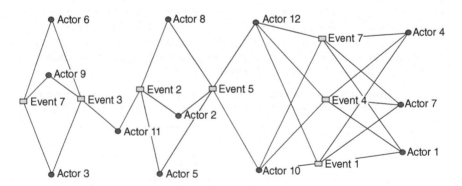

Figure 1.4 A two-mode network

Many of the whole network measures introduced above have two-mode equivalents, making it possible for a two-mode network to be analysed in its basic form. It is very common, however, to 'affiliate' two-mode networks, deriving two single-mode networks from them which can then each be analysed in the normal way. A people and events network, for example, might be affiliated to give us a network of people (linked where they attend the same events) and a separate network of events (linked where they are attended by the same people). Figure 1.5 visualises the single-mode participant-to-participant network which can be derived from Figure 1.4. In this case participants are linked to one another where they have attended at least one of the same events.

The data that we get when we affiliate two-mode data are weighted because participants might attend more than one of the same events. We might analyse the affiliated network in this weighted form. Alternatively, however, we might dichotomise it (simplifying it by deeming ties simply absent or present) on the basis of a threshold value. For example, we might decide to call two events connected when they share three or more of the same participants.

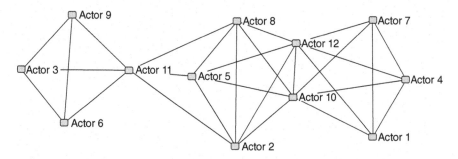

Figure 1.5 A single-mode network of participants derived from Figure 1.4

In historical research, using archival sources, it is often impossible to get whole, single-mode data and we may have to use an affiliated two-mode data source as a proxy. Indeed, there may be many reasons why we resort to two-mode data gathering as a means of deriving a single-mode network. If the resulting network is meaningful and fits with the theories driving the research this if often fine. Researchers should be aware, however, both that this method of data gathering tends to shape the resulting network in a number of ways and that the move from two to one mode (affiliation) involves a loss of information (Everett and Borgatti 2013). This latter problem may be avoided, in relation to some analytic routines, however, if both modes are analysed and the results of these two analyses recombined (ibid.)

Ego-Nets

Having briefly introduced whole and two–mode networks we can now turn to the main focus of this book: ego–nets. As explained at the beginning of this chapter, an ego–net is the network of contacts (alters) that form around a particular node (ego). Ego herself is sometimes removed for analytic purposes. That varies. Similarly, whilst it is often preferable to have data regarding (relevant) ties and the absence of such ties between alters, and whilst much of what we discuss in the book assumes access to such information, ego–net analysis may, in some cases, focus simply upon ego's ties, bracketing the question of ties between alters. For present purposes, however, we will assume that an ego–net involves ego, her alters and all relevant ties between alters.

Ego–nets can be abstracted from whole networks. Each node in a whole network is or has an ego–net. Each has, potentially, a number of alters, and those alters are either connected to one another or not. Thus, in Figure 1.6 we have abstracted four ego–nets from the whole net represented in Figure 1.3 (the egos are the slightly larger, grey vertices).

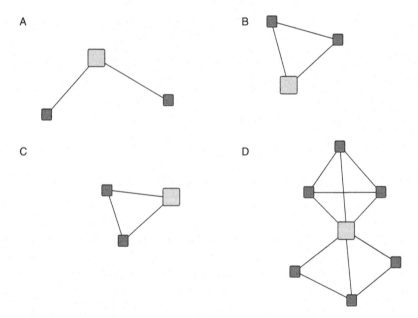

Figure 1.6   Four ego-nets (extracted from Figure 1.3)

Note that each ego–net varies in size. A, B and C each have 2 alters but D has 6. If our egos ever needed extra muscle for a job they were contemplating then D would be better placed to get it, all other things being equal, than the others. On the other hand, she probably has many more people asking her for favours and making demands upon her time, which may not always be a good thing.

The structures of the nets also vary. Although A, B and C are each of the same size, B are C are each cliques, according to SNA's technical definition, whereas A is not. A clique, it will be remembered, is a subset of nodes, each of whom enjoys a tie with each of the others. This is true of B and C, but A's alters are not tied to one another. This will reduce the likelihood of solidarity and consensus in A and may make coordination more difficult. It may also sometimes work to A's advantage, however, as she controls the flow of information and resources between her two alters (at least as far as we can tell (see below)) and she may benefit from that. She may take credit for the good ideas of one alter when passing them on to the other, for example, and/or may be rewarded in kind by the recipient when passing on resources from one alter to another.

Furthermore, the independence of her alters from one another means that they are more likely to provide access to different flows of information, which is an advantage. In a very famous paper on the information flows involved in securing a new job, Mark Granovetter (1973, 1982) observed that transitive ties (which were discussed above) are often 'redundant' in informational terms because ego's alters will tend to give her the same information. Whilst transitive ties are more conducive to the development of trust, cooperation, consensus and solidarity (Coleman 1990), which can be an advantage (see Chapter Two), the closure of contacts precludes access to external nodes and thus external sources of ideas and information, resulting in constant regurgitation of the same ideas and information and, potentially thereby, stagnancy (Burt 2005). For this reason they can be less useful to those involved in them. New information is much more likely to come from intransitive ties; ties to alters who are not connected to the ego's other alters.

Note that ego-net D, which is bigger than either A, B or C, combines elements of each of their respective structures. Ego D has access to two independent 'pools' of information, like A. D occupies a similar 'brokerage' position, albeit mediating between two groups of alters rather than just two alters. One of these two groups (located above her on the plot) is a clique, like ego-nets B and C. The other is one tie short of a clique. Perhaps ego D will enjoy both the benefits of transitivity and brokerage? She enjoys solidarity and trust with each of her two clusters of alters and also both the opportunity to broker between them (with the benefits that brings) and access to two distinct pools of information and other resources. However, her position may create its own constraints. Her two clusters may compete for her loyalty, for example, pressuring her to take sides, and they may make competing demands upon her time, energy and other resources (see, for example, Crossley 2008b).

The Pros and Cons of Ego-Analysis

It is always possible to extract ego-nets from a whole network. Where this is done the ego-nets can, of course, be recombined into a whole network, allowing the researcher to move between the level of the whole and the level of individual ego-nets. However, it is not always possible and not always desirable to gather whole network data. Researchers often elicit ego-net data in ways which do not allow us to put the whole back together (although it is always there tacitly). There are three good reasons to do this.

Firstly, ego-net analysis affords a means of analysing big networks. If we are interested in a relatively small population of actors, such as participants in a local music scene, protest group or pupils in a school, then it is feasible for us to conduct a census survey of our node set and we can therefore do whole network analysis. If we are interested in processes affecting bigger populations, such as a whole town or 'the general public', however, then a census survey will not be possible in most cases, ruling out whole network analysis. Generally we are constrained to sample large populations, denying ourselves access to the information required for a whole network analysis. Ego-net analysis is entirely compatible with a sample survey, however. Indeed it will ordinarily involve a sample survey, and as such it is possible to use it in relation to much bigger populations.

It is important to add here both that randomisation and other strategies employed in sample surveys are entirely compatible with an ego-net approach and that questions which elicit ego-net data, of the type discussed in Chapter Three, can be added to any standard questionnaire. Indeed, it is becoming increasingly common for a small number of ego-net questions to be added to the various regular large national surveys conducted in many countries. Ego-net questions inevitably add bulk to a questionnaire and for this reason their inclusion has to be given careful consideration, but a small ego-net module will add no more bulk than any other module and may prove very enlightening.

Secondly, because ego-net analysis is compatible with the range of sampling strategies routinely used in (quantitative) social science it is also compatible with most of the techniques of statistical analysis and modelling employed in such research. Whole network data contradict the assumptions of standard statistical approaches and, for this reason, can only be analysed, statistically, by means of a range of specially adapted methods (Borgatti et al. 2013, Lusher et al. 2013). Most obviously, for example, cases (nodes) in a whole network survey are not randomly sampled from a wider population (as is assumed in inferential statistics) and the connections between them contradict the assumption of case-wise independence. There are no such problems with ego-net data, however, at least where appropriate sampling techniques have been employed. We should add here, furthermore, that ego-net analysis generates a range of measures, discussed in Chapter Four, which may be included, alongside other, more conventional measures, in such research.

This will be particularly salient where networks are one amongst a number of foci within a research project, each of which must be accommodated within a single research design. Whole network analysis makes very specific demands upon the researcher and allows little room for compromise. As such it cannot easily be added to a project which has a remit beyond networks. Ego-net analysis, by contrast, is often quite easy to slot into a more conventionally structured project.

A final advantage of ego-net research relates to what Simmel (1955) calls 'intersecting social circles' and what White (2008) calls network domains or 'net doms'. Both writers observe that in modern societies most people interact and form ties across a number of distinct 'social circles' or 'domains' whose membership, with the exception of ego herself, does not overlap. For example, the typical adult may have alters in their family, neighbourhood, workplace, gym and local pub. They are a point of intersection between these different circles but they are most likely the only point of intersection in many cases. Their gym buddies will probably know one another but won't know anybody else in ego's network and likewise for members of each of the other circles. These patterns of separation and intersection, which are essential to a proper understanding of the networked character of human social life, are much easier to get at by means of an ego-net survey. If we are interested in one domain, such as the gym, then a whole network approach may make sense because we have a relatively contained population (everybody who goes to the gym) (Crossley 2008b). If we are interested in many domains, however, some of which only overlap through a single node, then the size and complexity of the task at hand, coupled with the demands of bounding our object of study, will often rule out a whole network study. We need to ask individual egos about the different social circles in which they mix and the different sets of alters with whom they enjoy ties in each of those circles.

Note here that focusing upon a single domain, as we typically do in a whole network analysis, may result in a distorted picture of the social world because it separates that domain from others. Studies of social influence within the whole network of a school or a gym population, for example, may miss important actors from outside of that domain who influence those within it. Ego's activity in the gym may be affected by her relations to alters in a different domain, such as her family or workplace. Similarly, nodes who appear isolated may only be so in the one domain observed and only because they connect more strongly to alters in other domains not captured in the node set of a whole network study. By moving outwards from the individual and allowing us to tap into each of the various circles in which they mix, ego-net analysis helps to circumvent this potential problem.

Having said this, there is a comparable problem with ego-net analysis, which is avoided in whole network analysis. To give an example: when discussing the ego-nets in Figure 1.6 we referred to A's brokerage position and the advantages this creates for her. However, what if her two alters each have a tie to a common, fourth node who has no direct tie to A and who would not show up, therefore, in an ego-net study (see Figure 1.7)? Each of A's alters now has an alternative source of information and other resources, which reduces A's bargaining power. In Figure 1.7, A's two alters are each in a position to play a brokerage role too, mediating between A and this fourth node. Indeed, each node in this mini network is in exactly the same position vis-à-vis the others: each connects two otherwise unconnected nodes and is indirectly connected to one further node by each of their alters. Exactly how this will play out is not clear, but what matters for our purposes is that where our ego-net analysis (Figure 1.6) suggested that A was in an advantageous position, compared to her alters, a fuller analysis suggests that she is not. She is in the same position as each of her alters. And that is only how she appears on the basis of this snapshot. If we were to add further nodes then the picture may change again. Additional information, beyond that regarding A's ego-net, changes the picture that we derive from A's ego-net. This is only one example of the kinds of complications and qualifications (to an ego-net analysis) that might arise if we have access to what is, in this respect at least, the fuller structural information that we derive from a whole network study.

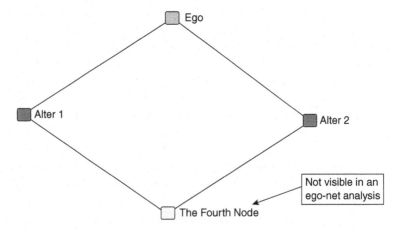

Figure 1.7   The fourth node

Beyond this we may be interested in the properties of the whole network and/or its broader sub-groupings. Some of these properties could be inferred from a sample of ego-nets. If we are confident that the number of alters ('degree') is normally distributed across a population, for example, and that our sample of ego-nets is truly random, then we may infer the average degree, and by means of this, the density of a whole network from our sample. Furthermore, again on condition of assumptions regarding distribution and randomness, the density of individual ego-nets may be used to infer likely levels of clustering in the wider network. However, our assumptions may not hold. A body of literature has emerged in recent years pointing to the existence of a class of networks whose degree manifests a so-called 'power-law distribution'. In lay terms this means that a very small proportion of nodes in a network have a huge number of alters, whilst the vast majority have only a small number. Where this occurs the network has a very distinctive, centralised, structure but one that will probably elude a random sample survey because random sampling is unlikely to pick up the tiny minority of 'hub' nodes in the population. Again this is just one example, amongst many, of whole network level properties that are difficult and/or impossible to get at by means of a sample of ego-nets.

Quantity and Quality

The discussion in this chapter hitherto has been largely framed in quantitative terms. We have spoken of random samples, measures and models. Network analysis, in all of its forms, is amenable to a mixing of methods, quantitative and qualitative, however, and we intend to reflect this in this book. Matrices are a good means of capturing who knows whom. They allow us to distinguish between types of ties, different strengths of connection and sometimes also between positive and negative ties. But we may wish to know more about the meaning of specific alters for ego, what they do together and the 'story', as White (2008) calls it, of their relationship. We may wish to embellish our data regarding ego's network with wider qualitative information about their life and outlook, gleaned through qualitative interviews, and/ or to embed our ego-net data within an ethnographic understanding of its context. Indeed, much early and pioneering research on SNA emerged out of an ethnographic context, with graph theoretic methods being used to build upon, organise and systematise qualitative-observational data, and the authors of that work often included both quantitatively and qualitatively defined properties in their concept of a 'network' (e.g. Mitchell 1969).

This is significant for the present authors because several of these pioneers were members of the 'Manchester School' – a research cluster (to use the contemporary jargon) based in our own institution. Indeed, our own research centre, the Mitchell Centre, is named after one of these pioneers, and he, in turn, was the PhD supervisor of one of us (Martin Everett). Our vision of SNA, both in this book and more generally, reflects the pragmatic and mixed approach of the original Manchester School, combining methods where it makes sense to do so and moving freely between qualitative and quantitative data.

Conclusion and Chapter Plan

In this chapter we have introduced the idea of ego-net analysis, comparing it with analysis of whole networks and considering both where it is most appropriate and what its respective strengths and weaknesses are. We have also introduced the vocabulary of SNA and a number of concepts and measures which will be revisited in greater detail in later chapters. It only remains for this chapter to briefly map out the content of these chapters.

Chapter Two – Social Capital and Small Worlds: A Primer: Many recent developments in ego-net analysis have originated in the context of debates in two central substantive areas of research: social capital and small worlds. In order to facilitate proper understanding of these developments we use Chapter Two to briefly introduce these two areas of substantive research, explaining where and why they connect to innovations in ego-net research.

Chapter Three – Getting Ego-Nets: Here we consider a number of the most common ways of gathering ego-net data.

Chapter Four – Analysing Ego-Net Data: We discuss all of the main measures of ego-net properties typically used by network analysts, explaining where and why they should be used.

Chapter Five – Narratives, Typologies and Case Studies: This chapter introduces qualitative approaches to ego-net analysis and discusses the advantages of adopting a mixed-method approach.

Chapter Six – Multilevel Models for Cross-Sectional Ego-Nets: In this chapter and also Chapter Seven, we build on the discussion of ego-net measures in Chapter Four but also slightly shift our focus and gear, by considering a number of recent statistical developments in ego-net analysis. In Chapter Six specifically we focus in particular upon the way in which ego-net data might be used in the context of multilevel modelling.

Chapter Seven – Statistical Analysis of Network Dynamics: Sticking with a more advanced statistical approach, this chapter considers methods for modelling change within ego-nets across time.

2

SOCIAL CAPITAL AND SMALL WORLDS: A PRIMER

Learning Outcomes

By the end of this chapter you will:

1. Understand three different operational definitions of 'social capital' and various related concepts, including 'structural holes' and 'brokerage'.

2. Be familiar with both the small world phenomenon and the early social scientific research which underlies more recent interest in it.

3. Have been introduced to a number of techniques for eliciting network data, including the 'position generator', 'resource generator' and 'reverse small world experiment' (the first two are discussed further in Chapter Three).

4. Understand the background context to a variety of ego-net measures (which are discussed in Chapter Four).

Introduction

There has been a huge growth in research on or involving social networks in recent years. Two areas of research in particular have become very prominent: social capital and small worlds. These are substantive areas of interest but each has sparked methodological innovations in SNA and in particular in ego-net analysis. There are many reasons, beyond an interest in social capital or small worlds, to study ego-nets and *a fortiori* social networks more generally, but the tailoring of some methods to the requirements of addressing these issues means that a basic familiarity with them is necessary for a proper and full understanding of what follows in this book.

In this chapter we offer that grounding. The chapter is not intended as a sophisticated discussion of the complexities of either concept nor a comprehensive and up-to-date review of their uses (on social capital see Field 2008 and Halpern 2004; on small worlds see Crossley 2005, 2008a, Schnettler 2009a,b, and Scott 2011). We aim only to provide sufficient exposition to make the measures and methods discussed later in the book meaningful. We begin with social capital.

Social Capital

'Social capital' is defined and used in different ways in the literature. For purposes of exposition we will distinguish three versions of the concept: one focused upon access to resources; one focused upon social cohesion; and one focused upon 'brokerage' across 'structural holes'.

Social Capital as Indirect Access to Resources

The resources version of the social capital concept originates in the work of Pierre Bourdieu (1986), who understands social capital as one amongst a number of forms of 'capital' unevenly distributed in contemporary societies, which afford those who own and control them leverage in pursuing their various projects and aims. Some are richer than others in terms of their financial assets (e.g. income, savings, property, etc.), for example, a continuum which Bourdieu captures with his concept of 'economic capital'. Some enjoy a greater volume of what he calls 'cultural capital'; that is, such cultural resources as educational qualifications, ownership of 'high' cultural artefacts (e.g. literary novels, classical music CDs, art prints) and/or a 'cultured' disposition and demeanour ('embodied cultural capital'). Some enjoy greater status and recognition ('symbolic capital'), often in virtue of these other forms of capital but to some extent also independently of them. And some are better connected than others. They enjoy a relative advantage in virtue of their ties to other people. It is this latter resource that Bourdieu terms 'social capital'.

Bourdieu makes reference to other forms of capital in his various books and papers but these four – economic, cultural, symbolic and social – are the main forms that he discusses, and of these he makes particular use of the concepts of economic and cultural capital. Social capital remains underdeveloped and arguably under-used across his major works. He says enough about it, however, to merit further discussion.

The various forms of capital are each transferable, for Bourdieu. Indeed their value is largely exchange value. Each is important because of the advantage it bestows upon the actor in their efforts to procure the others (on some readings the ultimate goal of these 'exchanges' is the procurement of symbolic capital (i.e. status and recognition)). This is particularly true of his concept of social capital. Social capital, as Bourdieu understands it, involves ties to others which either have a symbolic value and thereby provide the individual with symbolic capital, or afford them indirect access to an alter's portfolio of capital.

Knowing and being known to know an elite can be a status marker, for example, and may be valued as such. Actors like to be seen to move in and belong to exclusive circles. Connection to an elite may also be useful, however, because that elite may be persuaded to use their resources in a way which serves ego's advantage. If a contact serves on an important committee (bureaucratic or political 'capital'), for example, they may be persuaded to steer the decision of that committee in a way which advantages ego. Alternatively, they may be prepared to invest their money (economic capital) in one of ego's schemes, to bring their expertise (cultural capital) to bear upon it or lend their status (symbolic capital) and backing to it.

This conception of social capital informs Bourdieu's (1984) much-discussed interest in lifestyle activities and consumption. If the well-to-do are inclined to go to the opera, then going to the opera will increase an actor's chances of coming into contact and forging ties with the well-to-do. It will increase their social capital. This may not be a conscious decision. Bourdieu's conception of habitus[1] suggests that actors are conditioned through early experience to act in ways which tend to reproduce their social position, irrespective of reflective intentions and awareness. Children of well-to-do families might acquire a love of opera from their parents, for example, which motivates them to attend the opera without any need for more utilitarian motivations. This will still bring them into contact with other well-heeled individuals, however, thereby generating social capital for them and helping to maintain their social position. Furthermore, their shared tastes (e.g. for opera) and the embodied cultural capital (e.g. airs and graces, accent and comportment) which will also form a part of their habitus on account of their upbringing, increases the likelihood of them hitting it off and forming ties (i.e. social capital) with other elites when they do meet. Echoing a theme of much work on homophily in social networks, Bourdieu argues that actors prefer to form bonds with others who share their interests, dispositions and embodied orientations, because this makes interaction easier. They have interests in common which they enjoy discussing and they communicate in the same way, making the process of communication easier and more enjoyable (on the concept of homophily see Chapter One; on measures of homophily see Chapter Four).

What happens at 'the top' also happens lower down. Bourdieu envisages society as a 'social space', multi-dimensional in principle but with two key axes.

a vertical axis representing individuals' overall volumes of capital, when all forms (economic and cultural in particular[2]) are combined, and a horizontal axis representing the composition of that volume; that is, the ratio of economic to cultural capital in each individual's portfolio (see Figure 2.1). Every individual within a specified population has a position within this space, according to Bourdieu, and those who are more proximate are more likely to be similar in disposition (habitus), thereby more likely to come into contact and more likely, in virtue of their shared dispositions and interests, to form ties when they do. It is on this basis, he argues, that social classes, as 'real' social groups, are formed (Bourdieu 1993). Individuals with comparable portfolios of capital gravitate together, form bonds and networks, and these networks are the basis, or at least one basis[3] upon which social groups or classes begin to shape.

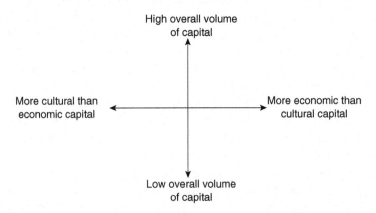

Figure 2.1   Bourdieu's conception of social space

Ties per se do not constitute social capital, for Bourdieu, however; only ties which afford indirect access to other forms of capital. And the more resources they afford, the greater their value qua social capital. An individual who has 'friends in high places' has more social capital than an individual whose friends are located towards the bottom of social space. Indeed a friend who does not afford the individual access to desired resources does not contribute to the individual's social capital at all, by Bourdieu's definition.

His conception of 'fields' does allow for some qualification of this, however. Fields are relatively discrete (but sometimes overlapping and often nested) domains of activity which add further differentiation to the structure of the social world. Education is a field, for example. Higher education is a sub-field within it. Science is a field, biology a sub-field within it, etc. Fields themselves are located in social space. The field of classical music is located high in social space, for example, compared to 'popular music', and its more avant-garde sub-field is located towards the cultural pole of the composition axis (the highly cultured enjoy avant-garde art music, according to Bourdieu (1984), whilst the merely wealthy prefer the classics). Specific forms of capital emerge within fields, however, prompting conflicts and strategic manoeuvring which mirror those in the wider space, and this applies as much to fields located towards the bottom of social space as to those at the top. An ability to breed and train pigeons or membership of a committee of a national body for pigeon fanciers may have little value in social space writ large, for example, and may consign those who have and/ or pursue it to a lowly social position. In so far as pigeon fanciers form a social field, however, such know-how and membership will count as forms of capital within that field, and a tie to somebody who has such capital will be an important form of field-specific social capital.

As noted above, Bourdieu did not develop his concept of social capital to any great extent. His basic point, that ties provide indirect access to the resources of others, is echoed in the important work of Nan Lin (2002), however. Lin's position resembles Bourdieu's in many respects. He assumes a hierarchical and pyramid-shaped social structure with a small elite at the top. Furthermore, he stresses the importance of the inheritance of privilege through family lines, observing that children of the well-to-do often enjoy more profitable ties than those of a more lowly birth (see Lin, Ensel and Vaughn, 1981; Lin, Vaughn and Ensel, 1981). Elaborating the concept of social capital much further than Bourdieu, however, Lin observes that low-status individuals tend to profit more from weak ties, while high-status individuals benefit more from strong ties. This is because high-status people, being at the top of the pyramid, benefit from ties within their own social group. As 'in-group ties' these ties tend to be strong. Lower-status people, by contrast, benefit from ties outside of their own social group, to individuals in higher social groups. These tend to be weak ties in virtue of the circles in which high- and low-status individuals, respectively, mix (Lin, Ensel and Vaughn, 1981; Lin, Vaughn and Ensel, 1981). Low-status individuals do not ordinarily mix in elite circles and any ties they enjoy to elites are therefore usually intransitive (see Chapter One) and weak.

Lin has been a key methodological innovator in social capital research, devising means of measuring social capital, in this sense of indirect access to resources by means of social ties, which have been widely used by many researchers. Specifically, he pioneered the *position generator*: a questionnaire item which asks respondents about any ties they may have to alters in a range of social positions (generally a range of occupations). The position generator has been adapted for inclusion in a number of national surveys, allowing researchers to include social capital amongst the battery of variables that they routinely monitor in their work.

The rationale for the position generator follows directly from the social capital concept as we have discussed it above. It measures respondents' ties to potentially influential others. And it does so in much the same way that we might measure respondents' incomes or educational attainment (their economic and cultural capital). We discuss the position generator further in Chapter Three, alongside other types of 'generator', including the 'resource generator'. The *resource generator* is another tool which allows us to capture 'social capital' in the way that concept is understood by thinkers such as Bourdieu and Lin. It is a questionnaire item which seeks to determine whether respondents have ties to others to whom they might turn in an effort to secure various resources (in some cases also specifying the nature of the tie and/or other attributes of the alter(s) involved).

Social Capital as Social Cohesion

Although the term 'social capital' is of relatively recent origin, the second version of the concept that we will consider, focused upon social cohesion, has roots which track all the way back to the origins of sociology as a discipline. The focus on the transition from pre-modern to modern societies in the pioneering work of Tönnies (2003) and Durkheim (1964) was motivated in large part by a concern that urbanisation and industrialisation were destroying traditional, close-knit communities (i.e. Tönnies' '*gemeinschaft*'), in which each individual knew a high proportion of others, sharing preferences, lifestyles, a collective identity and strong affective bonds (i.e. Durkheim's 'mechanical solidarity'). The newly emerging urban centres which these early sociologists were observing had much larger populations than the villages of their ancestors and involved uprooted populations whose members were largely anonymous to one another and apparently lacking any collective identification. Traditional forms of social integration and support were swept away in the emergence of a new society (i.e. Tönnies' '*gesellschaft*'). A new form of social integration, which Durkheim (1964) called 'organic solidarity', was emerging to take their place, however. In the new order, as Durkheim envisaged it, individuals possess different resources and skills which they exchange in a division of labour. This creates interdependency between them and thereby integrative bonds.

Whether or not this new form of solidarity will fulfil the functions of its predecessor, either for the individuals involved or at the collective level, was an issue on which the classical theorists wavered and sometimes disagreed but there was at least some consensus that the process of transition itself often had negative effects at both levels, a claim explored most famously in Durkheim's (1952) study of suicide. Interaction and relations between individuals stabilise the human personality, for Durkheim, adjusting and regulating their expectations to fit their environment and providing numerous forms of support (emotional, intellectual, material, etc.) that are necessary to well-being and, indeed, survival. Furthermore, such interaction and bonding plays a crucial role in maintaining macro-social order and survival. Individuals cooperate and work together, benefiting from the pooling of their efforts and resources. Rapid social change disrupts these ties and patterns of interaction and thereby has a negative impact upon both individuals and the wider social order.

In making these observations, Durkheim directly anticipates the second of our conceptions of social capital, pioneered by Robert Putnam (2000). Social capital, for Putnam, entails strong bonds between social actors and the trust, cooperation, mutual support, sense of solidarity and belonging, etc. which such bonds tend to cultivate. Like Durkheim, Putnam believes that the existence of such bonds is beneficial to both individual and wider society, including democracy and the economy, and like Durkheim, but writing more than 100 years later, he believes that he has found evidence both of its decline and of the detrimental effects of that decline.

This 'bonding capital', as he calls it, is one of two forms of social capital that Putnam identifies. The other form, 'bridging capital', overlaps with the third definition of social capital that we will discuss: social capital as brokerage. We will briefly discuss both here before moving on to our third definition.

'Bonding capital' refers to the aforementioned benefits, individual and collective, generated by strong and close-knit ties. Individuals who belong to dense social networks (involving positive ties of cooperation, solidarity, etc.) have bonding capital for Putnam. Similarly, their network or wider community itself may be characterised as high (or low) in bonding capital, and Putnam predicts other collective goods, such as economic prosperity, where it is high. Bonding capital is not only a possession of individuals on this conception, as it is in Bourdieu's and Lin's conception. It is a property of collectives: neighbourhoods, towns, regions and even nation-states. Furthermore, its value derives from the intrinsic benefits of (positive[4]) connection between individuals rather than, as in Lin's conception, the indirect access to other resources which connection might afford.

'Bridging capital' refers to links which reach across groups or communities, facilitating a flow of ideas and resources between them and affording each community access to goods which it might not otherwise enjoy. Again this may be an individual or a collective property. An individual who moves in various different social circles enjoys bridging capital by virtue of this. They bridge their various circles and thereby benefit from access to various pools of ideas, resources, etc. In addition, however, the circles to which they belong will benefit because the individual will serve as a conduit through which resources, ideas and innovations can flow. Each of the communities to which the individual belongs will enjoy indirect access to certain of the goods of the others through the mediation of the individual and will benefit from this. Furthermore, bridges are often beneficial for Putnam because they offset segregation between distinct communities, integrating and contributing to stability and order at the level of the whole. They help to prevent strongly bonded communities from coming into conflict, to the detriment of all involved, by mediating between them.

Putnam defines social capital in a more structural fashion than either Bourdieu or Lin. Social capital, for him, is less a matter of whom you know, more a matter of patterns of connection. This is why it makes sense, from his point of view, to speak of social capital in relation to both individuals and collectives. Furthermore, for this reason, his conception is also less dependent upon a conception of wider social inequalities. Put crudely, it is better to have 'friends' than not, for Putnam, even if they are not 'friends in high places'. Poverty-stricken communities may still enjoy high levels of bonding capital even if nobody involved in the network has access to high levels of any other type of resources. In addition, bridges across communities are valuable because they contribute to peace and order, irrespective of whatever resources are exchanged across divides. If different communities or their representatives talk and strive to achieve mutual understanding, then, all things being equal, this will benefit them. Networks have intrinsic social effects and value in Putnam's conception of social capital.

Putnam does not generally use SNA measures to test and explore his thesis. He measures participation in public activities, using this as a proxy for networks. His ideas resonate with the work of other writers who do work more directly within the SNA tradition, however; who use direct network measures to explore their ideas and, in some cases, have devised new and innovative ego-net measures for doing so.

The concept of bonding capital resonates with James Coleman's (1988, 1990) important work on social capital, for example. Coleman develops a sophisticated argument to explain why and how dense and closed networks tend to cultivate trust, cooperation and mutual support between actors, creating an environment which, though constraining in certain respects, creates opportunities which would not otherwise be available for those involved. When each of an actor's alters is connected to everyother, closing their network and making it dense, he argues, that actor has a strong incentive to cooperate with their alters, offering support and proving trustworthy. To do otherwise will give them a bad reputation, which will spread quickly because of the network's high density and will prove a severe impediment to them. Everybody will become aware of ego's treachery, leading to ostracism and potentially cutting ego off from others upon whom she depends. If ego mixed in a number of different circles which were not connected, except through her, then this would be less of a problem because her bad reputation would only diffuse to a subset of her alters and she could maintain good relations with the others. When most of her alters know one another, however, which is what we mean by a dense network, all of her alters are likely to be in contact and she may be ostracised in all of her relationships, which is a considerable sanction. Mindful of this, ego has a strong incentive to cooperate.

These are constraints upon ego rather than opportunities. To the extent that each of her alters is similarly constrained, however, ego will find herself in a cooperative, supportive and trusting environment, and she will benefit from this. Her alters are constrained to help her.

One example which Coleman uses to illustrate his argument centres upon diamond traders. Their job is made much easier if sellers can lend buyers precious stones for a specified period, such that buyers can examine the stone, consider its likely resale value, etc. In many contexts this would be impossible because buyers would simply take the stone and run. A huge amount of trust is required if stones are to be lent because the risks incurred by the lender are equally huge. The diamond trading community is a very dense network, however, where everybody knows everybody else and depends upon their alters in order to operate and make a (very lucrative) living. As a consequence, the cost of 'defection', to use Coleman's game-theoretic language, outweighs any short-term gains it might entail. Traders have a strong incentive to respect the trust shown to them and, in fact, stones are often lent without any written record being kept. In other words, the diamond trading network is able to function effectively because it is dense and closed. It has social capital, as Coleman calls it, or what Putnam calls 'bonding capital', and this allows its members to behave in ways that would not otherwise be possible.

There is an element of rational choice cynicism in this argument, assuming, as it does, that individuals in a dense network only cooperate because it is strategically advantageous for them to do so; that is, because the costs of non-cooperation, in the form of sanctions, are greater and the potential benefits lower than can be achieved by cooperation. Other conceptions suggest, alternatively, that dense networks can cultivate a sense of duty amongst their members and/or a sense of solidarity and *esprit de corps*, again leading to cooperation but in a rather different way (Blumer 1969, Mead 1967). However, Coleman's argument might be thought of as a bottom line. Even if the density of a network doesn't give rise to a sense of duty and *esprit de corps*, even if network members adopt a strategic, utilitarian stance towards one another, they still have incentives to cooperate in a dense network.

Density is often measured on whole networks and in the above example that might be our preference. We might wish to take a census of diamond traders, for example, exploring who knows or trades with whom and calculating the density of this network, i.e. the total number of ties expressed as a proportion of all possible ties. As we explain in Chapter Four, however, we can measure the density of individual ego-nets too and this may be an equally useful way of exploring these issues and measuring social capital, especially if the population that we are interested in is too big to allow us to conduct a census survey. Density, whether measured on a whole network or individual ego-nets, is a measure of social capital in this respect.

In addition, a simple measure of ego-net size might help us to operationalise the concept of social capital, defined in this way. At the very least it allows us to identify egos who have a lot of connections, and thus perhaps a large supportive network to draw upon. Furthermore, it allows us to identify communities whose members typically enjoy contact with a large number of alters. If we know the size of the population and the average ego-net size within it then we can estimate the density of ties within the larger population. Furthermore, we might compare ego-net sizes across time to test claims regarding declining social capital. If samples of egos from the same population have successively fewer ties when measured at points across time this would suggest that social capital is declining – although, of course, we would have to consider other potential interpretations.

BOX 2.1

Three Ego-Net Generators Introduced in this Chapter

(Discussed further in Chapter Three)

Position Generator: Survey respondents are asked to indicate where they know others who occupy a range of social positions (e.g. occupations and/ or statuses).

Resource Generator: Survey respondents are asked to indicate who, if anyone, they would turn to in order to access a range of specified resources.

Name Generator: Survey respondents are asked to list (usually anonymously) the individuals with whom they enjoy a particular type of relation. They are usually also asked to indicate which of their alters enjoy the same (specified) type of relation with one another. They are also often asked to indicate alter attributes. The number of alters ego is allowed to specify may be restricted (e.g. to five) but this denies us the possibility of capturing ego-net size.

If these are the measures that we are going to use then we might elicit data using a simple *name generator*; that is, a questionnaire item which asks respondents to list their key alters and indicate whether those alters know one another. The question usually allows for the anonymity of alters (we are interested in their ties and possibly their attributes but not specifically who they are), and in some cases the number of alters which egos are allowed to nominate may be restricted – although that obviously prevents any proper estimate of ego-net size. In some cases, where ego-net size is very important, the diary- and directory-based methods discussed both later in this chapter and in Chapter Three may be used.

Social Capital as Brokerage

As noted above, Putnam's discussion of 'bridging capital' anticipates our third conception of social capital. Specifically, it echoes Mark Granovetter's (1973, 1974, 1982) celebrated work on 'The Strength of Weak Ties'. Focusing upon the information and favours that individuals draw upon when moving jobs, Granovetter notes that alters with whom we enjoy 'strong ties' are often less useful than those with whom we enjoy 'weak ties'. The reason for this is that those to whom we are strongly tied tend to be tied to one another (this is the phenomenon of 'transitivity' introduced in Chapter One) and therefore have access to exactly the same information as we do. We each move in the same small and insulated bubble. Alters to whom we are only weakly tied, by contrast, tend to move in different circles to us, which means that they have access to different pools of information, which may prove useful.

Ego-net research is particularly suited to capturing weak ties, when compared to whole network research (see Chapter One on the distinction), because alters to whom we are only weakly tied are unlikely to belong to the population surveyed in a whole network study and listed on the roster of names typically used in such research. They are outsiders to the main community to which ego belongs, 'hidden' and therefore best discovered through a research approach which allows individuals to nominate their alters freely, without the constraints which whole network approaches inevitably entail. Tie strength can be measured in a variety of ways in ego-net research, moreover, some of which are discussed in Chapter Three.

For the same reason and also because weak ties may not be the first people who come to ego's mind when surveyed about their contacts (on account of weak connection), the qualitative approaches to ego-net research outlined in Chapter Six might also be useful for digging out weak ties. Granovetter draws upon qualitative data in his classic work and some of the weak ties he discusses are so vaguely and tentatively related to ego (e.g. the sister of somebody who attended university with ego ten years previously) that they are only ever likely to surface in qualitative research focused upon the specific processes in which weak ties are mobilised (such as 'Getting a Job', to cite the title of Granovetter's 1974 book). We can identify some weak ties by way of a standard (quantitative) survey, however, as we discuss in Chapter Three.

A similar but more general argument to Granovetter's is made by Ronald Burt (1992, 2005) in his celebrated work on 'structural holes' and 'brokerage'. A structural hole, as defined by Burt, is a gap or absence of ties between clusters of nodes (between 'components' (see Chapter One)) within a network. A broker is an individual who manages to bridge one or more such holes, mediating between the parties involved, usually to the mutual benefit of all involved (but perhaps to their own benefit most of all). A broker is the conduit through which resources, ideas and information can pass from one cluster or community to the other. Burt believes that dense and closed networks, of the kind which Coleman celebrates, have a tendency to stagnate because they are closed to the inflow of new ideas and other resources. Echoing Granovetter, he claims that ties within them are 'redundant' because they all lead to the same, restricted destinations. Brokers change this. They facilitate new inflow. This is beneficial to the groups to whom they belong, who get access to this inflow (of ideas, information or other resources) and it is beneficial to the individual herself. She will often be rewarded for affording her alters access to otherwise inaccessible resources and information and may sometimes be mistakenly attributed status as the source of ideas and innovation which, in fact, she is only passing on. Brokerage, for Burt, is a form of social capital.

In the earlier of his two main accounts of this process Burt (1992) appears to pit his concept of brokerage as social capital against the focus upon density and closure in the work of Coleman and others. In more recent work, however, he has argued that 'brokerage' and 'closure' each have both strengths and weaknesses such that either might count as social capital in a given situation and such that the ideal situation is one in which both occur together, with a single broker linking two or more otherwise closed and dense networks (Burt 2005).

As with density and closure, Burt's concepts of structural holes and brokerage can be mapped and measured in the context of whole networks. Much of his own work has adopted an ego-net approach, however, and in Chapter Four we discuss a number of the measures which he has introduced for the purposes of capturing and quantifying the extent to which an ego bridges structural holes and is well placed within their network to play a brokerage role. Specifically we discuss effective size, a measure which seeks to distinguish redundant and non-redundant ties, and we discuss constraint, which builds upon the concept of ego-net density to further specify the room for manoeuvre which actors have within their networks.

BOX 2.2

Three Definitions of Social Capital

	RESOURCES	COHESION	BROKERAGE
Brief description	Social ties afford indirect access to resources which ego does not directly possess (i.e. the resources of others).	Dense networks of strong ties support ego in various ways and contribute to social integration.	Ties which bridge structural holes facilitate the flow of ideas, resources, etc. across those holes, benefiting the communities bridged and also the bridging individual.
Key writers	Bourdieu (1986), Lin (2002).	Coleman (1988, 1990), Putnam (2000) (on 'bonding capital').	Burt (1992, 2005), Granovetter (1973, 1974, 1982), Putnam (2000) (on 'bridging capital').
Key methods of (ego-net) elicitation	Position generator, resource generator.	Name generator, diary- and directory-based methods.	Name generator.
Key measures	Number of positions/resources, especially 'high' positions and rare resources, accessed.	Ego-net size and density.	Effective size and constraint.

Is Social Capital Declining?

Before we conclude this discussion of social capital it is important to briefly note that Putnam's claims regarding the decline of social capital, like the claims of Durkheim and Tönnies before them, have been hotly contested and are by no means universally accepted. The claims of the classic writers were offset, albeit indirectly, by Simmel (1955, 1971), whose work explores the multiple relational forms and contexts of modern societies, and more directly by the writers of the Chicago School, who were influenced by Simmel (Bulmer 1984). Claude Fischer (1975, 1982a, 1982b, 1995), a contemporary network analyst who draws strongly upon the Chicago School in his own work, captures the main message of their work, at least with respect to this theme, when he argues that the modern city is not a community but rather a patchwork of multiple communities (he also sometimes says 'worlds' or 'sub-cultures'), all rubbing up against one another. Urbanisation has created opportunities for genuine community formation in Fischer's view because minorities (e.g. ethnic, sexual or interest-based minorities) tend to exist in large enough numbers, within the huge, concentrated population of the city, to form the critical mass necessary to give rise to a community. Traditional *gemeinschaft* were communities of convenience which were often insensitive to the needs of minorities within them, from this perspective, and minorities had no choice but to try to fit in because they did not exist in big enough numbers to do otherwise. In big cities, by contrast, minorities can hook up and form their own communities, communities which are more meaningful because of this.

Fischer's work belongs to a long tradition of research on urban networks in SNA, much of which has challenged the idea that individuals in contemporary societies are less connected than they once were (Laumann 1973, Wellman 1979, 1985, Wellman and Whitaker 1974, Wellman et al. 1991). As the concept of social capital has gained currency in social science (and beyond) and as writers such as Putnam have argued that it is in decline, these researchers, often adopting an ego–net approach and comparing their findings to the findings of early work, have sought to rebut these claims too. The nature of social relations may very well have changed as a consequence of increased geographical mobility and new technologies, it is conceded, but the average individual is no less well-connected than she ever was.

Small Worlds

The small world idea is perhaps best known under the rubric of 'six degrees of separation'. The idea is that any two individuals picked at random from a population will be linked, *on average*, by a chain of only five intermediaries (and thus a path of six ties or 'degrees'[5]) in a chain of mutual acquaintances (see Box 2.3). This idea, which has a long history, has been an important focus in complexity science in recent years (Crossley 2005, 2008a, Newman et al. 2006, Scott 2011). Accepting the empirical truth of the six degrees claim, believing it to hold across a range of large complex systems and being interested in it because it would help to explain coordination in such systems,[6] complexity scientists have asked how it is that a system or network involving hundreds of millions of nodes could be characterised by such short path lengths? Six degrees sounds very short and many scientists claim that they would have guessed a much longer average path length. Two plausible models have been suggested to explain this counter-intuitive finding, the first centred upon Granovetter's notion of weak and intransitive ties (Watts 1999, 2004), the second centred upon the notion of network hubs which provide a central link-point between a huge number of others (Barabási 2003). More relevant for our purposes, however, is the role which social psychologist Stanley Milgram, plays in this story.

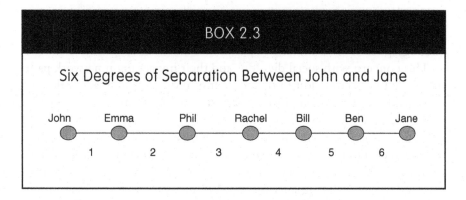

It was Milgram who produced the empirical evidence to suggest that any two individuals picked at random from a national population (in his case the USA) are separated, on average, by a mere six degrees of separation. He conducted a series of experiments in which individuals were invited to initiate a chain letter with the purpose, ultimately, of reaching a target individual in another city. Assuming that the randomly picked 'starter' didn't directly know the 'target' on first-name terms (in which case they would contact them immediately), they were instructed to post on a folder of documents to somebody whom they knew on a first-name basis and who they thought might know the target individual or might know somebody who knew them. This second individual was then asked to do the same and so on until the target individual was contacted. Where the chain completed, Milgram found, its average length involved 5.2 intermediaries.

The completion rate was not great. In one run, for example, only 217 out of 296 starters actually started and only 64 chains completed (Travers and Milgram 1969). However, Milgram found similar results across several studies, his findings have been confirmed by subsequent studies (Kochen 1989, Dodds et al. 2003) and the complexity scientists referred to above have found similar results in other, similarly large networks in the non-human world (Barabási 2003, Newman et al. 2006, Watts 1999, 2004). Milgram was certainly on to something.

The purpose of Milgram's experiment was to explore the properties of the social structure of the USA. In part this was a matter of measuring basic network properties, especially average path lengths. However, Milgram and his colleagues were also interested in the division of the social body into different status groups and the contact or lack of contact between those groups. They observe, for example, that letters generally crossed geographical distances much more easily than they traversed the 'social distance' constituted by racial divisions. Often a letter which was required to cross both a large geographical distance and a racial divide would make it to the town of the target individual quite quickly but then circle repeatedly without ever crossing the racial divide. Geographical space proved much easier to traverse than social space and for Milgram and his colleagues this revealed an important property of social structure, namely, racial division and segregation.

This concern with social divisions and their impact upon network paths has tended to become lost in the context of more recent 'small world' discussions. In so far as complexity scientists have maintained an interest in social structure they have tended to reduce it to basic network metrics, and in particular path lengths. The identities and status differences that mediate ties between human actors, making them more or less likely, has received almost no consideration. They were central for Milgram, however: part of the *raison d'être* for his small world studies and integral to what he meant by 'social structure'. And one reason for discussing Milgram here is to flag their general importance for ego-net research in social science. Often in ego-net research we will ask ego to indicate a variety of statuses (gender, ethnicity, age, etc.) for both themselves and their nominated alters, and we will be interested in the extent to which their ties traverse status divides. As noted earlier in this book, where individuals disproportionately form ties with others who are similar to themselves in some respect, we term this 'homophily'. We discuss ways of measuring homophily in Chapter Four.

In addition to identifying the importance of homophily, Milgram's work is important for our introduction to ego-net analysis for a number of other reasons. Firstly, it introduces a particular method of snowballing from multiple ('starter') ego-nets for purposes of exploring 'whole network' properties that would not ordinarily be available to an ego-net study. In Chapter One we claimed that one of the advantages of ego-net research is that it allows us to study big networks by sampling from their node populations. One way to do this is by way of random sampling, which has the advantage of meeting the assumptions of most standard forms of statistical analysis and modelling, thus allowing us to integrate network considerations into a broader survey study. Milgram suggests another approach, however, and this approach has the advantage of allowing us to explore whole network properties, principally path lengths, which a random sample does not.

Secondly, Milgram shows us that when ties are loosely defined (i.e. people whom you know on a first-name basis), everybody in the world is connected to everybody else, often at a relatively short distance. This highlights the importance of drawing boundaries in network-focused studies and of being careful how we define ties. If we do not give careful consideration to boundaries and the definition of the ties which interest us, then the networks we find ourselves analysing may become very big indeed! Furthermore, Milgram alerts us to the importance of correctly ascertaining the meaning of ties. His experiments defined ties in a very loose way, allowing participants to call upon alters whom they did not know very well, were not very strongly connected to and did not interact with on a regular basis. Had ties been defined in a different, stricter way then a very different network structure might have been suggested. Milgram underlines the significance of this point himself:

> Almost anyone in the United States is but a few removes from the President, or from [super rich] Nelson Rockefeller, but this is true only in terms of a particular mathematical viewpoint and does not, in any practical sense, integrate our lives with [theirs]. (Milgram 1967: 117)

This quotation underlines the importance of reflecting upon and analysing the meaning and 'content' of the ties we analyse. As we explain in Chapter Six, qualitative approaches are often the best way to achieve this.

Finally, Milgram's work is important because it begs important questions about the size of individuals' networks and the ways in which they use and search within those networks for the purposes of (in this case) trying to reach a target individual. Prior to Milgram's study researchers had addressed some of the questions regarding social structure that he addressed by way of a reflection upon size of individual ego-nets. If we know both the size of a population and the average ego-net size of the members of that population then we can begin, albeit making certain assumptions and encountering various problems, to estimate certain properties of the network linking members of that population. Milgram moved that particular research agenda on but the question, 'How many people does the average person know?', though undoubtedly a very sticky question which hangs on exactly what we mean by 'know', remains important within network analysis.

Various methods have been devised for addressing this issue. These can be subdivided into *techniques of elicitation*, which help respondents to construct often very large lists of alters, and *techniques of scaling up*, which extrapolate from the constraints (e.g. time constraints, respondent patience, sampling, etc.) of such exercises and estimate how long a list might have been if produced in their absence (see Bernard et al. 1990 and Killworth et al. 1990 for a good overview). Elicitation methods include diary-based approaches, where individuals note all of their contacts over a specified period, and directory-based methods, where respondents are presented with a (usually large) sample of individuals from a particular sampling frame and are asked either to indicate whether they know anybody from the sample or anybody with the same or a similar name.

In the days of telephone directories, for example, respondents were typically presented with random pages from a directory and asked to indicate if they knew one or more people with a surname on the page. Researchers counted how many people they claimed to know and then scaled this up, determining how many people would have been nominated if the respondent had looked at every page of the directory. Degenne and Forsé (1994) suggest that the average network size estimated in such studies was 5,520 (see also Freeman and Thompson 1989). However, variations in estimates gleaned by using different telephone directories pointed to potential biases in this approach. As telephone directories are a thing of the past and readers are unlikely to use them, we will skip over these problems and the fixes suggested for them. It must suffice to point out that any study of this kind, like any study more generally, is only as good as its sample and sampling frame.

One very interesting way of exploring network size that we should briefly discuss before concluding this chapter, however, is the 'reverse small world experiment' devised by Killworth and Bernard (1978/9, Killworth et al. 1984). As its name suggests, this method reverses, or at least partially reverses, the procedure adopted by Milgram. Where Milgram asked a large number of starters to initiate a chain centred upon a single target individual, Killworth and Bernard presented 58 starters with 1,267 different (fictional) targets each,[7] asking them who they would approach as a first link in a chain intended to reach this target (these first links were not contacted and there was no intention to continue chains any further or measure path lengths). Targets were said to reside in different locations and clues suggested that they represented a variety of different statuses (ethnic, occupational, gender, etc.). From the responses given, Killworth and Bernard were able to: 1) measure network size by counting the number of different 'first links' starters nominated overall; 2) observe the frequency with which different 'first links' were used; 3) explore the ways in which starters used and searched their networks (did they match on geography or status for example?); and 4) observe how status divides were negotiated.

Many of the methods used to address the 'How big?' question suggest that ego–nets are very big. Killworth and Bernard report an average of 210 first-links in their work but the telephone directory studies discussed above, as noted, regularly point to network sizes in excess of 5,000. This is a lot of contacts and it is fairly obvious that the vast majority of these ties will be 'weak ties', in Granovetter's sense, and mostly latent; that is, characters from an individual's past, whom they no longer see on a regular basis but whom they might recognise and start up a conversation with were they to meet them in the street. This is a very loose definition of a tie and were we to tighten it the number of alters would drop dramatically. How far it would drop would depend upon just how we tightened and specified 'tie'.

Individuals have many fewer strong ties because strong ties generally have to be maintained by those party to them, using up scarce resources, not least time and energy. Furthermore, some have argued that there are cognitive limitations to the size of a network that any one human being can know with any degree of reliability, and thus with the size of network of meaningful, strong and stable ties we can maintain. There have been various estimates of this size and they vary markedly. The best known of the estimates, however, is 'Dunbar's number'. Anthropologist, Robin Dunbar estimates that humanbeings are capable, cognitively, of maintaining an ego–net comprising 150 alters (Dunbar 1992).

Summary

In this chapter we have laid the foundation and explored the background for much that follows in the book by discussing two key foci in recent work on social networks: social capital and small worlds. We have introduced a number of techniques for eliciting data on ego–nets (e.g. resource and position generators, the reverse small world), and a number of measures of ego–net properties (e.g. ego–net density, effective size and constraint). In what follows we will return to and build upon these foundations.

Notes

1. Bourdieu develops his concept of habitus across a number of works (see, for example, Bourdieu 1984 and Bourdieu 1992). Habitus are intelligent and purposive dispositions which social actors acquire through experience of particular types of situation, initially in childhood. They are ways in which actors are formed by the situations into which they are born and they operate beneath the level of conscious reflection.
2. Although Bourdieu refers to a large number of forms of capital across his various works, much of his theoretical work and his concept of social space in particular seems to centre exclusively upon economic and cultural capital.
3. Bourdieu also focuses upon the way in which representations of social groups, formed by political parties, academics and the media, in so far as they mobilise a sense of group consciousness, contribute to the formation of a group. He suggests, for example, that trade unions and labour parties contributed to the formation of the working class.
4. Obviously ties can be negative (warring nations have a tie, as do bullies and their victims). Negative ties would not ordinarily contribute to social capital.
5. Ties are referred to as 'degrees' in this context. If two individuals, John and Jane, are linked by five intermediaries then there are six ties (six degrees) separating them.
6. If, as one might imagine, nodes in a large network were separated by very long paths then communication between them would be slow, inefficient and liable to error. This would hamper coordination. The shorter the average path length within a network the less likely, all other things being equal, these problems are and the greater the probability of good coordination.
7. Needless to say, respondents completed this exercise in a number of sessions over time.

3

GETTING EGO-NETS

Learning Outcomes

By the end of the chapter you will:

1. Understand the three key methods for eliciting ego-net data which were briefly introduced in the previous chapter (i.e. position, resource and name generators).

2. Have the knowledge to construct your own data collection tool, choosing the method most appropriate for your research questions, the type of boundaries and the reachability of the population that characterises your study.

3. Be able to critically reflect upon various ways in which ego-net data can be collected: surveys, qualitative interviews, ethnographic observations, archival data and electronic sources.

4. Be capable of reflecting upon the accuracy of ego-net data collection strategies.

Introduction

In this chapter we present some of the most popular methods and techniques for gathering ego–net data. The main technique focused upon is the *name generator*, which is the most common, at least where researchers need or want information on network structure. A brief introduction to other popular methods, including *position generators* and *resource generators*, is also provided, however, and, in addition, we consider means of gathering data from both electronic and more open-ended, 'qualitative'[1] sources.

Where relevant we will link our discussion of these various methods to the theoretical discussion of social capital in the previous chapter, demonstrating how they operationalise that concept, in its various forms, empirically. Ego–net data is not only gathered for purposes of exploring social capital, however, and the name generator in particular opens out the possibility of network-focused research oriented to different research agendas. We will try to draw out this possibility too.

The chapter is organised as follows. Section one provides an overview of data collection tools that allow one to measure social capital in the first of the senses discussed in Chapter Two; namely, as indirect access to resources. The two tools discussed are the position generator and the resource generator. These tools do not allow one to collect full structural data. However, they constitute a relatively quick and effective way of exploring indirect access to a wide range of statuses and resources amongst a large sample of individuals, and they can be relatively easily added into standard questionnaires. As this suits the needs of many researchers and corresponds to what they mean by 'social capital' and 'networks' they are often ideal tools.

Section two presents the name generator tool, which allows the collection of structural data (ego–alter ties, and alter–alter ties) for a selected number of egos. This method allows us to capture the density of ego–nets and also the presence of structural holes (see Chapters Two and Four), therefore constituting the best instrument to investigate social capital, where it is conceptualised in terms of either social cohesion and/or brokerage (see Chapter Two). Again, egos can be randomly sampled when researchers use this tool and results can therefore be generalised in accordance with standard statistical guidelines.

Section three discusses various more 'qualitative'[2] ways of gathering ego–net data, e.g. using qualitative interviews, ethnographic observations, archival material, and online/electronic sources. Such methodological approaches are discussed in light of the advantages and limitations that they offer for ego–net studies, in particular reflecting upon boundary specifications and the reachability of populations.

The chapter concludes with some observations on the accuracy of ego–net data, an area of research that has produced interesting results and can be extremely useful in planning and conducting a network study.

Indirect Access to Resources

The Position Generator

As noted in Chapter Two, one conception of social capital, associated both with Pierre Bourdieu and Nan Lin, understands ties to others to be of value in so far as they provide indirect access to resources which ego does not directly own or control. An important tool for measuring social capital, defined in this way, is the 'position generator', first suggested by Lin and Dumin (1986). The instrument looks like a normal questionnaire item (see Table 3.1). Respondents are asked to indicate where they have a tie to another who holds any of a list of 20 occupations (Lin and Dumin 1986: 371). As the authors point out, the operationalisation of 'access to social resources' through a selected set of occupations had already been adopted by Laumann (1966) in his examination of social distance. Lin and Dumin name this approach, however, and are commonly identified as its originators.

Having elicited a list of alters in this way, researchers may ask further questions regarding the attributes of those alters and/or the nature of their relation to ego. Is alter a family member, for example, or a friend? Is she female? How old is she (approximately)? By comparing alter attributes against ego's own attributes, which will usually have been collected elsewhere in the questionnaire, moreover, the researcher can reflect upon and measure homophily in their egos' networks (on homophily measures see Chapter Four).

The list of occupations used in a position generator has to be adapted and validated for the specific social context in which the research takes place. For example, Lin and Dumin compiled their list of occupations after an examination of the frequency distributions of occupations in the American labour force from the 1970 Census of Population, Classified Index of Occupations (Lin and Dumin 1986: 371). Anybody wishing to a use a position generator for a different context will have to undertake similar checks for that context – although the widespread use of position generators in large national surveys in many countries these days provides a useful source of 'off the peg' options. Furthermore, lists of positions may be manipulated to suit specific research interests and questions.

The position generator is directly rooted in Lin's conception of social capital (as indirect access to resources), which was discussed in Chapter Two. It also provides a useful way of operationalising Bourdieu's conception of social capital for purposes of empirical research, not least as Bourdieu's and Lin's respective conceptions of social capital are quite similar (see Chapter Two). Note, however, that the position generator asks about ties to alters who occupy particular social positions (on the assumption that they will be in possession of certain key resources) rather than asking directly about (indirect) access to resources. This may be advantageous if we are interested in the circles in which ego mixes or the reflected glory that derives from knowing prestigious alters. If we are specifically interested in access to particular resources, however, then a more direct approach may be preferable. One such approach is the *resource generator*.

The Resource Generator

A similar tool to the position generator, the resource generator, first devised by Van der Gaag and Snijders (2003), measures the access to specific

Table 3.1 Position generator for measuring accessed social capital: an example (Lin 1999: 39)

Here is a list of jobs (show card). Would you please tell me if you happen to know someone (on a first-name basis) having each job?

Job	1. Do you know anyone having this job?*	2. How long have you known this person? (# of years)	3. What is your relationship with this person?	4. How close are you with this person?	5. His/her gender	6. His/her Ethnicity	7. Do you think you may find such a person through someone you know? (Person M)	8. Repeat #2–6 for Person M
Lawyer	Yes	3	Relative	Very close	F	Asian		
Policeman	No						Person M	#2–6
Teacher	No						No	
Etc.								

*If you know more than one person, think of the one person whom you have known the longest (or the person who comes to mind first) resources which their ties to others afford egos. Like the position generator, the resource generator measures potential access to social resources instead of their effective mobilisation. Unlike the position generator, however, which relies exclusively on the assumed importance of job prestige for the interpretation of results, resource generators directly investigate the link between ties and resources (Van der Gaag and Snijders 2003: 3). It does so by asking respondents about their access to a fixed list of resources representing concrete items of social capital, e.g. do they know anyone who can fix a bike, who owns a car, who can play an instrument, who reads professional journals, who is active in a political party, who owns a holiday home abroad, who knows about governmental regulations or financial matters, who has contact with the media, who can do small jobs around the house, and so on, for a total of 37 items. The strength of the tie involved is often measured by its type, i.e. is alter a family member, friend, acquaintance, etc? An example of what the instrument looks like can be seen in Table 3.2.

The resource generator assumes that the connections constitutive of social capital are multiplex, a claim which Putnam (2000) makes too. Where Putnam suggests that this entails that social capital can only be indirectly observed by the common tendency of its indicators to collectively increase or decline, however, Van der Gaag and Snijders suggest that we explore the correlations between various strands:

> positive correlations between resource items in some group of items indicate that individuals who access one of these items also have a high probability of accessing other items from that group. (Van der Gaag and Snijders 2003: 10)

Using this approach and focusing upon data from the Netherlands, Van der Gaag and Snijders identify four distinct domains of social capital: 1) prestige and education related; 2) entrepreneurial; 3) skills-focused; and 4) personal support social capital.

The position and resource generators are both good instruments for measuring social capital when it is defined as indirect access to resources, especially where weak ties are involved (Marsden 1990). In addition, they are valid tools for investigating questions related to, for example, social support, power and influence (Bidart and Charbonneau 2011); they have the advantage of being firmly rooted in theory (Van der Gaag and Webber 2008); and each can be adapted to address different research questions and social contexts. Grounded in the idea of a hierarchically modelled society, for example, the position generator can be robustly operationalised and

Table 3.2 Resource generator for measuring accessed social capital: an example (Van der Gaag and Snijders 2003: 42)

		If yes, access through:			And yourself?
Do you know anyone who:	Yes	Acquaintance	Friend	Family member	Yes
Can repair a car, bike, etc?	✓		✓		
Owns a car?	✓			✓	✓
Can play an instrument?					
Reads professional journals?					
Is active in a political party?	✓	✓			
Etc.					

systematically adapted to 'every society in which occupations, occupational prestige or job-related socioeconomic indices have been catalogued' (Van der Gaag and Webber 2008: 40). Similarly, the check list of resources employed in the resource generator can be modified to accommodate both different research foci and different social worlds. Both tools are limited, however, in the respect that they only measure network diversity and range. Neither provides information on network structure. If we want information on network structure, as is required by the other definitions of social capital that we considered in Chapter Two and, indeed, as may be important for various other purposes, then we must look to the name generator.

BOX 3.1

Position and Resource Generators

Position and resource generators are data collection tools that allow us to explore the ways in which social ties afford ego indirect access to resources she may either desire or need. As such they operationalise the concept of social capital, as theorised by both Pierre Bourdieu and Nan Lin (see Chapter Two). They differ in the respect that the position generator asks ego whether they enjoy ties to alters in any of a range of nominated social positions, whilst the resource generator asks if they would have anybody to turn to should they need to access one or more of a range of resources.

The Name Generator

The name generator usually involves three elements (Agneessens 2006):

- **Alters**:The name generator collects information on ego's relevant alters.

- **Structure**: It collects information about relationships between these alters.

- **Alter Attributes**: It collects basic information about the alters.

The first and the second elements (alters and structure) are essential for this approach. The third isn't essential but is commonly included. In what follows we consider each element in turn.

Alters

Interviewees are asked to list either all or a set number of people with whom they enjoy a particular type of relation, for example: all of the people they consider friends; all the people they might ask for advice about a particular issue; all the people they would trust enough to lend money to, and so on. Name generators can investigate emotional and intimate support, by asking whom ego would discuss important matters with, or whom they feel close to. They can focus on companionship, by asking whom ego likes to socialise with. They can map material support, by asking who helps ego in looking after the house, or gives them a lift to work. They can track information exchange, by asking whom ego seeks information from about specific topics. Furthermore, the direction of the relationship can be reversed, e.g. by asking ego whom they provide these forms of support to.

Most network studies in this tradition have focused on positive rather than negative ties (Wellman 1981). Ties are not always beneficial, however. People can be overwhelmed, annoyed and/or exploited by their alters, and there are some studies that have investigated relations with alters who are overly demanding, who are highly likely to let ego down or who upset or anger her (Leffler et al. 1986). These latter studies fit with a broader stream of work on the effects of 'negative ties' (Dewall 2013, Labianca et al. 1998, Labianca and Brass 2006, Read 1954, Smith et al. 2014). A focus upon negative ties may be entirely appropriate for some research purposes. In contrast to much of what we have discussed hitherto, however, such research is unlikely to be focused upon 'social capital'. It is social network analysis, or ego–net analysis but it explores other aspects of networks than that captured by the concept of social capital.

Respondents usually need to work with real names when filling in a name generator, in order to identify for themselves who they are talking about. However, the researcher generally has no need for these proper names and accessing and storing them raises ethical problems which are best avoided if possible (not least as alters are not generally approached for their consent). Consequently, interviewees are usually asked to erase names before passing data on or to use initials or meaningful (to the respondent) pseudonyms which reduce the likelihood of identification by the researcher.

Name generators may allow respondents to nominate as many alters as they wish or feel to be relevant. However, as noted above, in some cases researchers limit the number of alters that ego is able to nominate. The latter approach has the advantage of limiting the time that will be required to complete the questionnaire. The former may require a lot of time. However, the former, open-ended approach has the advantage of allowing the researcher an opportunity to derive a better sense of ego's network size and may also reach further into ego's network, beyond their immediate circle and towards weaker ties. A further way of limiting the number of alters that ego nominates is to specify a time-frame within which ego and alter have enjoyed contact, e.g. 'people you have talked to about x within the last six months' (Burt 1984).

Name generators can focus upon one or more of a number of types and aspects of ties. They can focus upon *the content of exchange* between people, by asking whom ego discusses important matters with, or socialises with (exchange approach); *the role of the relationship,* by asking ego to list friends, neighbours, co-workers, and so on (role-relational approach); *the strength of the relation,* by asking whom ego feels especially close to (affective approach); *the frequency of communication,* by asking whom ego is in contact with (how often, via which media) over a certain period of time (interactional approach); and *the locality of ties,* by asking who lives nearby or in the same geographical area (geographical approach).

Some scholars have investigated the effects of using these different approaches on the type and quality of data obtained. Van Sonderen and colleagues (1989), for example, compared the size and overlap of ego-nets obtained using the affective, exchange and role-relational approaches. They found that the exchange approach elicits a larger number of alters, due to its ability to reach weaker ties. Of the exchange ties elicited in their study, 46% were also obtained from the affective approach. Conversely, 73% of names obtained from the affective approach were also named in the exchange approach. Similar results were obtained by Campbell and Lee (1991), who observed that the affective approach elicits smaller networks than either the content or role-focused approaches. They extended their analysis to the composition of the networks but did not report any differences associated with a specific name generator. However, they did note that the 'density' (see Chapters One and Four) of the ego-net increases when alters are characterised by residential proximity and closeness to ego, meaning that the closer they live and the stronger the tie to the focal actor, the more likely it is for alters to know each other.[3] Spatial proximity also increases the frequency of contacts.

In related research, Marin and Hampton (2007) observe that the names elicited with the interaction approach are not correlated with the ones obtained from the affective approach, and that the affective approach is good for measuring strong ties. They also note that the role-relational and affective approaches may be open to different interpretations, especially where there is no common agreement over the meaning of particular terms, e.g. 'friend' or 'close friend' (see also Fischer, 1982b). By comparison, the exchange approach seems to be less prone to the ambiguity of terms, improving the validity and reliability of the instrument (Marin and Hampton, 2007). Questions asking about tie attributes are referred to as *tie interpreters*.

Researchers might decide to explore a single tie type. Alternatively they may use the name generator several times in the same interview, to cover different areas of an ego-net. If they do ask about multiple relations, moreover, they will typically design questions in such a way as to capture overlap and thus multiplexity; that is, they will seek to identify which alters enjoy what combination of tie types with ego. Finally, tie strength can also be measured by asking the respondent to indicate how close they are to each of the persons named or by asking about the frequency of interaction (Table 3.3).

The questions asked on a name generator and the type of relation explored may overlap, in practice, with those covered on a resource generator. We may, for example, ask whom ego relies upon for financial support. The difference between the two, in part, derives from the further questions which the name generator asks about structure (see below). In addition, however, where the resource generator typically only records whether ego has a single alter who can provide a certain resource, the name generator allows ego to record numerous alters who may afford access to the same resource. Furthermore, as noted above, it allows us to identify alters who provide indirect access to a range of resources, enabling an analysis of multiplexity. Finally, the types of ties elicited by means of a name generator are not all necessarily related to access to resources, nor indeed to social capital. At least this may not be the rationale for asking about them. From the point of view of certain sociological theories ego will only ever enter into a relationship if they get something out of it and it is to their advantage. This is not always how egos see things, however, and the name generator does not require us to make that assumption.

Structure

Once a list of alters is elicited the respondent is asked to report about relationships that link every pair of alters named (Table 3.4). Questions about the type of relationship may vary. Wellman, in his first East York

Table 3.3   Example of name generators

Could you please list the names of all the people/up to six names of the people

| | With whom you discuss matters important to you/have discussed in the last 6 months | | | You often socialise with in your spare time/have socialised in the last 6 months | | | You ask for advice on working-related matters/asked in the last 6 months | | |
| | How often? | | | How often? | | | How often? | | |
	Daily	Weekly	Monthly	Daily	Weekly	Monthly	Daily	Weekly	Monthly
Bill	✓			✓					
Bob			✓					✓	
Carol					✓		✓		
Ann									
…/up to six									

study (1968), asked which alters are close to each other, by listing every possible pair. Fischer (1982a), in a similar study in California, asked (for each pair) if person one and person two knew each other well. In other cases, the question may simply ask if two pairs of alters have a relationship independent from ego; for example, by asking if they would acknowledge each other if casually meeting in the street. Burt (1984), in the design of ego-net questions for the General Social Survey, asked for the strength of alter-alter ties, measured on a three-point scale of 1) strangers, 2) moderate friends and 3) close friends.

Eliciting alter-alter ties is crucial if we are to identify and explore the structure of an ego-net. Most of the measures discussed in Chapter Four rely upon this information.

Table 3.4   Example of alter-alter questionnaire

	Yes
Does Bill know Bob?	✓
Does Bill know Carol?	✓
Does Bill know Ann?	✓
Does Bob know Carol?	
Does Bob know Ann?	
Does Carol know Ann?	✓

Alter Attributes

Once the structure of the ego-net is elicited, researchers often ask about the characteristics of alters. If role relations have not already been asked about, for example, then they may ask about this: is each alter a friend, family member, co-worker, neighbour, etc.? They might ask about demographic characteristics and status: gender, age, place of residence, place of birth, educational background, e.g. occupational status, income, etc. Indeed, questions can relate to any aspect of alter's life, outlook and/or behaviour that ego is likely to know about, e.g. attitudes, tastes, hobbies, habits, etc. Such information might be used to explore the composition of an ego-net and it can also be compared both with ego's characteristics and across alters in order to investigate homophily within the network (Table 3.5) (on the concept of homophily see Chapter One; on homophily measures see Chapter Four). Questions asking about alter attributes are referred to as *name interpreters*.

Table 3.5 Example of name interpreters

Is:	A relative	A friend	A co-worker	Gender	Age
Bill	✓			M	40
Bob		✓		M	36
Carol			✓	F	25
Ann			✓	F	55

BOX 3.2

The Name Generator

The name generator is a data collection tool which asks egos to nominate alters with whom they enjoy a particular type (or types) of relation and which further elicits both information on relevant ties between alters and also information on alters' salient attributes. Because it generates information on the structure of ego-nets, the name generator can be used to capture both the cohesion and the brokerage-focused conception of social capital which were discussed in Chapter Two. Importantly, however, ego-net data gathered by means of a name generator may be used for a variety of research purposes beyond the exploration of social capital, including a focus upon negative and damaging relations.

Social Capital and Beyond

In Chapter Two, in addition to discussing conceptions of social capital focused upon indirect access to resources, we discussed conceptions centred upon: cohesion and ego-net density (Coleman's conception); brokerage and structural holes (Burt's early conception); and advantageous combinations of cohesion and brokerage (Burt's later conception). Because they do not record alter–alter ties, position and resource generators do not allow us to operationalise these latter conceptions. Name generators do, however, because they do record alter–alter ties. They give us the structure of an ego-net.

In Chapter Four we discuss a number of measures, which can be derived from name generator data, which capture both ego-net cohesion and structural holes/brokerage. We should state explicitly here, however, that, again distinguishing data from the position and resource generators, data gathered by means of a name generator may serve a variety of research agendas beyond those specifically focused upon social capital. Debates on social capital have stimulated a huge amount of research on ego-nets (and social networks more widely), which is why we provided an overview of the concept in the previous chapter, but work using the name generator pre-dates interest in social capital and the tool is multi-purpose, facilitating investigation of a wide range of network-focused network topics.

Second-Order Zones[4]

An ego-net is sometimes referred to as a 'first-order zone' (Barnes 1969). An ego's second-order zone would involve the alters nominated by their alters (e.g. their friends' friends). If ideas about transitivity (see Chapter One) are correct then we would expect many of ego's friends' friends to be ego's own friends and thus included in her first-order zone. However, we would not expect perfect overlap, and introduction of new alters into the picture, at a distance of two degrees from ego, might prove very interesting. Ego might be found to have indirect access to more and greater resources than is apparent from a survey of her first-order zone, for example, or might be found to be vulnerable to previously unseen dangers (e.g. infectious diseases).

Tracking ego-nets into their second-order zones is a very difficult and both time- and labour-intensive task, however, and is sufficiently rare in practice that we will not pursue it further in this book. For readers wishing to take this possibility further some interesting examples of research exploring second-order zones can be found in Heath et al. (2009), Schweizer et al. (1998) and Uehara (1994).

Name Generators in Survey Research

Name generators are mostly used in the context of large sample surveys. Their earliest use dates back to the late 1960s. In 1965, for example, Laumann (1973) conducted a survey of 1,013 native-born white men between the ages of 21 and 64, living in the greater metropolitan area of Detroit. He asked them about their three closest contacts. At more or less the same time, Wellman (1969) was creating a survey schedule (for his PhD) that asked Pittsburgh ninth-grade adolescents about their network. Building upon this, Wellman subsequently designed the sociological component of the well-known East York studies, in collaboration with the psychiatrist Donald Coates (Wellman 1993). In these seminal studies, administered in 1967 and 1968, Wellman surveyed 845 respondents, asking for the names of all the people living in their household, and the initials of the people outside the household whom they felt closest to (whether friends, neighbours or relatives). Structural information was only gathered on the first six people nominated but the list of further names allowed Wellman to explore and measure network size. Alongside these lists and structural information on the first six alters, Wellman also asked about a wide range of alter attributes (role, sex, occupation, where they lived) and the frequency, means and reason for contact between ego and alter (how often they were seen, how often they were contacted by phone or letter, whom they got together with informally, who provided help for everyday matters or in case of emergencies) (Wellman and Whitaker 1974, Wellman 1985, Wellman et al. 1991).

While the East York study adopted a single name generator, Fischer (1982a), in his study of personal networks in 50 urban and rural Northern California communities, surveyed 1,050 adults about their support networks (emotional, companionship, material). He used ten different name generators and 19 name and tie interpreters. Eight of the interpreters asked about all named alters, while 11 asked about the first five only (gaining details about how long they had been known by ego, the frequency of contact, how they met). For each pair of names Fischer also asked if they knew each other well, obtaining alter–alter ties. Interestingly, name generators and their corresponding interpreters are not grouped in a specific subsection of Fischer's questionnaire. They are included in between questions which investigate many other aspects of the individual's life.

It is increasingly common for name generators to be included in the regular round of large, government funded national surveys common in most countries. The earliest example of this, which has to some extent set the standard for subsequent inclusions, is Burt's (1984) work on the US General Election Survey. In this survey one name generator was used, eliciting the names of people whom ego had discussed personal matters with during the previous six months. While no size constraints were imposed at this first stage, alter–alter ties (whose strength was measured on a three-point scale) were only elicited for the first five alters nominated. In addition, the questionnaire asked about frequency of contacts, years of acquaintance, relationship content (discussion topics), and role (kin, friend, etc.). The purpose of including these measures in the survey was to measure social integration, that is, the extent to which a respondent had personal contact with incumbents of a variety of social categories (Burt 1984).

Other Methods

Beyond questionnaire-based surveys, name generators can also be implemented in the context of most of the various types of qualitative interview commonly employed in contemporary social science, including semi-structured, unstructured, thematic and life-history interviews. Beyond this, moreover, ego-net data more generally can be gathered by more direct means. Researchers may observe relations in an ethnographic context, for example, or an archive, and the growth of online communication over the last 20 years has opened up a range of new opportunities for exploring ties and networks. In what follows we discuss these possibilities, beginning with a discussion of the use of visual aids in an interview context. Before we begin, however, a brief note on the definition of network boundaries is required.

Boundaries: Nominalist and Realist

Questionnaire and interview-based means of data gathering generally allow egos to define their own ties and networks, albeit within the constraints imposed by the researcher. As we move away from interviews and questionnaires, towards methods based in observation and a fortiori archival analysis, however, it is increasingly the researcher who decides which alters do and do not belong within a network. Reading through the diary of a long since dead political activist, for example, the researcher must distinguish between significant contacts and individuals whom ego just happened to enjoy some contact with (Edwards and Crossley 2009). Furthermore, if their focus is political activity then they may wish to further distinguish between alters who had an impact on ego's political activity and those who did not, perhaps only including the former in their mapping and analysis of ego's network (ibid.).

Laumann et al. (1983) call this latter approach, where the researcher makes decisions about inclusion, a nominalist approach. They contrast it with what they call the realist approach, that is, the former approach discussed above, where ego herself decides who does and does not belong to her network.

Realist and nominalist approaches each have their own respective strengths and weaknesses, with no one approach being obviously better for all purposes. Which approach one adopts is most often a pragmatic decision based upon what is possible. In studies of 'average individuals' in contemporary contexts we often have no options but to ask them about their ties, and it makes most sense, in that situation, to allow them to draw relevant lines around sections of their network. When doing historical research, by contrast, we often have no choice but to consult archives and make inclusion decisions on behalf of those whom we study. It is important to be aware of this distinction, however, and to reflect upon the implications of taking one approach or another within the context of a specific project. With this said we turn to the use of visual aids.

BOX 3.3

Realist and Nominalist Approaches to Network Definition

The Realist Approach: Actors decide for themselves who belongs to their network for the purposes of a research project (within the constraints set by the researcher).

The Nominalist Approach: The researcher decides who belongs to an ego's net (which alters to include and which, if any, to exclude) for the purposes of their research.

Visually Aided Data Collection

Alongside name generators, researchers have sometimes used visually aided data collection tools. Visualisation is very common in social network analysis, but it is more often used in analysis than in data collection. This is partly because, in whole network studies, the final picture of the overall structure of relationships can only be obtained at the end of the process of data collection, when information is gathered from everyone who belongs to the network. In the case of ego-nets, however, each respondent produces a subjective account of her own alters and their ties, which can be constructed and visualised as the network information unfolds (Hogan et al. 2007). Fitzgerald

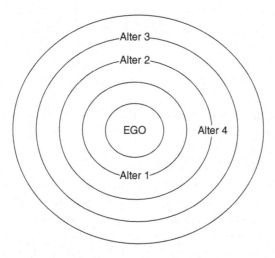

Figure 3.1 An example of target

(1978), for example, used a creative process for collecting relational information in Africa. She asked her respondents to write names of alters on plastic chips and to arrange them according to the strength of the tie.

The most common means of visualisation used in data gathering is probably the instrument known as the 'target', which consists of a series of concentric circles (with ego in the middle). Ego is asked to place the names of alters within the circles, putting those to whom they are closer more centrally and weaker ties further towards the outside (Figure 3.1). This tool was originally designed by Kahn and Antonucci (1980) and was recently adopted by Spencer and Pahl (2006) in their study of friendship. However, neither of the projects collected alter-alter ties, depriving the researchers of structural information and therefore also precluding any visualisation of structure.

Hogan and colleagues (2007) developed an improved version of the target, in which alter-alter ties are included. In their approach, the whole process of data collection is entirely visual, and directly involves respondents in the activity of drawing the network. A name generator which asks about 'somehow close' and 'especially close' alters is administered, and respondents have to write names on differently numbered and coloured Post-It notes, where the number keeps track of the order of naming, and colours represent the strength of the tie. Eight name interpreters, describing roles, are subsequently administered. Once all names and interpreters are elicited, respondents place these Post-It notes on a target of four concentric circles, and then draw alter-alter ties (Hogan et al. 2007: 127): the visually aided process facilitates the enumeration of alter-alter ties because respondents can simply draw the existing relationships, without being asked about every possible tie. In addition, they can group people together when they belong to cliques, reducing the burden of listing all ties in highly cohesive sub-groups.

Another approach to visually aided data collection was developed by Bellotti (2008a, 2008b) in her research on friendship networks. In this case name generators and interpreters were administered in a brief preliminary interview and their results then imported into UCINET (Borgatti et al. 2002) and visualised with NetDraw (Borgatti 2002). The visualisation was then used as a prompt in in-depth interviews (see Figure 3.2 for an example). Interviews usually took place one week after the first meeting.

The use of network visualisation as an input for the interview both allows and invites the respondent to talk about all of the people named. It also stimulates discussion about alter-alter ties. Interestingly, some of the people interviewed in Bellotti's study were aware of the shape of their social environment and reasoned in network terms by grouping friends together, and defining the criteria that differentiated the groups. Others, by contrast, tended to talk about one friend per time, and then moved on to a dyadic level, discussing alters' relationships with other friends.

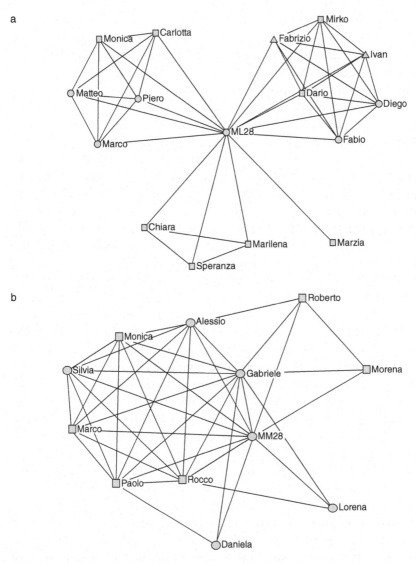

Figure 3.2 Examples of ego-networks' visualisations, with egos (ML28 and MM28) included

Qualitative Interviews

Both visually aided data collection tools and name generators can be administered (separately or together) within qualitative interviews, usually accompanied by a range of more open-ended questions which explore the content and meaning of relationships, and the meaning of the overall structure of individual social environments. According to Hollstein (2011), qualitative interviews are useful for investigating new and unexplored networks; concrete acts, practices and interactions; actors' perceptions and assessment of relationships and networks they are part of; network outcomes; and network dynamics. By recording the subjective accounts of network structures, they aim to gain an insider view of the interactional processes which generate those structures (Edwards 2010).

Qualitative interviews have accompanied administration of name generators since the very earliest ego-net studies. Wellman, for example, conducted semi-structured interviews[5] with a subsample of the first East York study's respondents (Wellman 1990), investigating general life events and changes, household composition and daily life, and detailed descriptions of close relationships. Since then, numerous studies have combined various forms of name generators with qualitative accounts. Bidart and Lavenu (2005) interviewed 66 young people living originally in Normandy (France), who were questioned every three years about the evolution of their personal networks and the events marking their entry into adult life. Hollstein (2014) combined fuzzy set analysis of qualitative material and network data to investigate youth transitions from school to work. Bellotti (2008a, 2008b) interviewed 23 single young adults living in Milan (Italy) about the composition, dynamics and outcomes of their friendship networks. Bernardi et al. (2007) interviewed 64 young adults living in two cities in Germany in order to investigate the social mechanisms at work or the variation in the composition of the networks of informal relationships in relation to fertility behaviour. In this last study, the authors mix a semi-structured interview with a standard name generator, a target and a brief socio-demographic questionnaire. They also go on to interview a subsample composed of three relevant members of each ego's social network: their parents, current partner and a close friend (when these were available). Although they then focus the analysis on dyads of close friends, they collect a large amount of qualitative material which they regard as 'best suited not only to explore the meaning of parenthood but also to identify the relationships salient for contributing to the construction of this meaning and for their translation into intentions and behaviour related to family formation' (Bernardi et al. 2007: 24).

There has been a growth of interest in using qualitative interviews in social network analysis in recent years. Debates regarding this innovation are captured in a recent book edited by Hollstein and Dominguez (2014) and a special issue of the journal, *Sociologica*, edited by Bellotti (Bellotti 2010, Crossley 2010, Kirke 2010, McCarty 2010, Molina 2010). An overview of mixed methods techniques can be found in Bellotti (2014), Edwards (2010), Hollstein (2011), Molina et al. (2014).

Software for Ego-Net Data Collection in Interviews

There are several software packages which facilitate the collection of ego-net data in interviews. We cannot offer an exhaustive list of them here, but in this section we will briefly describe two.

Egonet, which was designed by Chris McCarty and is freely available online (http://sourceforge.net/projects/egonet/), is intended to facilitate the construction and administration of a name generator and has the further advantage that it tends to standardise the administration format across interviews, thus minimising the bias that may emerge when interviews are conducted by different researchers. It is easy to use, with a user-friendly interface and it offers a visualisation tool that can be used directly during the interview, serving as a visual aid in the manner discussed above. Furthermore, it creates general global network measures and data matrices that can be used for further analysis by other software packages. Its main flaw, presently, is that it does not appear to have a manual.

EgoNet.QF, designed by Straus, Pfeffer and Hollstein (2008) and again freely available online (www.pfeffer.at/egonet/) allows one to collect data electronically using the aforementioned concentric circle method. In addition, it creates a visualisation which can be manipulated during the interview. However, it does not create data matrices, a shortcoming which limits its analytic potential. In this case an English-language manual is available free of charge (www.pfeffer.at/egonet/EgoNet.QF%20Manual.pdf).

Ethnographic Observation

Ethnographic observation is probably the oldest of all network data gathering approaches. The pioneering studies conducted at the Department of Social Anthropology and Sociology at the University of Manchester during the 1960s, for example, mostly used ethnographic observation. As Clyde Mitchell recalls: 'in many ways [...] the most reliable and adequate information is most likely to be obtained through direct observation. The observer over a period of time is able to make his own assessment of the interaction of an individual with others around him and to record its characteristics' (Mitchell 1969: 31). Following Mitchell (and also based in the Manchester school), Epstein used direct observation to study the spread of gossip (Epstein 1969a and 1969b); Kapferer used it to map interactions between a group of African mine employees who were engaged in surface work in the Cell Room of the Electro-Zinc Plant of the mine (Kapferer 1969: 184); and both Wheeldon (1969) and Boswell (1969) constructed networks from observation. While both Epstein and Kapferer were non-participant

observers, moreover, Wheeldon (1969) and Boswell (1969) were active participants in the interactive situations they were studying, and therefore had
to account for their role in influencing the network dynamics. Wheeldon
(1969) studied a community in Southern Africa, focusing on six leaders
who were frequently named by other members of the community. His
methodology is a mixture of observations, informal discussion, interviews
and survey materials, where the aim is not the systematic collection of network data, but the observation of the structure and function of leadership in
a specific community. Boswell (1969) observed the mobilisation of personal
networks during periods of crisis in the African city of Lusaka. He selected
difficult situations, like the death of a kin relation, and compared the ways
in which selected individuals dealt with them with the general expectations
of what is supposed to be done in such situations. It is also worth noting
that while Epstein and Kapferer observed whole networks, Wheeldon and
Boswell focused on ego-nets.

The use of observation is more common in whole network analysis.
Direct observation of ego-nets is rare. However, there are notable examples additional to the work of Wheeldon and Boswell. For example, in his
famous study of an Italian slum in Boston, *Street Corner Society*, William
Foote Whyte (1943) began by spending several weeks following a local man,
Doc, through his daily and weekly routines (a common ethnographic technique referred to as 'shadowing'). Doc was the leader of a group of 'corner
boys' but also liaised with a club of college boys and their leader, Chick. By
recording his daily interactions over an extended period of time, Whyte was
able to map Doc's personal network, subsequently extending his observations to interaction between a number of other people Doc was related to.
Working in this way, snowballing outwards from Doc, he was eventually
able to map a large part of the whole network within the slum.

Similarly, Mische (2008), in her analysis of youth movements in Brazil,
adopts the technique of shadowing key actors, following them in their daily
activities and reconstructing their life and political trajectories. These actors
are used as cases to exemplify some interesting positions in the wider network of youth affiliation to political groups. In both studies, observations
are the main source of data, but they are accompanied with other techniques, including interviews and consultation of secondary sources, which
are extremely useful for framing ethnographic data within a specific social,
economic and political context.

A mixture of observations, shadowing and interviews is also adopted
by Uzzi (1997), who collected ego-nets of 23 garment firms, and by
Dominguez and Watkins (2003), who conducted participant observation
and longitudinal ethnographic interviews with five African-American
and five Latin-American women. In both cases, the researchers not only
interviewed the relevant actors about their relationships, but also followed

them in their daily activities. According to Dominguez and Watkins (2003), the ethnographic approach has some important strengths. Firstly, when interactions are observed over an extended period of time, they unfold as 'processes through which the respondents develop and utilize relationships for the acquisition of resources' (Dominguez and Watkins 2003: 115), and show how these processes may change according to specific circumstances. Secondly, observations reveal behavioural patterns over time and allow one to capture not only what respondents say but also what they do.

Diaries

A similar outcome to the technique of shadowing is obtained by using contact dairies as a tool for data collection. This method consists of asking one or more individuals to fill in a daily record of all the people they have been in contact with: they can be divided according to the means of communication, be it face-to-face interaction, telephone, text, email or whatever. This method was first adopted by Gurevitch (1961), who collected information from 18 people on the socio-demographic characteristics of their contacts over 100 days. It has subsequently been adopted and developed, for example, by Lonkila (1999) and Fu (2005).[6]

Recording interaction in diaries can be partial and biased, especially if participants fill their diaries retrospectively, at the end of the day. In an effort to avoid these problems, some researchers have elicited contact diaries by way of repeated interviews. For example, Shelley et al. (1990) interviewed 21 respondents every other day for 30 days to record whom they contacted and how long they spent with these contacts. Given that the respondents did not need to record the contacts themselves, the researchers had better control over the quality of data collection (Fu 2007).

The main advantage of this method is that it does not aim to measure only a specific subset of personal networks (the intimates, the material supporters, and the like). By recording every interaction, it allows us to observe infrequent as well as frequent contact, strong and weak ties, and a wide variety of contacts independently from their content. In other words, it gives an approximation (although partial and incomplete, given the limitation to a specific time frame) of the global network, defined as 'all the people known to an individual, given a suitable definition of "knowing"' (Bernard et al. 1990: 180).

Archival Sources

Historical archives are another valuable source for the collection of network data. They have been widely used in whole network research, and they are gaining increasing importance due to the vast possibilities of data mining from electronic resources. The peculiarity of archival resources is that the information is not created for the purpose of the research, and pre-exists the data collection process. This means that the researcher has a minimal influence in the production of the data, especially compared to other forms of direct inquiry, like surveys and interviews. However, the impact of the researcher on the production of the information still exists. Given the fact that data were not produced to answer specific research questions in the first place, they are normally embedded in documents and need to be selected by the researcher over other non-relevant information. This process of selection is guided by the aims of the research and inevitably entails a constant and active decision-making process about who and what should be included and who/what excluded.

The typical examples of network studies based on archival sources are those belonging to the established tradition of the analysis of interlocking directorates, where the aim is to detect directors who sit on multiple boards of corporations[7] (this is an example of two-mode analysis, which was briefly introduced in Chapter One). This is done by searching on the lists of names of boards of directors and creating affiliation matrices[8] for those sitting on the same boards. Another good example of archive-based research is Padgett and Ansell's (1993) classic study of the Medici. Padgett and Ansell used archival sources to investigate the structure of relationships between family oligarchies in Florence during the Renaissance (Padgett and Ansell 1993). In this case a wide range of sources was examined, from previously produced historical accounts to direct search of archival data like tax assessments and neighbourhood co-residence. Similarly, the recent work of Crossley (2008c, 2009, 2015) on the emergence of the punk and post-punk music worlds of Liverpool, London, Manchester and Sheffield between 1975 and 1980 has made extensive use of historical material (consulting authoritative secondary sources, biographies, autobiographies and online archives). Finally, Bellotti's analysis of the structural advantages in obtaining funding in academic disciplines is also based on archival sources (Bellotti 2012, 2014). By consulting the description of funded research projects in physics and philosophy in Italy, information about both the formal structure and the academic content of collaboration was collected.

The list could go on, but all of the archival studies mentioned so far are whole network studies. Ego-net studies using archives are less common. One example, however, is Edwards and Crossley's (2009) work on the ego-net of suffragette Helen Kirkpatrick Watts. They draw upon 23 letters (dated 1900–14) written by Watts or her family concerning her activism, and also eight of her written speeches (dated 1909). They analyse this material in three stages. The first stage mapped the flow of letters as a network, observing who wrote letters to whom, when and with what frequency. In addition, it involved a qualitative analysis of the content of the letters (Edwards and

Crossley 2009: 43). This first stage produced network data on connections between Watts and her correspondents. The second stage analysed the connections between people named in the letters, looking at the relationships that are described in the letters and adding further alters and further alter-alter ties on this basis. In the third stage, the ego-net constructed through the first two stages was cross-checked with information obtained by local and national newspapers, as well as secondary sources on fellow prisoners and co-attendees of events (Edwards and Crossley 2009: 49). In all the stages, qualitative analysis on the nature and the content of relationships between the people with whom Helen Watts interacted during her involvement in the suffragette movement and the radicalisation of activities, is brought into dialogue with a binary mapping of network structure (ibid.).

Internet Studies

The final source of ego-net data that we will consider is the internet, a space which offers apparently endless opportunities to collect and analyse social network data. These include email communication; social networking sites; movie, music and book databases; citation databases; internet sites including web pages, Wikis, digital news sites, and so on. The collection of data from most of these sites is no different from collecting any other archival data, except that it can all be done electronically. The Internet Movie Database (IMDb) is a good illustration of this. It contains information on nearly every film ever made in machine-readable form. These data include cast members, film crews, plot-lines, news articles, movies that reference a given movie, and so on.

The collection of data from online databases presents no new challenges for the network researcher, beyond a basic level of technical competence. One area in which this is not true, however, involves data from social media sites. There are many social media sites and each allows different levels of access to the researcher. This access is controlled by companies and is liable to change without notice depending on the organisation's need. Some sites are clearly network orientated; for example, Facebook and LinkedIn, which focus entirely on personally constructed networks. Others, such as Twitter, are close to a broadcast medium as 'followers' do not need to gain permission from the actors they are 'following'. Some sites do not look as inherently network orientated, but can be mined for network data – for example YouTube or Flickr.

Since organisations have complete control over data access for social media sites it can be difficult to collect data from them. LinkedIn, for example, allows very little access to data. It is possible to ask someone to construct their ego network by simply looking at whom they are connected to when

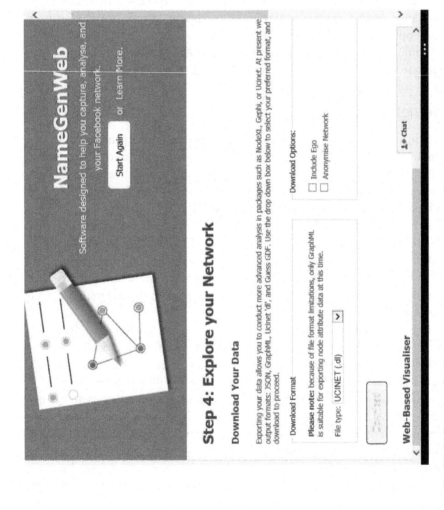

Figure 3.3 NameGenWeb download page

they are logged in, but they would not have information on alter-alter ties and this may be a problem. Currently the two largest social media sites, Twitter and Facebook, do allow some kind of limited access. In what follows we consider two tools developed to help the researcher collect data from these organisations: NameGenWeb which can be used to gather Facebook data, and NodeXL, which is useful for obtaining Twitter data.

Facebook

NameGenWeb was developed by Bernie Hogan at the Oxford Internet Institute and is a Facebook app available at https://apps.facebook.com/namegenweb/.[9] To run this for a particular ego they need to log into their Facebook page. The software creates an ego–network using the Facebook friends relation with alter-alter friendship ties. Hence if two friends of ego are friends on Facebook they will have an edge connecting them. The software allows for visualisation online or the data can be downloaded in UCINET dl text format,[10] amongst other formats (on UCINET see Chapter Four). It also allows for alter attributes, which can be selected from a list. In Figure 3.3 opposite we have a screenshot of the fourth step just before the data is downloaded. We have selected the UCINET dl format which is a text version of the dl spreadsheet editor in the edgelist format.[11] We can see

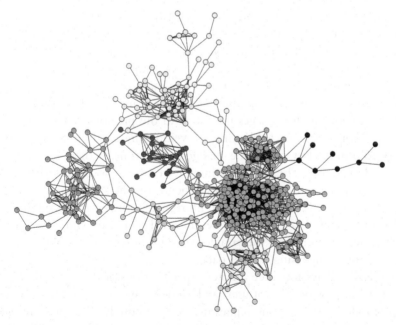

Figure 3.4 A Facebook ego network with ego not shown

on the right that we have the option to remove the names and anonymise the data and the option to include ego. If we scrolled slightly further down the page we would see an option to visualise the network directly on screen.

To obtain the data simply click the download button and choose the save option. In the download's folder there will be a text file but it will have the form *name_facebookidnumber.dl*. The name will be the user's (that is ego's) Facebook name. The 'facebookid' is a number used by Facebook to uniquely identify its users, which means that friends of ego with the same name will not get mixed up. The extension dl means it is a text version of the dl format. This file can be looked at using notepad but can be read straight into NetDraw or UCINET. In UCINET use the command Data|Import Text File|DL and in NetDraw use File|Open|Ucinet DL text File|Network (1-mode). Both programs will allow the user to store this as a standard UCINET or vna file for later use in the software. Figure 3.4 is an example of the Facebook friends of one of the authors of the book. In this we see typical clustering in which there are dense groups relating to certain activities or physical locations. The grey nodes indicate people known from home, the different shades of grey (which appear as different colours on a computer screen) represent different clusters of contacts: e.g. neighbours, work colleagues, holiday friends etc.

Twitter

NodeXL is a free add-on to Excel that has its own visualisation and network analysis tools but is focused on collecting data from social media (again it is able to export data for analysis in UCINET dl format and so can be used in conjunction with UCINET and NetDraw). It has built-in tools for collecting Flickr, YouTube and Twitter data. We focus upon Twitter here.

There are two types of Twitter interface that can be used by NodeXL: a search interface and a streaming interface. The search interface allows a user to search through all messages published in the previous week but with a rate limit set by Twitter. At the time of writing, the rate limit is 180 queries every 15 minutes but this can be changed at any time by them and has been changed previously. The streaming interface captures tweets in real time but this too is restricted by Twitter and depends on the volume of activity. It can be as low as 1% of all tweets. Unfortunately the sampling method for either of these interfaces has not been released by Twitter and so we do not know how representative the samples are. This poses many problems when interpreting or analysing Twitter data.

NodeXL allows for three different specifications of the network. Firstly, the user can provide a list of users and NodeXL will construct the relationship of follows or mentions/replies in tweets. Secondly, this can be reversed and the user supplies a hashtag or a search term and NodeXL will look for users who use these tweets and the relation can be follows or mentions/replies.

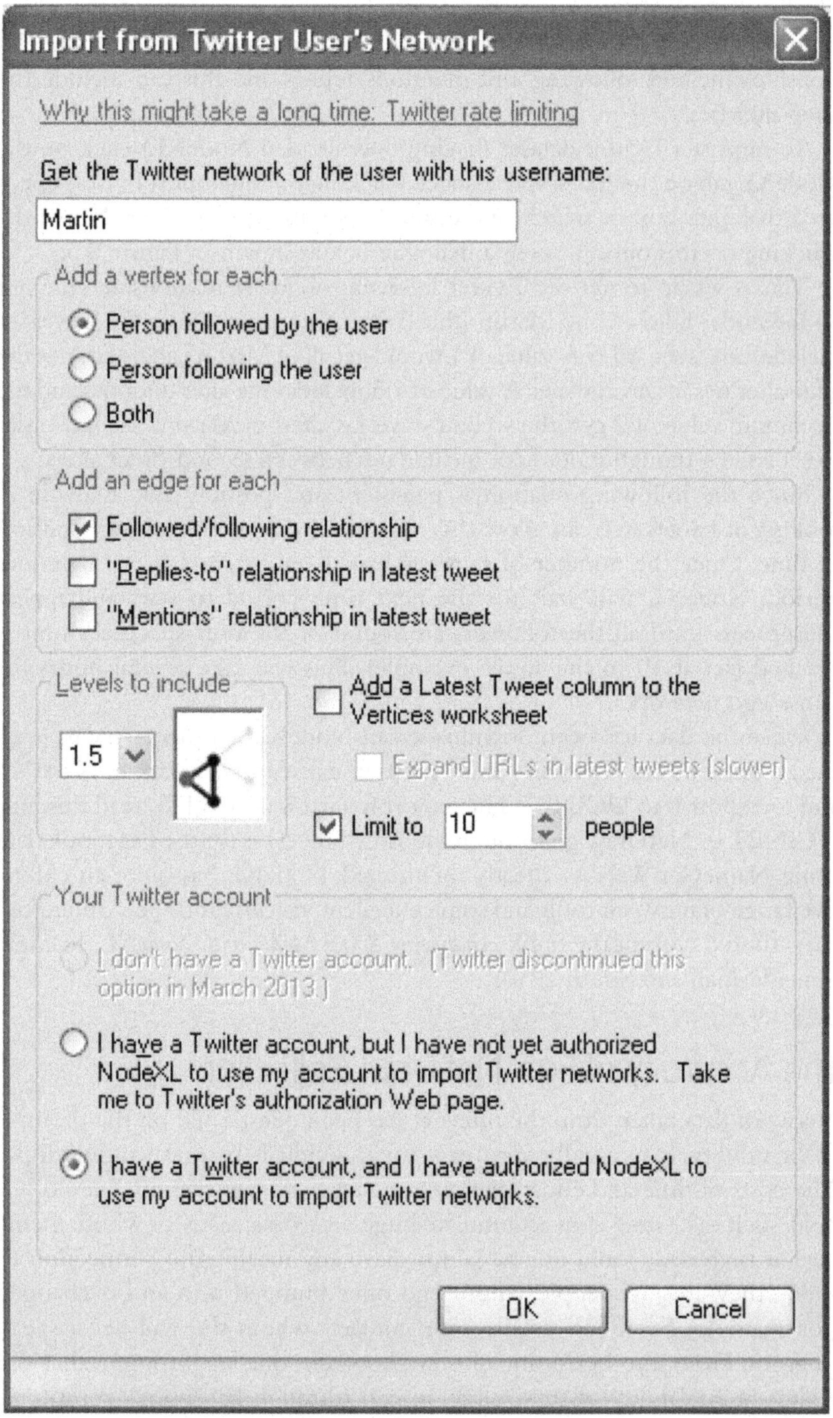

Figure 3.5 Twitter import function from NodeXL

Finally, there is the specification most relevant to ego-net analysis, which captures all people followed by and/or following ego. The types of relationships include following and mentions/replies and this can include the alter–alter ties.

To import a Twitter dataset (having downloaded NodeXL) click on the NodeXL tab on the Excel spreadsheet. Clicking on the import button opens up a dialogue box in which one option is 'From Twitter User's Network'. Clicking on this option opens a dialogue box as shown in Figure 3.5.

This is set up to get the Twitter following/follower relationship amongst all the nodes followed by Martin (the Twitter username). Note the 'Levels to include' box is set at 1.5. A value of 1 would get all of Martin's alters but not the alter-alter ties in this ego-net. A value of 1.5 includes the alter-alter ties and the maximum value of 2 gets the second wave, i.e. alters in Martin's second-order tweet zone – though it does not include ties between second-order alters.

Since the following relation is persistent and possibly not as dense as looking at tweets, we can allow the collection to run over a longer period of time. Once the number of requests have been reached in a 15-minute period, NodeXL will wait for the next time period to start and repeat the process until all the followers are found or the user-specified limit is reached (set at 10 in the above example). This can take several hours for dense ego networks.

Once the data has been downloaded in NodeXL it is necessary to press the autofill button. This will allow you to visualise the network in NodeXL and to export it to UCINET. The export format is again dl. To read this into UCINET or NetDraw go through the same process as for the Facebook data using NameGenWeb. As already mentioned, NodeXL has quite an extensive range of network tools and some excellent visualisation tools. Interested users should consult the book *Analyzing Social Media with NodeXL* (Hansen, Shneiderman and Smith 2010).

The Accuracy of Ego-Net Data Collection

Network data taken from the internet has been questioned on the grounds of its validity. It is usually very easy for individuals to make online links. The costs of time and effort that circumscribe ego-net size off-line do not hold, such that some egos accumulate huge networks, many of whose members, it is argued, could not be said to have any meaningful connection to ego – they are just people whom ego once bumped into and exchanged (for example) Facebook details with; contacts whom she will never speak to again. From another point of view, however, one might argue that the enduring availability of these alters to ego (through Facebook) constitutes them as weak ties whom ego may decide to call upon at some point, and who may prove useful. Furthermore, the other forms of network elicitation discussed in this chapter each have their own problems. In the final section of this chapter we offer a brief generic overview of some of these problems.

The accuracy of information gleaned by way of name generators has been questioned by a number of researchers. Laumann (1969), for example, investigated the accuracy of alter attributes, as described by egos, in his above-mentioned classic study. Having been given the phone number of alters by egos in his original study he followed them up. He discovered that certain attributes, specifically the ones describing public characteristics of friends like age and occupation, are much better recalled than less visible attributes, like attitudes toward politics. Comparable results have been obtained by Wilcox and Udry (1986), who compared the sexual attitudes and behaviours of adolescents with the attitudes and behaviours imputed to them by their best friends. They found that when people report on attitudes they are much more influenced by their own position regarding a topic than the opinions of their alters.

The accuracy of reporting on the existence and frequency of relationships with alters is even more problematic. In a series of experiments, Bernard et al. (1984)[12] tested various aspects of recall accuracy, comparing it with data gathered by means of diaries, observation and electronic monitoring. They conclude that, for both number of contacts and frequency of contact, people recall less than a half of their communications. Furthermore, this figure is not improved if people keep records of their behaviour, or if they are aware of being observed or previously alerted of the data collection. The only improvement in the measurement is obtained if people are asked to recall recent events: the more recent the time frame, the more accurate they tend to be (Bernard et al. 1984: 499). Similarly, Freeman and Romney (1987) note that people are better at reporting typical social relations rather than occasional ones, and typical rather than specific event attendance. They may be good at recalling who usually attends a specific, regular event, for example, but when asked who attended on a particular occasion they will tend to draw upon that typical situation rather than knowing the specificity of the particular occasion. Finally, focusing upon the content of ties, Shulman (1976) studied the correspondence between interviewers and their alters on the description of the relationship, and found that the rate of agreement varies between 55% and 72% on five different types of exchange, with less agreement for weak ties.

Accuracy regarding reciprocity is another element that has been investigated in the context of ego-net studies – although its measurement is not as straightforward as it is in whole networks. When interviewing all the people who belong to a network in a whole network study, reciprocity is easily observed by simply matching each pair's response for the tie that links them. In an ego-net study, by contrast, reciprocity can only be investigated if alters are contacted and asked about their relationship with ego (a sample of alters may suffice if the purpose is to test for accuracy). Studies which have done this include the previously discussed work of Laumann (1969), who found that 43.2% of alters nominated the ego who nominated them when asked to complete the name generator themselves. The percentage was slightly lower (36.2%) in a study by Shulman (1976) on the reciprocal naming of six closest intimates. This study also showed that reciprocation declines steadily with strength (or 'closeness') of tie. Higher levels of agreement were found in a study of mental health patients by Barrera et al. (1985). They find 69.4% agreement for 'intimate interaction' and 97.4% for 'physical assistance' (Barrera et al. 1985: 13). Note, however, that in this case egos put the researchers in touch with their alters, an approach which inevitably 'reminded' alters of their contact and to some extent framed their interaction with the researchers by way of this contact. Finally, Antonucci and Israel (1986) analysed reciprocity across a number of types of supporting and role relations, with results ranging from 49% to 60%. Their results suggest that reciprocity is dependent upon the type of relationship measured and the kind of support exchanged.

Some of the work on data accuracy in ego–net studies has been inspired by Krackhardt's (1987) path-breaking work on Cognitive Social Structures (CSS – that is, nodes' mental representations of the networks they are involved in). Batchelder (2002), for example, compares the data obtained from three different measurements of cognitive social structures, where 22 students were asked to report on the ordinary ties, the close ties and the top three ties they believed to link each other pair of students. The analysis indicates that the three cognitive tasks produce highly comparable results, suggesting that they can be used interchangeably to measure CSS. Given the lack of observational data though, it is impossible for this kind of study to estimate how much the perception of the network structure is an accurate representation of the actual one.

BOX 3.4

Reliability, Validity and Accuracy

Reliability: Instruments are reliable when the data that they gather are not affected by such contextual factors as the time at which they are administered or the individual administering them.

Validity: Instruments are valid when they capture what the researcher aims to capture.

Accuracy: Refers to the extent to which people confidently recall and report their social ties without intentional or unintentional omission.

Summary

In this chapter we have given an overview of various approaches to collecting ego–net data. We have described the multiple quantitative, qualitative, visual and electronic tools that can be implemented to elicit ego–net data; and we have critically discussed issues relating to the accuracy of ego–net information. In the next chapter we discuss the key measures that can be applied to these data.

Notes

1. That is to say, sources more commonly associated with qualitative research.
2. See note 1.
3. This characteristic is known as the transitivity effect: for a more precise definition and an extensive discussion, see Wasserman and Faust (1994: 243).
4. Barnes (1969) distinguishes between first-order zone actor-centred networks, where data are collected only from a focal actor about his/her relationships and the relationships between alters, and second-order zone networks, where data are also collected from each alter named by the original focal actor, about their relationships with their alters, and their alters' ties.
5. The original interview schedule for the second East York study (1977/1978) can be found on Barry Wellman's website.
6. A good review of the use of diaries as tools for data collection can be found in Fu (2007).
7. This is not the place to review the vast literature on interlocking directorates. A good starting point is the review article by Mizruchi (1996) and the book by Scott (1997).
8. In this case we would begin with a matrix whose rows represent directors and whose columns represent the firms on whose boards they sit. From this we would then derive two further matrices, one linking those directors who sit on one or more of the same boards, the other linking firms who share one or more of the same directors.
9. As the book goes to press it has been announced that namegenweb will no longer be supported. To download data researchers can use the nodeXL routine social net importer see: http://socialnetimporter.codeplex.com/.
10. A dl file is a Data Language file which allows one to import text data in UCINET (Borgatti et al. 2002), which automatically transforms them into relational data.
11. Edgelist dl is a file format read by UCINET (Borgatti et al. 2002) and NetDraw (Borgatti 2002) in which adjacent actors, say, name1 and name2 are coded one edge per line as a pair separated by a space. See Borgatti et al. (2013) and Chapter Three in this book for more details.
12. The whole set of experiments is reported in a series of articles on informant accuracy: Killworth and Bernard (1976); Bernard and Killworth (1977); Killworth and Bernard (1979/80); Bernard et al. (1979/80); Bernard et al. (1982). The whole set of results is summarised in Bernard et al. (1981, 1984).

4

ANALYSING EGO-NET DATA

Learning Outcomes

By the end of the chapter you will be able to:

1. Calculate and interpret standard measures for ego-nets.

2. Analyse and visualise ego-nets in UCINET, NetDraw and E-Net.

3. Combine ego-net data with other attribute data using standard statistical models.

Introduction

In this chapter we look at descriptive methods and tools for analysing ego-net data. Having outlined a number of important measures for ego-net analysis we focus on two software packages designed for social network analysis: namely, UCINET (Borgatti et al. 2002) and E-Net (Borgatti 2006). The package UCINET is designed for looking at whole networks and not ego-nets but it can be used to analyse ego-net data. E-Net, as the name suggests, has been specifically designed for ego-nets. However, as mentioned in the first chapter, ego-nets may be extracted from whole networks. If we have a whole network then UCINET can be used to analyse each extracted ego-net in turn. We can also use the feature to analyse a collection of ego-nets by merging them into a dummy whole network.

Ego-nets are often collected using sampled egos from a larger population. The sampled egos provide all the data (they specify alters, alter-alter ties and all the attributes) and so this is like a standard survey instrument. Properties of the ego-nets are attributed to ego and this can then be used as a variable in standard statistical analysis such as regression. We still need to make sure that the assumptions of any statistical model are not violated and hence our egos will need to be randomly sampled from the whole population and the ego–nets should be independent of each other. In this chapter we look in detail at the measures that can be used as variables in such an analysis. We first discuss the measures and then look at how to compute them using UCINET and E–Net.

Ego-Net Measures

In their book, *Analyzing Social Networks*, Borgatti et al. (2013: 217) provide a classification of ego–net measures that we shall use here. These measures tend to fall into one of two groups. They either capture social capital, which we discussed at length in Chapter Two, or they measure homophily, a concept, introduced in Chapter One, which captures the tendency for social actors to more often forge ties with alters who are similar to themselves in some salient respect, e.g. individuals may pick friends of a similar age to themselves or who belong to the same ethnic group as them. In some cases, such as selection of sexual partners amongst heterosexuals, the opposite tendency, 'heterophily', is in play. Homophily measures will capture this opposing tendency too. Some of the measures discussed require alter–alter ties. Some do not. Similarly, some require attributes (either continuous or categorical) whereas others are purely structural. Table 4.1 gives a brief description of each measure, together with the type of data required.

Table 4.1 Summary of ego-net measures

Measure	Description	Ego-alter ties	Alter-alter ties	Attributes
Tie central tendency	Total number or mean of ties	X		
Tie dispersion	Distribution or variation of ties	X		
Alter central tendency	Proportion in each attribute category or mean	X		X
Alter dispersion	Distribution of alters across attribute categories or variation	X		X
Ego-alter similarity	Similarity of ego attributes to alter attributes	X		X
Structural shape	Measures determined by the pattern of alter-alter ties	X	X	

We now examine each of these measures in a little more detail.

Tie Central Tendency

The most obvious and straightforward measure that we can apply to an ego-net is size or 'degree'; that is, the number of alters in the network. Ego-nets often vary markedly in their size and this can be a very important difference, closely correlated with other variables of interest. Where our data are binary then our measure of ego-net size is straightforward. We simply report the number of ties per ego. Where our data are valued (e.g. we have measured frequency of interaction or have used a Likert scale to capture tie strength), we may use any of the standard statistical summaries, such as mode, mean, median, etc., to capture central tendency, e.g. we may report that ego-net A has a mean tie-strength of 4, where ego-net B has a mean value of 2. Alternatively we may find that ego-net C has a modal value of 2, compared to ego-net D, where the figure is 5. Often in ego-net research, we will ask about a range of tie types (e.g. close friends, work colleagues, family ties) which we may subsequently wish to compare. Again the standard statistical measures of central tendency can be used in this context.

As already mentioned, ego-net measures are measured alongside individual attributes in much research, with a view to exploring their effects upon those attributes (or vice versa). For example, we may hypothesise that having a lot of friends contributes to an individual's sense of subjective well-being. If we have data on number of close friends in our ego-net and also a measure of subjective well-being we can test this hypothesis by looking for a correlation between the two measures and regressing one upon the other, as we would in a standard quantitative social science project.

We can see from Table 4.1 that tie central tendency only requires ego-alter ties. It ignores alter–alter ties where they are present.

Tie Dispersion

Tie dispersion examines how ties are spread. Again we see from Table 4.1 that we do not require information about alter–alter ties for this measure. For valued data this could simply be the standard deviation or variance.

For binary data clearly we do not have dispersion in any one relation but we could look at dispersion over a number of relations. For example we may be interested in the number of work ties and the number of friendship ties, or the number of close friends and the number of family ties. We may hypothesise that those with few family ties have more close friends who are able to provide emotional support or resources. Alternatively, reflecting the work of Granovetter (1973), egos with a mixture of strong and weak ties may have better access to new information and resources than those with just strong ties.

Blau's H and Agresti's IQV are summary measures of dispersion. The IQV (which stands for Index of Qualitative Variation) is just a normalised version of the Blau index. Suppose we have r different relation types and P_i is the proportion of ties in relation i then the Blau index H is simply:

$$H = 1 - P_1^2 - P_2^2 - P_3^2 - \ldots\ldots - P_r^2$$

BOX 4.1

Calculating Blau's H and Agresti's IQV

- Total number of alters is 4+12+9=25
- Hence proportions are 4/25, 12/25 and 9/25, i.e. 0.16, 0.48 and 0.36
- From the formula $H = 1 - 0.16^2 - 0.48^2 - 0.36^2 = 0.6144$
- Since there are 3 relations $IQV = 0.6144/(1-1/3) = 0.9217$

This measure has a value of 0 if all the ties are in one group and a maximum of $1-1/r$ if each group has the same number of ties. The IQV measure is H divided by $1-1/r$. Box 4.1 shows how to calculate these measures for an ego-net with 4 actors as close friends, 12 actors as work colleagues and 9 actors as close family.

Alter Central Tendency

This is analogous to the tie central tendency but using the alter attributes. If we have categorical attributes such as gender, ethnicity or socio-economic status then we can simply count the number or proportions of each alter in each of the categories. We could well hypothesise that individuals with connections to people with diverse skills (marketing, HR, finance, etc.) are in a better position to start up companies than those with less diverse networks. Also, people who have connections to people from a wide range of ethnic groups would have a better understanding of integration than someone who only has connections to a small number of groups. As mentioned in the previous chapter, these data are often collected using the position generator. If the attributes are continuous, such as age or income, then we can, as in the tie dispersion case, use standard statistical measures such as mean or median. We can also have the situation that the ties are weighted, in which case we can weight the alters by the tie strength.

Alter Dispersion

Alter central tendency looks at the size and proportion of the alters whereas dispersion looks at how this is spread. We are interested if these are spread evenly, i.e. we have similar numbers of alters in each of the categories if we have categorical data. If ego were a student and the categories were year of study then we would be measuring the extent to which ego knew the same number of students in each year. As in tie dispersion we can use H and IQV as summary measures. If we have continuous categories such as age or income then again we can simply use standard deviation.

Ego-Alter Similarity

The previous two measures examine the attributes of alters but do not compare these to the attributes of ego. However, such comparison is often important. It is very common for actors to associate with people who have similar attributes to themselves and we may wish to measure whether this is so within our own population. For example friends tend to be from the same educational background, similar income groups, of the same ethnicity, etc. – a process referred to as 'homophily'. Social network analysis gives us various ways of measuring homophily which we explain below.

Before we do, however, note that unless we have longitudinal data or are looking at unchangeable node attributes it can be difficult, even using these measures, to distinguish in practice between a situation in which a pre-existing similarity between nodes has contributed to drawing them together in a tie and a rather different process whose outcome is much the same: mutual social influence. Where attributes are changeable (e.g. behaviours, expressed attitudes and tastes), contact between social actors can lead each to adopt those of the other. If ego has alters who are all smokers, for example, this may encourage ego to smoke. Measures of ego–alter similarity allow us to test whether one or the other (or both) of these processes are in play, but in the absence of longitudinal data or node attributes which can be regarded as unchangeable, they cannot tell us which. Clearly we require data regarding both alters and their (relevant) attributes for these measures.

If the data are continuous we can measure ego-alter similarity by taking the average of all the absolute differences between the ego attributes and the alter attributes. There are a number of other alternatives, the choice of which really depends on the nature of the data (whether for example it is highly skewed or contains outliers) and the research question being examined.

One of the most popular categorical measures is the EI index of Krackhardt and Stern (1988). Here the E stands for the number of external ties – that is, the number of ties ego has to alters in a category different from their own. The I stands for the number of internal ties – that is, the number of ties ego has to actors in the same category as they are in. E+I is the total number of ties or degree of ego. The EI index is defined as:

$$EI = \frac{E - I}{E + I}$$

Hence it is the number of external ties minus the number of internal ties divided by the total number of ties. It varies from −1 to +1. A score of −1 means that ego only has ties with alters in the same category as themselves, showing perfect homophily, and a score of +1 means that ego only has ties to alters in different categories, showing perfect heterophily. Perfect homophily occurs when ego only has ties to people who support the same sports team as them or are members of the same political party. Heterophily on the other hand can be important in areas of social support – it is better for a recovering addict that they have ties to people who are not addicts.

As a simple example of the measure, suppose ego socialises with 25 work colleagues: nine are White, eight are Black, four are Asian and four belong to other or mixed groups. If ego was Asian then the EI index would have I=4 and E=21 so that EI would be (21–4)/25 = −0.68. This would indicate a high degree of heterophily.

However, care needs to be taken in interpreting this as it could well happen that the organisation which has 100 staff has an ethnic breakdown which is 35 White, 30 Black, five Asian and 30 other or mixed race. In this case we see that the Asian ego socialises with four out of the five possible Asian colleagues indicating homophily not heterophily. The problem is that the EI index only looks at ties that have been formed and does not consider the pool from which the ties have been drawn. If we know that the number of non-chosen alters in the same category as ego is X and the number of non-chosen alters in a different category to ego is Y then we can use Yules Q to take account of these considerations. We can summarise our example in a simple crosstab as follows:

	Same category as Ego	Different category to Ego
Ego has tie with	4	21
Ego does not have tie with	1	74

Using the notation above, this table becomes:

	Same category as Ego	Different category to Ego
Ego has tie with	I	E
Ego does not have tie with	X	Y

Yules Q can be defined using this table as:

$$Q = \frac{IY - EX}{IY + EX}$$

In our example this yields a value of (4×74−21×1)/ (4×74+21×1) = 0.87 which gives a strong homophily score (positive scores indicate homophily for Yule Yules Q and negative scores indicate heterophily). Unfortunately we do not usually have the information about non-ties when we collect ego-net data and this is usually only available when we do an ego-net analysis of a whole network.

Structural Shape

An ego-net with alter–alter ties is a network in its own right and any of the standard whole network measures can be applied to the ego-net. Note these measures sometimes include ego and are sometimes calculated with ego removed. In either case we need to be careful in any interpretation since the networks have a boundary defined as being at a distance of one degree from ego. Hence two alters may both be connected to ego but they may also both be connected to a number of other actors who are not connected to ego and so are not in the ego network. To cover all the possible measures in which we consider the ego network as a whole network would detract from the focus of this book and so we will restrict ourselves to measures which have been commonly used in this way. Readers who are interested in the wider range of methods should consult Borgatti et al. (2013).

The most obvious and certainly one of the most common measures in this category is density. Since ego has a tie to every alter this is usually calculated amongst alters only. Ego-net density is the number of ties between alters divided by the number of possible ties. In other words, it is the density of the network with ego removed. High density shows that ego's alters are well-connected and this could be viewed positively if ego was in need of social support. However, in other situations it may be seen as something that constrains ego. The power to manage self-presentations, which Goffman

(1959) deems central to agency, is considerably curtailed when all of ego's alters know one another, for example, because her alters will tend to confer and swap information. Ego cannot assume different personas in different situations or at least this is more difficult – a situation which Goffman (1961) explored in detail in his work on total institutions.

The straightforward ego-net density measure is a relatively blunt structural instrument which fails to explore differentiation within the ego-net and which can disguise the fact that some parts of it are, in some cases, denser than others. One way to overcome this is to find the components in the alter network (again we look at the network with ego deleted) – perhaps measuring their individual densities. If there is just one component then this would indicate that the alters are from similar social circles and as such ego may not have much access to alternative viewpoints or information. If on the other hand ego is connected to alters from many components then they could well have access to diverse resources and this could be of benefit. This is the argument put forward by Ron Burt (1995) in his book *Structural Holes*, and he proposed a set of structural measures for capturing this that we now outline.

Using Burt's terminology, when two alters are not connected there is a structural hole between them. He goes on to argue, backed up by examples, that unconnected alters can offer ego different pieces of information or that ego can play them off against each other. In both cases there is much benefit to ego. Burt proposed three measures to capture this situation (each defined for valued networks): effective size, constraint and hierarchy. We will describe the first two in detail.

Effective Size

As its name suggests, 'effective size' provides another way of measuring the size of an ego-net. It differs from the other measure considered earlier in this chapter (i.e. degree) in the respect that it takes into account the redundancy of certain ties: that is, the fact that certain of ego's alters may duplicate one another in terms of the goods they afford ego access to. Alters who duplicate in this way do not contribute to the effective size of ego's network for Burt.

Effective size for undirected binary data is ego's degree minus the average degree of the alters (not including ties to ego). If there are no ties between the alters then the average degree of the alters is zero and hence the effective size is ego's degree. In this instance we see that ego has connections to unconnected alters and so this network has the maximum number of structural holes. If all the alters are connected to each other, then, since we do not include ego, the average degree of the alters will be one less than the degree of ego and hence the effective size would be one. Note that if ego has no alters then it has an effective size of zero.

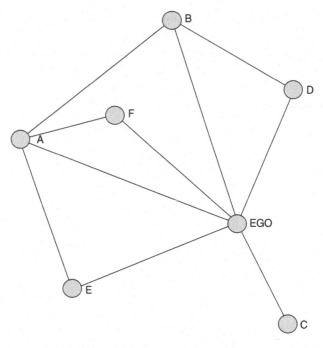

Figure 4.1   A simple ego-net

We can see how effective size is calculated looking at the network in Figure 4.1.

BOX 4.2

Effective Size

Let $p_{iq} = \dfrac{(a_{iq} + a_{qi})}{\Sigma_j(a_{ij} + a_{ji})}$, $i \neq j$

and

$$m_{jq} = \frac{a_{jq} + a_{qj}}{\max_k (a_{jk} + a_{kj})}, \quad j \neq k$$

Then effective size is given by:

$$\sum_j \left[1 - \sum_q p_{iq} m_{jq} \right] \quad q \neq i, j$$

Where the sum over j is all the alters of ego.

We see EGO has degree 6 and if we look at the alters then they have degrees (not including connections to EGO as follows A=3, B=2, C=0, D=1, E=1 and F=1. This means the average degree of the alters is 8/6 so that the effective size 6–4/3 = 4.6667. As already mentioned, this is the calculation for a binary symmetric matrix. The formula for a valued and directed matrix A whose elements are a_{ij} is given in Box 4.2.

Constraint

The constraint measure focuses upon the alternatives that alters have to exchanging resources with ego. If they are connected to one another, such that they can trade with one another in preference to trading with ego then they are in a position to constrain ego in their interaction with her. If they are not connected to one another then it is assumed that they have no (or few) alternatives and ego is less constrained. The measure of constraint focuses upon investment (of time and energy) in relations. For binary data it is assumed that time invested is equally divided amongst alters and hence a function of ego's degree. We calculate how much constraint each alter has on ego. Ego constraint is the sum of these constraints.

Returning to Figure 4.1, to give an example, we noted that there are six contacts for EGO. From this we infer that ego spends 1/6th of their time with each alter. We denote by P_{ij} the time that i (ego) invests in each j (alter). The general formula for the constraint that alter A has on EGO is given by:

$$(P_{EGO,A} + \sum X P_{EGO,X} P_{X,A})$$

where the summation is over all X that are connected to A. Hence in Figure 4.1 $P_{EGO,E} = P_{EGO,A} = 1/6$ and $P_{A,E} = \frac{1}{4}$ so that the constraint on ego from E is $(1/6 + 1/6 \times 4)^2 = 0.0434$. The total constraint on EGO from all the alters is 0.4. This measure is an inverse measure of structural holes as less constraint means more structural holes. It should be noted that this measure can have values larger than one. This is particularly true for smaller networks.

Software: UCINET and Ego-Nets

Turning now to software, UCINET (Borgatti et al. 2002) is a network analysis package designed for analysing whole networks. It has a number of routines which calculate ego–net metrics from whole networks. Also associated with UCINET (but a separate program in its own right) is NetDraw (Borgatti 2002). This allows visualisation of ego-nets drawn from whole networks. Both UCINET and NetDraw have flexible data entry methods and have capabilities beyond what we require. Both packages and documentation are available on the Analytic Technologies website (www.analytictech.com). We shall cover the simplest form of data entry which will demonstrate the basics, but anyone interested in exploring the full potential of this software should look at the book, *Analysing Social Networks* (Borgatti et al. 2013) and the book's companion website that gives details on how to do all of the examples given in the text.

Data Input for UCINET

In Chapter One we saw how to represent networks in an adjacency matrix. Whilst this is a useful method, it is not very practical if we have large networks. An alternative is to use link lists. We briefly outline these here. The simplest link list is a nodelist format. This lists each actor in the network on a new line followed by the actors they are connected to on the same line. Hence if we were to represent our ego-net in Figure 4.1 in this format we would have:

EGO A B C D E F

A EGO B E F

B EGO A D

C EGO

D EGO B

E EGO A

F EGO A

The first line tells us that EGO is connected to all the other actors. The third says that B is connected to EGO and also to both A and D. Note that each edge is represented twice. To avoid this repetition we can tell UCINET that the ties are all reciprocated. This allows us to reduce our data input to:

EGO A B C D E F

A B E F

B D

Note this format works for any binary whole network and is in essence a simple representation of the network with each line representing an ego-net with no alter-alter ties. Figure 4.2 is a screenshot of UCINET with the DL editor launched. The DL editor allows input for linked list formats.

The editor can be launched by clicking the fourth button from the left on the UCINET tool bar (annotated in the diagram) or by clicking on Data|Data editors|DL editor from the menu buttons above the toolbar.

Figure 4.2 UCINET and the DL editor

The format required is called nodelist 1 and the box has been ticked to indicate that the edges are symmetric (i.e. all ties are reciprocated). Finally the data have been entered into the editor in a spreadsheet format with each node in a separate cell. This can now be saved as a UCINET dataset.

Analysing Ego-Nets with UCINET

We will first show how to use UCINET to do some ego-net analysis on whole networks. UCINET has a number of datasets included and so we will use these as an illustration. We first use an example with no alter attributes – as our data source is a whole network alter-alter ties are necessarily present. The ZACKAR dataset in UCINET is data collected by Zachary (1977) in a karate club. There are two matrices. The first is a simple binary matrix (ZACHE) representing the existence of ties. The second includes tie strengths which count the number of interactions that occurred between the actors with values from 0 to 7. In UCINET we ran Network|Ego Networks|Egonet Density and entered ZACKAR as the dataset as shown in Figure 4.3.

If we now run this by clicking OK we get the output as shown in Figure 4.4 (we just show the first 14 actors) where ZACHE is the binary matrix and ZACHC is the valued matrix.

In this output each row represents a different ego-net and the columns give the ego-net size, the average degree of the alters (not including ego) and the density of the network (again with ego removed). For the valued

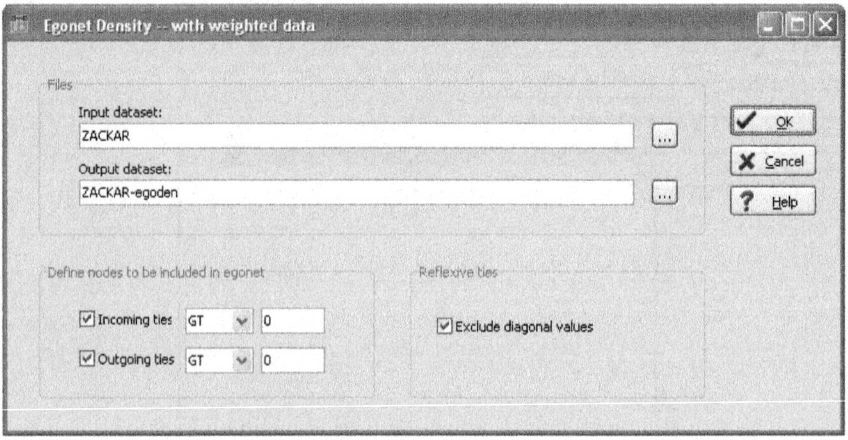

Eponet Density -- with weighted data

Files

Input dataset:
ZACKAR

Output dataset:
ZACKAR-egoden

✓ OK
✗ Cancel
? Help

Define nodes to be included in egonet

☑ Incoming ties GT ∨ 0

☑ Outgoing ties GT ∨ 0

Reflexive ties

☑ Exclude diagonal values

Figure 4.3 UCINET Ego Density routine

	Matrix: ZACHE				Matrix: ZACHE		
	1	2	3		1	2	3
	Size	AvgDeg	Density		Size	AvgDeg	Density
	------	------	------		------	------	------
1	16.000	2.250	0.150	1	16.000	7.500	0.500
2	9.000	2.667	0.333	2	9.000	7.778	0.972
3	10.000	2.200	0.244	3	10.000	7.000	0.778
4	6.000	3.333	0.667	4	6.000	12.333	2.467
5	3.000	1.333	0.667	5	3.000	3.333	1.667
6	4.000	1.500	0.500	6	4.000	4.000	1.333
7	4.000	1.500	0.500	7	4.000	4.500	1.500
8	4.000	3.000	1.000	8	4.000	12.000	4.000
9	5.000	2.000	0.500	9	5.000	7.200	1.800
10	2.000	0.000	0.000	10	2.000	0.000	0.000
11	3.000	1.333	0.667	11	3.000	4.000	2.000
12	1.000	0.000		12	1.000	0.000	
13	2.000	1.000	1.000	13	2.000	3.000	3.000
14	5.000	2.400	0.600	14	5.000	9.600	2.400

Figure 4.4 UCINET Ego Density for the Zachary dataset

data the size remains the same but the average degree is the average value of all the alter ties and density is the sum of all edge values divided by the total possible number of edges. For binary data the effective size is simply column 1 minus column 2. Since actor 12 has only one alter the density would be undefined and is represented by a blank.

As already noted, it is common to have some information on alter attributes. There was a fission in the karate club which resulted in two new clubs being formed. The UCINET dataset has the information telling us which club each actor subsequently joined after the split. We can use this to look at homophily in the ego-nets. To what extent did each actor associate with actors who ended up in the same club as they did after the split? To explore homophily in UCINET we run Network|Ego Networks|Egonet Homophily on the Zachary dataset selecting club as our attribute as shown in Figure 4.5.

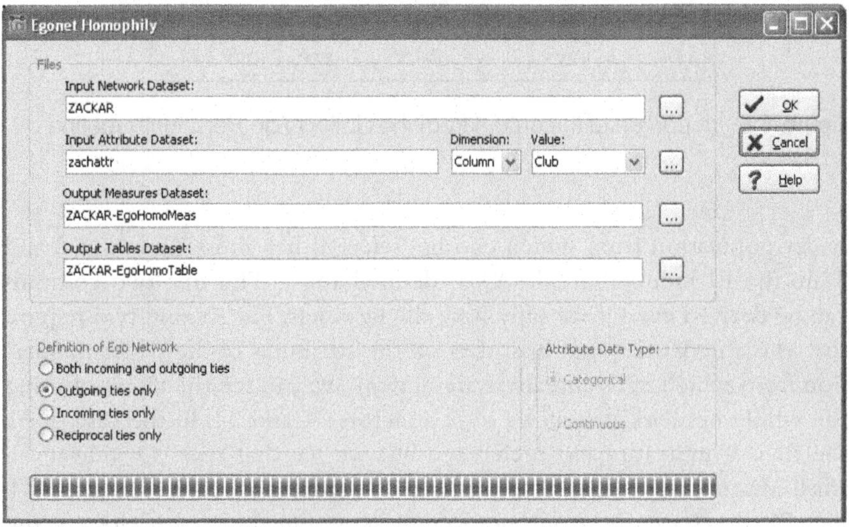

Figure 4.5 UCINET Ego Homophily

Note the definition of the Ego Network is irrelevant as the ties are undirected. The output has eight different homophily measures but we show just the first four on the last 14 actors in Figure 4.6.

The first column is the proportion of ego's ties that are in the same category as ego. The third column gives the proportion of matches, taking into account the proportion of nodes falling into each category in the

```
Matrix #1: ZACHE
Ego Net Homophily

              1           2          3          4
           PctHom      EI Ind     Matche     YulesQ
           ------      ------     ------     ------

    20      0.667      -0.333      0.545      0.391
    21      1.000      -1.000      0.576      1.000
    22      1.000      -1.000      0.576      1.000
    23      1.000      -1.000      0.576      1.000
    24      1.000      -1.000      0.667      1.000
    25      1.000      -1.000      0.606      1.000
    26      1.000      -1.000      0.606      1.000
    27      1.000      -1.000      0.576      1.000
    28      0.750      -0.500      0.576      0.574
    29      0.667      -0.333      0.545      0.391
    30      1.000      -1.000      0.636      1.000
    31      0.500       0.000      0.515      0.034
    32      0.833      -0.667      0.636      0.758
    33      0.833      -0.667      0.758      0.852
    34      0.824      -0.647      0.848      0.941
```

Figure 4.6   A portion of the output from the UCINET Ego Homophily routine

wider population from which ego has selected her alters. Columns 2 and 4 are the EI index and Yules Q as defined above. The first two columns can be derived even if we only have the ego-nets. The second two require the whole network (or at least data on the attributes of the wider population from which egos and alters are drawn). We can see the effect of using the whole network data if we look at actors 31 and 34. In the case of 31 the EI is 0 indicating no preference but we see that Yules Q indicates a small amount of homophily. The effect is more noticeable for actor 34. Her EI shows a fairly strong homophily score but this moves close to the maximum when the composition of the wider population is considered, in the Yules Q measure. No actor shows any heterophily which is to be expected as people were likely to stay in the club that their alters ended up in. We can look at alter dispersion in UCINET by running Network|Ego Networks|Egonet Composition – there are then choices for categorical or continuous attributes.

Our final example of using UCINET will be to look at Burt's structural hole measures. We again use the Zachary data and the routine is Network|Ego Networks|Structural Holes. This routine gives all of the

Burt measures plus a number of other brokerage type measures which are in the same vein as Burt's measures. UCINET offers the ego–net model which is the one we have discussed but in addition allows the user to select the whole network model. This later model is similar to the ego–net model but includes actors who are not connected to ego but are connected to two or more alters. We give just Burt's measures for the first 14 actors of the Zachary data in Figure 4.7.

```
Matrix #1: ZACHE
Structural Hole Measures

           1        2        3        4        5
        Degree   EffSiz   Effici   Constr   Hierar
        ------   ------   ------   ------   ------

  1     16.000   13.750   0.859    0.178    0.102
  2      9.000    6.333   0.704    0.342    0.165
  3     10.000    7.800   0.780    0.244    0.057
  4      6.000    2.667   0.444    0.528    0.050
  5      3.000    1.667   0.556    0.840    0.074
  6      4.000    2.500   0.625    0.642    0.035
  7      4.000    2.500   0.625    0.642    0.035
  8      4.000    1.000   0.250    0.766    0.000
  9      5.000    3.000   0.600    0.554    0.022
 10      2.000    2.000   1.000    0.500    0.000
 11      3.000    1.667   0.556    0.840    0.074
 12      1.000    1.000   1.000    1.000    1.000
 13      2.000    1.000   0.500    1.125    0.000
 14      5.000    2.600   0.520    0.530    0.037
```

Figure 4.7 Burt's structural hole methods for a portion of the Zachary data

The first column is degree, a measure of actual size. The second is effective size which, as we have said, takes account of redundancy. We see that most ego–nets have an effective size much smaller than their actual size.

Column 3 is efficiency. This is effective size divided by degree. The idea here is that maintaining ties requires resources and that it is inefficient to maintain ties with alters who are connected to one's other alters. It would be better to have ties with others who are not connected, thereby increasing the number of structural holes in one's network and the opportunities which they afford. This probably does not make much sense for the situation here but could be important in a more competitive environment. In fact, to emphasise that his theory is about competition, Burt does not call the nodes actors but players.

The fourth column is constraint and the fifth is Burt's final measure, hierarchy. This is a centralisation type measure based on constraint. It takes into account the distribution of constraint amongst alters.

UCINET provides a number of other ego-net measures. Probably the most important are those, intended for ego-net panel data, which measure change in ego-nets across time. Given a network at two time periods (stored in a single dataset with two matrices), they count number of ties gained, lost, kept, etc., and record whether contacts in each of these categories had ties with the alters in the earlier ego-net. We do not provide details here but we do discuss methods for analysing change in ego-nets further in Chapter Six.

NetDraw

NetDraw (Borgatti 2002) is a stand-alone network visualisation tool but it is also integrated with UCINET. It can directly read UCINET data-files although it does have its own data structures. We shall only consider it as part of UCINET and it can be launched directly from the UCINET main screen. It can be launched by clicking on Visualize | NetDraw or by clicking the button directly below 'Visualize' just to the right of the button marked 'Alg'. The UCINET quick start guide gives a brief introduction to NetDraw and we will not go into details here other than demonstrating routines we require. If we launch NetDraw and then click on File | Open | Ucinet dataset | Network and enter Zackar and click OK we obtain the image shown in Figure 4.8.

The layout is the default and is based on the idea that nodes should repel each other, lines should be of a similar length and nodes that are separated by many steps should be far apart. The Zachary data are not directed and the arrow-heads can be removed by clicking the button marked '→'. Once the network is loaded we can bring in any attribute files and these can be used to shape, colour or position the nodes. A good discussion on network visualisation is contained in Chapter 7 of *Analysing Social Networks* (Borgatti et al. 2013). For the Zachary data we imported the attribute file and shaped the nodes with respect to which club they joined.

NetDraw allows us to examine ego-nets from the whole network. If we click the ego button it brings up the Ego Network Viewer which is shown in Figure 4.9. All nodes are listed and the ego-net to be viewed is determined by ego. In this case we have ticked actor 3. We also ticked colour and have shaded ego black and the alters grey for easy identification. We can scroll through all the egos using the buttons below the right window pane.

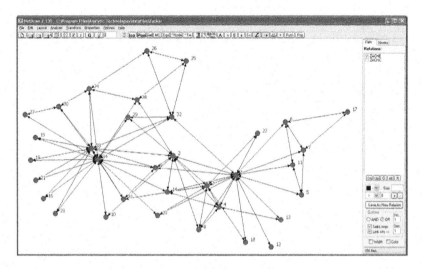

Figure 4.8 A visualisation of Zachary data using NetDraw

The ego-net corresponding to actor 3 will be displayed but it may be rather small as the actors will be in the same position as they were when the whole network was displayed. Clicking on the button with the lightning bolt will

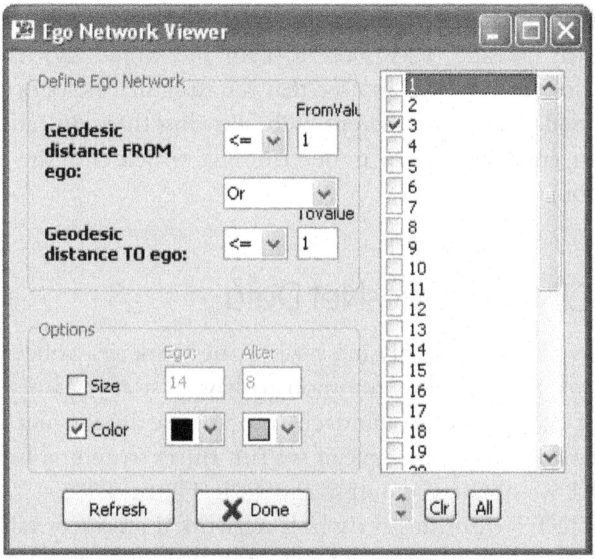

Figure 4.9 NetDraw Ego Network Viewer window

apply the general layout algorithm to just the displayed network and so will give a better visualisation. This is shown in Figure 4.10.

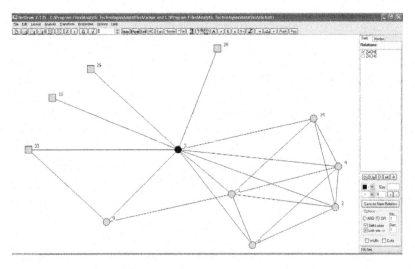

Figure 4.10   Ego-net for actor 3

We can see actor 3 had connections to actors who went to both clubs in nearly equal measure (IQV score is 0.96) and would also have a homophily score close to zero. We also see that the structural holes occur between actors who ended up at a different club, showing that constraint may well have been an important factor in determining which club the actor finally decided to join.

Using UCINET on Ego-Net Data

So far we have looked at analysing a whole network as a collection of ego-nets. However it is far more common to have just an ego–net or rather a collection of ego-nets. One approach is to analyse an ego–net as if it were a whole network. So, for example, if we run Burt's structural hole measures on Figure 4.1 we obtain the output shown in Figure 4.11.

Since UCINET treats this as a whole network it produces values for both ego and the alters but the alter values are not valid and only the ego line has the correct values. Clearly if we have only a few ego-nets then this method is

```
Structural Hole Measures

                 1        2        3        4        5
               Degre    EffSi    Effic    Const    Hiera
               -----    -----    -----    -----    -----

  1   EGO      6.000    4.667    0.778    0.400    0.095
  2   A        4.000    2.500    0.625    0.684    0.168
  3   B        3.000    1.667    0.556    0.840    0.074
  4   C        1.000    1.000    1.000    1.000    1.000
  5   D        2.000    1.000    0.500    1.125    0.000
  6   E        2.000    1.000    0.500    1.125    0.000
  7   F        2.000    1.000    0.500    1.125    0.000
```

Figure 4.11 Burt's structural hole measures on Figure 4.1

feasible but it would be tedious if we had a large number. We can overcome this problem by loading a collection of ego–nets as separate components in a larger network. We can then run ego methods on the large network and extract just the results for all the egos. It is worth obeying a few simple conventions to help manage this process. Firstly it is worth naming egos as ego1, ego2, etc., or if we have names then egoname1, egoname2, etc. It is important to make sure that each ego name is unique. Different alters for different egos may have the same name and this again can cause problems and so it is worth using a naming convention that includes ego. If we have ego1, ego2, etc., then the alters could be 1name1, 1name2, 1name3, 2name1, etc., where the first number indicates the ego that the alter is connected to. Even if ego and alters have names that are known it is recommended to use a number coding as well as a name. We will show how this works in a very simple example. If the data are already in UCINET, all in separate UCINET files, then the routine Transform | Graph Theoretic | Union can be used to create one dataset. Normally though the researcher would not have these coded as UCINET files and would need to import them using the DL editor. As an example we shall construct an overall network of four ego-nets, the first of which will be Figure 4.1. We will name the egos as Ego1,2,3,4, etc. For the alters we will use letters but with the convention described above. The DL screen is shown in Figure 4.12.

These are then saved as a UCINET dataset and if we view the result in NetDraw we obtain the networks as shown in Figure 4.13.

We also use the spreadsheet editor to type in some attributes. We have the categorical attribute for sex and the continuous variable for age. In addition we have created an ego indicator matrix (an attribute file indicating which

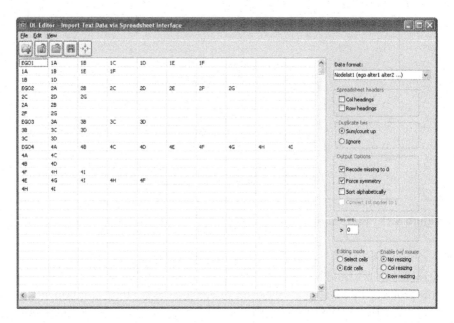

Figure 4.12   The DL screen for four ego-nets

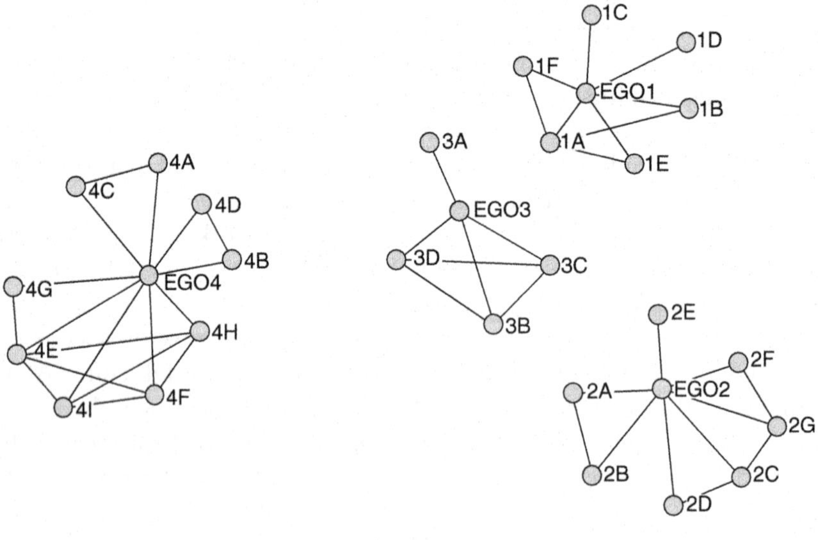

Figure 4.13   Imported ego-nets

egos are nodes and which alters), where 0 indicates that a node is an alter and 1 indicates that they are ego. We show the first 17 entries of this matrix in Figure 4.14.

		ind	Age	Sex
		---	---	---
1	EGO1	1	23	1
2	1A	0	45	1
3	1B	0	63	2
4	EGO2	1	24	2
5	2C	0	33	2
6	2A	0	45	2
7	2F	0	19	1
8	EGO3	1	53	1
9	3B	0	26	1
10	3C	0	38	2
11	EGO4	1	44	2
12	4A	0	55	1
13	4B	0	63	2
14	4F	0	26	1
15	4E	0	45	1
16	4H	0	62	1
17	1C	0	65	2

Figure 4.14   Ego-nets attribute matrix

As an example we run the ego-net composition routine for continuous attributes and select age as our attribute as shown in the following screenshot, Figure 4.15.

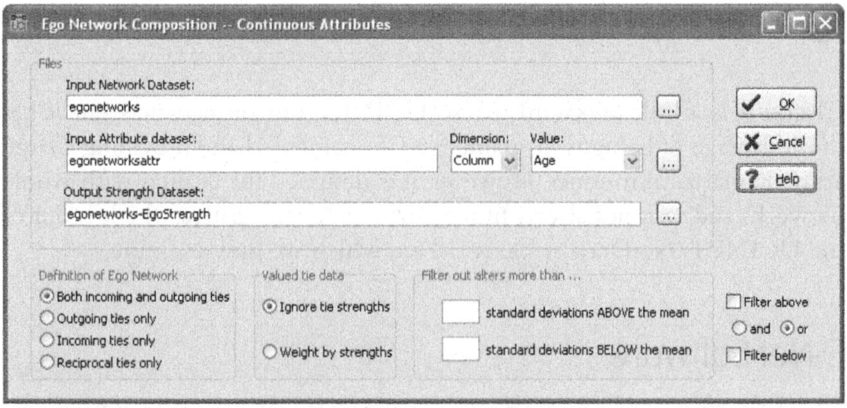

Figure 4.15   The Ego Network Composition screen

The output will contain redundant information for each of the alters and if we had a few hundred ego-nets this would be unwieldy. We therefore use the extract feature in UCINET to pull out the results just for the egos. That is we run Data | Filter | Extract | Submatrix on the output egonetworks-Ego Strength making sure we only keep the rows corresponding to ego specified by column 1 of our attribute matrix as shown in Figure 4.16.

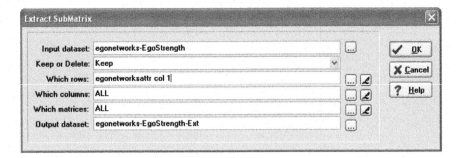

Figure 4.16   Extract screen for ego network composition

This results in the output for just the egos are shown in Figure 4.17.

		1 Avg ---	2 Sum ----	3 Min ---	4 Max ---	5 StdDev ------	6 Num ----
1	EGO1	55.333	332.000	34.000	71.000	12.658	6.000
4	EGO2	49.286	345.000	19.000	83.000	19.491	7.000
8	EGO3	35.500	142.000	26.000	50.000	9.526	4.000
11	EGO4	44.778	403.000	26.000	63.000	12.291	9.000

Figure 4.17   Output for just the egos

Clearly it is a little awkward to use UCINET just on ego-nets but it has the advantage of being well-maintained, documented and providing a large array of analytical routines. However, it is designed for dealing with whole networks and so is not always fit for purpose. An alternative which is out of the UCINET/NetDraw stable is E-Net, which we now examine.

E-Net Software

E-Net (Borgatti 2006) is designed to analyse ego-net data collected via personal network research design. E-Net allows for visualisation, has a standard suite of measures but importantly has a data management function in an SPSS style format. E-Net has three file types. Firstly, it can read UCINET files and so can bring in whole networks. Secondly, it has a text dl type row format (actually an extension of NetDraw's vna format) which has a similar structure to the format we have suggested in UCINET. Finally, it has a column-based Excel format which we will not discuss. A full description of the various data types is contained in the article by Halgin and Borgatti (2012).

Data Input in E-Net

In the row wise format, data are imported in three matrices specified in plain text. It is best to create these using Excel and then to copy and paste these into notepad or some other text editor. The first matrix contains all the information about the egos; each matrix has a header to tell the software what type of data will follow. The ego matrix has the names and the attributes of all the egos. If 1 represented male and 2 female, for example, as in Figure 4.14, then our ego data would be as in Figure 4.18.

```
*ego data
ID      Age   Sex
EGO1    23    Male
EGO2    24    Female
EGO3    53    Male
EGO4    44    Female
```

Figure 4.18   Row wise data for ego

The second matrix is the alter data. This says which alters are associated with which ego and allows for values on the edges as well. We can use this format to have a variety of different types of ego-alter connection such as friend or co-worker. We simply have a different column for each type of relation. Suppose that in our example in Figure 4.13 we had two kinds of relation, namely, Sibling and Friend, and these are differentiated in our alter data matrix. In this matrix each edge from ego to alter is on a separate line. The next two columns specify the relationship type and the last two columns give the alter attributes. We give a portion of the data in Figure 4.19.

Finally, we give the alter-alter connections. Again there can be more than one relation and these need not be the same relation as connects alter to egos. This again is in an edge list format and we can have values associated with the edges. In Figure 4.20 we show a portion of the alter-alter tie matrix for the network in Figure 4.13.

```
*alter data

From    To    Friend  Sibling  Age    Sex
EGO1    1A    1       0        45     Male
EGO1    1B    0       1        63     Female
EGO1    1C    1       0        65     Female
EGO1    1D    1       0        34     Male
EGO1    1E    0       1        54     Male
EGO1    1F    1       0        71     Female
EGO2    2A    1       0        45     Female
EGO2    2B    1       0        83     Male
EGO2    2C    1       0        33     Female
EGO2    2D    1       0        67     Male
EGO2    2E    0       1        47     Female
EGO2    2F    1       0        19     Male
EGO2    2G    1       0        51     Female
EGO3    3A    0       1        50     Female
```

Figure 4.19 Row wise data for alters

```
*alter-alter data
From    To    Knows
1A      1B    1
1B      1D    1
1A      1E    1
1A      1F    1
2A      2B    1
2F      2G    1
```

Figure 4.20 A portion of the alter-alter tie network

If we start up E-Net and import this file then we get a screen that looks like Figure 4.21.

There are five important tabs and the screen has opened on the ego tab. This gives all the data we entered in the first ego matrix. As we only had four egos this is fairly simple. Note we can filter our egos using SQL in the filter box on the right. Hence we could specify SEX='Male' or age > 25 to filter some of the egos. The alters tab and the alter=alters tabs are similar and give the information in the second two matrices and again allow filtering. The visualisation tab allows the user to scroll through each ego-net manually or automatically. When an alter is highlighted, information about the alter is displayed. We can see this in Figure 4.22 where we look at Ego 4 and the alter information on 4D.

If we click on the analysis menu we can select one of the standard ego-net analysis methods we have already described. The output from this can

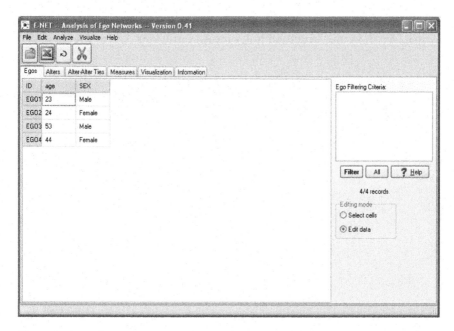

Figure 4.21 The E-Net Ego screen

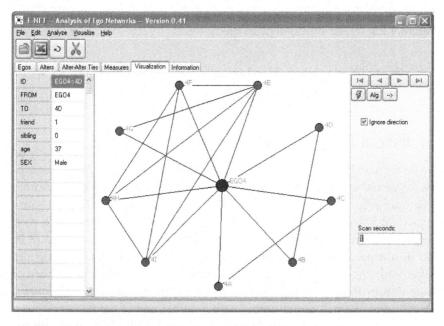

Figure 4.22 Visualisation of Ego 4 with 4D alter information

be displayed by clicking on the measures tab. This is shown in a spreadsheet format. We show the structural holes measures for our data in Figure 4.23.

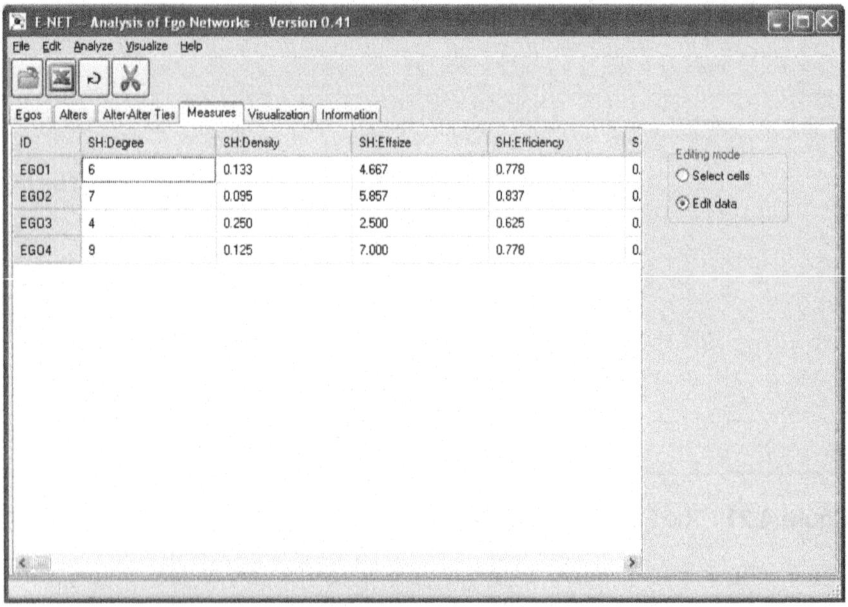

ID	SH:Degree	SH:Density	SH:Effsize	SH:Efficiency	S
EGO1	6	0.133	4.667	0.778	0.
EGO2	7	0.095	5.857	0.837	0.
EGO3	4	0.250	2.500	0.625	0.
EGO4	9	0.125	7.000	0.778	0.

Figure 4.23   E-Net structural holes measures

Cells can be selected or edited and clicking on the Excel button exports all the data from the spreadsheet into Excel.

Statistical Tests Using Ego-Net Measures

So far we have looked at purely descriptive measures for ego-nets but we may be interested in having some rigorous tests related to our ego-net measures. For example, we may want to test Burt's theory that people with more structural holes receive higher levels of remuneration, or that people with a greater range of friends are happier. These would be standard things to do in normal statistics, and under certain conditions we can also do the same with ego-net data. Standard inferential statistics makes a number of assumptions about the data allowing us to assume it is taken from a known distribution. We will not go into details here but one of the most common assumptions is that we have independent measurements. To achieve this we need to make sure that our ego-nets are all independent from each other. Note it is the networks that really need to be independent and not just the egos. We see how to relax this assumption in later chapters. For example, suppose in a given population (say everyone aged between 20 and 40 in the United Kingdom) we wanted to test whether women had a greater tie dispersion than men in their ego-nets, we could proceed as follows. Firstly, randomly draw a large sample of men and women from the given age group from the UK population. Ask everyone in our sample to construct their ego-net using the name generator and use this data to calculate Agresti's IQV measure as described earlier in the chapter. Perform a standard t-test to see if the average IQV score for the men's egos was lower than the average for the women's egos. We can use the same general approach to do any of the standard statistical methods such as ANOVA, correlation, regression, etc. In these cases we are treating the ego-net measures as attributes of the egos and provided the networks are independent we have not violated any statistical assumptions.

As already discussed we sometimes calculate ego-net measures from whole networks. In this case clearly the egos/alters are not independent and so we cannot apply standard statistical methods. In this case one alternative would be to apply permutation tests. This really falls under the heading of whole network analysis so we do not pursue it here. The interested reader can find more information in the book *Analysing Social Networks* (Borgatti et al. 2013). Equally our ego-nets might not be constructed from a whole network but they may still not be independent. We explore this further in the final two chapters of this book.

Finally we give a brief overview of a study that has used ego-net analysis in a statistical setting. We will not give details but merely outline what was done and summarise the main findings. Full details can be found in Podolny and Baron (1997). The study examines informal ego-net structures in the workplace and to what extent they can be used to predict mobility within the organisation. They collected data from a high technology organisation of some 25,000 employees, a random sample of 658 of these employees being provided by the human resources department. These employees were given a questionnaire and the researchers received 236 usable responses. The data looked at a one-year time period. During this time 57 of the respondents had a promotion (actually a 'grade shift' in terms used by the company) and this was the dependent variable. The independent variables were constructed mainly from the ego-nets. These consisted of ego-net size, number of alter-alter ties (which the authors call indirect ties) and average duration. The average duration was simply the average time ego had an association with all the alters. They collected these data on a number of different types of ego-net, for example the task-advice network (i.e. the formal ties), the strategic-information network (useful informal ties), fate-control networks (ties to people who had a role in determining their promotion) and support networks. They also included a number of non-network, mainly control, variables such as race, gender, age, tenure and time at current grade, as well as the existence of a mentor relation. The dependent variable, independent variables and the control variables were then modelled using a regression model. Since the dependent variable was 'having gained a promotion or not', logistic regression was used.

The results show that having large strategic-information networks improves promotion chances and this is further enhanced if this network has many structural holes confirming Burt's theory. In contrast, fate-control networks have a negative effect as size increases which is further exacerbated if the network has few alter-alter ties. This shows that it is important to have a small number of well-connected alters in the fate-control network. Finally, having a mentor had little effect unless they were also in the fate-control network. The paper gives further details on disaggregating certain types of tie, which we do not report here, but the point is that the importance of network structures is clear and this paper shows how they can be integrated into standard statistical methods.

Summary

Ego-net measures examine ties, alters and overall structure. Tie analysis tries to capture the central tendency and tie dispersion of ego-alter ties, whereas alter analysis looks at the central tendency and heterogeneity of the alters. Comparing the attributes of ego with the attributes of the alters provides us with measures of homophily. The patterning of alter-alter ties is captured by structural shape measures such as Burt's structural holes. Software packages such as UCINET and NetDraw can be used to extract and visualise ego-nets drawn from whole networks but equally well a collection of ego-nets can be assembled into something that resembles a whole network and these packages can then be used to calculate specific ego measures. If there are a large number of ego-nets, or sophisticated data-manipulation such as filtering is required, then E-Net provides these tools. If ego-nets have been independently and randomly sampled from a larger population then the ego-net measures can be attributed to ego, treated as a regular statistical variable and analysed by using conventional methods such as regression.

5

NARRATIVES, TYPOLOGIES AND CASE STUDIES

Learning Outcomes

In this chapter you will learn:

1. Why and how to draw upon qualitative data - not only in the construction of ego-nets (Chapter Two) but in the analysis of ego-nets as well.

2. The value of a narrative analysis of ego-nets, which explores 'network stories' and perceives networks as narrative constructions.

3. Mixed methods approaches to ego-net analysis, combining factors of network culture and network structure.

4. How typologies and case studies are useful in ego-net analysis.

Introduction

The previous chapter has discussed how ego-networks and their properties can be investigated using the formal methods of SNA. In addition to these techniques, there are ways to analyse ego-networks that seek to utilise qualitative data about ties and relationships, and to draw upon qualitative data as a central part of network analysis.

In this chapter we will consider key ways in which ego-net analysis can utilise qualitative data and how this analysis is carried out. Firstly, ego-nets can be analysed using the narrative accounts provided by qualitative sources, and, furthermore, they can be approached in analysis as 'narrative constructions'. Secondly, mixed methods approaches to ego-net analysis show how qualitative analysis can be usefully combined with formal SNA in order to take account of the ways in which 'network culture' and 'network structure' interact. In the course of the chapter we encounter some of the concrete ways in which qualitative and mixed methods ego-network analysis is performed, specifically through the use of typologies and case studies.

Qualitative data sources (like interviews, biographies, diaries, historical archives and so on) are particularly useful for ego-net analysis because of their flexibility. In Chapter Three we saw that they allow for information to be gathered about ego's ties to alters, as well as alter-to-alter ties (much like the name-generator survey). While these can be inputted into matrices for quantitative analysis, qualitative sources (unlike surveys) also give us access to something else: the actor's account of the network from their point of view. Qualitative sources therefore enable what has been referred to as a 'bifocal' approach to social networks that can involve both quantitative and qualitative forms of analysis (Coviello 2005). In this chapter we will engage with examples of research in which ego-nets have been analysed in solely qualitative ways, as well as examples of where qualitative analysis has been combined with the formal methods outlined in the preceding chapter.

Networks and Narratives

At the most basic, narratives are 'stories' that are told in written or spoken form, and provide an account of events and experiences and the ways in which they are connected together from an actor's point of view. Narratives are generated by a range of qualitative data sources, including interviews, letters, diaries, speeches, biographies and observations. In Chapter Three, we saw that qualitative data sources like these provide a crucial source for researchers when gathering ego-net data: here, we extend our focus by looking at how narratives can be used in the analysis of that data, both in their own right, and in combination with formal SNA.

In this section, we will suggest that 'network narratives' – the stories that are told about ties and relationships – are useful to analyse because they provide accounts of what ties 'mean' to network members from their subjective point of view. These accounts also assist the researcher in understanding and interpreting sociograms and network measures. In this sense, narratives provide us with a way to explore the *content* as well as the *form* of social ties, and, as we will see later in the chapter, there are good reasons to think that the two are mutually informative. Furthermore, narratives provide another way (in addition to the statistical techniques of Chapter Seven) to help us explore social networks as active and dynamic processes. Indeed, there is an argument that says that social ties are constructed through 'narratives' in the first place. This last statement is an important one: if telling stories about ties are important to the actual achievement of ties, then they clearly demand analytic attention (McLean 1998; White 2008; Yeung 2005). Let us consider each of these points in turn.

Accessing Meaning

In Chapter Four, we saw that the strength of formal SNA lies in its ability to visualise and explore the relational properties of ego-networks, and to extract ego-networks from whole populations. In the process, however, questions about the content, meaning and significance that social relationships have for ego are (necessarily) put aside (Crossley, 2010). In matrices, for example, we reduce social ties between ego and alters to numerical data which tells us whether ties of a particular 'type' are present or absent (0s or 1s in our matrix), and perhaps to some numerical indicator of the strength of ties (for example, reflected in the thickness of the lines in the sociogram).

This reduction of social relationships to numerical data aids a general view of the relational structure of ego-networks. It moves beyond a focus upon particular dyadic relationships by enabling us to situate an actor within the wider patterning of ties that results from mapping how alters are also tied to each other. In short, formal ego-net analysis gives us an 'outsider view' of the actor's network (Edwards 2010; Jack 2010). It locates the actor's social relationships within an overall structure of positions and ties by mapping all of the 'links between the links' and considering how this patterning affects the actor.

Once we have gained an understanding of this relational structure, however, it is likely that we will want to revisit the content of particular relationships and the meaning that ego attaches to ties in order to appreciate what the lines in sociograms actually denote. Rather than answering all of our questions, visualisation and measures often open up more questions about why ego-nets have the properties they do, if and how these properties change, and what effect they have on ego. One way to address these sorts of questions is to consider narratives, or 'network stories', which can reveal how ties are defined, understood and acted upon. Why so?

Symbolic interactionist perspectives in sociology argue that the meaning (or content) of social ties is important for ego, as well as the structure (or form) of social ties that is privileged in formal SNA (Fuhse and Mutzel 2011). They claim that there is a need to analyse social networks from a 'phenomenological' perspective, i.e. from the point of view of subjective experience (Fine and Kleinman 1983). One compelling reason for this is that network structure is itself rooted in, and shaped by, the meanings that ego attaches to ties and the ways in which they subjectively categorise them. Remember for a moment that lines in sociograms indicate ties of particular 'types' or relationship 'categories' between actors (friends, colleagues, foes, kin and so on). The researcher in formal SNA more often than not imposes the meaning of these categories and treats them as stable and fixed. In name-generator surveys, for example, actors are asked to name the people who provide them with various kinds of support, or with whom they discuss important matters, in order to explore networks based on 'friendship'. Categories like 'friendship' however do not have singular meanings, but are subjectively defined in different ways by actors themselves (Bellotti, 2008a). As McLean (2007: xi) puts it, social ties are 'not merely given, nor do they have a simple fixed meaning'.

Narrative accounts of networks from the actor's point of view can be useful therefore to the extent that they enable us to explore in analysis the various ways in which ties are categorised and defined by actors. A good example of a study in which interview narratives are used to open up the question of how relationships are subjectively defined and categorised is Bellotti's (2008a) research into the friendship networks of young singletons (aged 25–35) living in Milan, Italy. Rather than imposing her own understanding of how 'friendship' as a relationship 'type' should be understood, Bellotti asked interviewees for the names of their friends without defining a 'friend' for them in advance (or putting any limits on the number of people they could list). This enabled the research to explore the different definitions and models of friendship that people employ, and the significance that friends have within people's lives.

The narrative accounts produced in Bellotti's interviews revealed that actors operate with very different ideas of what a 'friend' is – some cite the importance of various kinds of support for example (and access to the various resources discussed in Chapter Two), while others do not; some cite 'old' friends they have little contact with, while others only talk of those they see on a daily basis; some put emphasis on one or two 'best' friends who provide exclusive support, others on a group of friends, or a series of groups, who offer different kinds of support (Bellotti, 2008a). Importantly, different ideas about the obligations that friendship entails created different 'styles' of relating to others, which were also reflected in the structure of the ego-networks (see Figure 5.2, discussed later). The relation between meaning and network structure will be revisited later in the chapter. For now, it is clear from Bellotti's research, that sociograms should be thought of as relational structures that are mapped in the first place on the basis of the subjective meanings of ego (in this case, whom they consider to be a 'friend' using their own subjective criteria of friendship). Analysing the stories that actors tell about their ties to others is a crucial part of unpicking the consequences of different friendship network structures. Significantly, how ties are defined by ego (i.e. the categories they employ to describe ties), create different expectations and obligations around their relationships. It should be noted that while narrative accounts of social ties can be readily captured in interviews, they could also be explored using less obvious formats like diaries, letters, speeches and biographies (Crossley 2015, Edwards and Crossley 2009, Edwards 2014, McLean 1998) in which actors routinely 'talk their ties' (Edwards and Crossley 2009).

Narrative accounts are therefore particularly adept at addressing questions about the meaning of social relationships. When we ask people to describe their social ties they tend to accompany these descriptions with evaluations of the strength, quality and significance of ties. In this way, narrating social ties reveals much more than the number and pattern of connections; it communicates the 'lived experience' of networks too (Emmel and Clark, 2009). Narratives can therefore reveal what ego-nets look like from the 'inside'. This 'insider view' addresses the content of relationships and ongoing communicative processes of 'networking' that produce and reproduce the network over time (Edwards 2010; Jack 2010). It focuses attention on the subjective meaning and interpretation of network ties, and the way the network is perceived by the actor, or by particular alters within it. This raises an interesting point: in qualitative research on networks, data analysis can actually start at the same point as data collection. As people narrate their ties as part of data collection tools, such as interviews for example, they provide much more than relational data on whom they have connections with. They also provide subjective evaluations of those relationships. They start to analyse the relationships and what they mean to them, providing valuable insights for the researchers' understanding and explanation of the network. A good example of this comes from the ESRC project *Connected Lives*, about the nature of people's social networks in inner-city neighbourhoods (Emmel et al. 2005–09, see also Box 5.1). One of the methods the researchers used was participatory mapping: a technique used within an interview, which involves the research participant drawing a map of their social ties using pen and paper. While essentially a tool to collect relational data, they found that the descriptions people gave of their social ties while drawing the map were accompanied by subjective categorisations and evaluations, which became an important part of the analysis itself. For example, one participant reflected her subjective evaluations of ties when she talked of putting her work colleagues in a 'scary square box', and her friends in a 'fuzzy nice box' (Emmel and Clark 2009: 17).

Another example comes from the work of Lubbers et al. (2010) who used EgoNet software in interviews with Argentinian migrants in Spain, constructing sociograms in the course of the interview that became objects for discussion about the possible reasons for network change. Interviewees were asked to name 45 people they knew, or knew by sight or name, and had had contact with in the last two years (and could still contact if they wanted to) (Lubbers et al. 2010: 4). Two interviews were conducted two years apart in order to ask interviewees to compare their ego-networks and to initiate narrative accounts about the mechanisms that may have created the changes they observed in network structure. These network stories about change were combined with statistical methods for investigating change in ego-networks (see Chapter Seven). It is clear from both these examples that the actors' *descriptions* of their social network form an important part of the *analysis* of that network (Knox et al. 2006).

Interpreting Network Measures

Exploring network stories can also be a crucial part of the analysis of ego-nets to the extent that it helps us to understand what sociograms and network measures actually mean (Coviello 2005; Crossley 2008b; Edwards 2010; Jack 2010). Knowing the structural pattern of relationships between ego and alters, and how dense the network is (and so on), does not provide automatic insights into how these properties affect agency. Network stories however can provide a context to the measures presented in Chapter Four, and this context enables a more nuanced interpretation of the measures themselves.

One of the aspects of ego-networks, for example, that you might want to deduce using formal SNA is the extent to which ego is embedded in distinct social circles (Simmel, 1955) and acts as a 'broker' between them. Blockmodelling techniques can be used to specify the various clusters in an ego-net and to statistically explore the extent to which they intersect via ego.[1] The consequences of the intersection of social circles is hard to interpret, however, without understanding the 'network story'. We might assume that if ego is a broker between their different social circles (i.e. the social circles represent distinct clusters that only intersect via ego), then ego is in a position of advantage. This might be because, for example, they have more flexibility to present multiple 'selves' in their different social circles because their contacts in these different circles do not know one another. They can take information from one social circle to another, acting as gatekeeper and appearing as innovator. In short, they enjoy a position of advantage and control.

Seeking out the network stories of brokers can suggest a different interpretation, however. By analysing narrative accounts and drawing upon observations, Crossley (2008b) argues, for example, that actors in broker-age roles between different social groups at a sports gym did not enjoy an advantageous position, but were torn between different groups and their demands. They experienced overriding tension rather than influence. We cannot interpret network measures in an accurate way, therefore, without bringing narrative accounts to bear in our analysis (Crossley 2008b).

The network stories gleaned from observation may be just as important here as interview accounts. Conti and Doreian's (2010) investigation of the network structure of police officers undergoing academy training found racially heterogeneous networks, with many ties between police officers of different ethnic identities. However, 'network stories' generated through their ethnographic fieldwork revealed that underlying these structures was a culture of racial tension in which racist language and attitudes persisted. The validity of our interpretation of ego–nets and their dynamics can therefore be improved by analysing narrative accounts of the network.

Measuring the structural properties of ego–networks also has limitations when trying to deduce how particular social ties actually influence. Just because an actor has many ties to alters who adopt certain social practices, for example, does not mean that they will be influenced to adopt them themselves (as some contagion and diffusion models suggest). Whether practices get taken up depends instead upon more cultural and discursive processes, which can be explored using the narrative accounts of network members. Strang and Soule (1998) suggest for example that the adoption of new ideas and practices depends primarily on whether ego can frame them as legitimate and acceptable using the cultural resources available within their network (Strang and Soule 1998). Edwards (2014) looks at this process of framing new political protest tactics as culturally legitimate within ego-networks drawn from UK suffragettes, who were adopting militant tactics (like trying to get arrested and, later, stone-throwing and arson) in the early twentieth century. Edwards (2014) argues that particular ties within ego-nets exert more influence on ego's decision-making. Interpersonal ties for example appear to carry most influence over ego's adoption of the tactics, and discussions with friends and family are decisive for framing militant tactics in positive or negative terms. Ego is also influenced most by alters who are perceived to be socially similar to themselves (in terms of class, status and prestige in the local community). Other studies support the idea that ego is not equally influenced by everybody they know, but is influenced most by the alters whom they define as 'like them' in class and status terms, while alters who they define as 'socially distant' do not have the same degree of influence (Bottero 2010; Burt 1987). The complexities of interpersonal influence can thus be accessed and explored further by analysing the actor's narrative account of their ties.

Process and Change

In addition to the statistical techniques that are used to look at network dynamics and change over time (Chapter Seven), network stories also pro- vide us with a way of exploring social networks as active, dynamic and ongoing processes of social interaction. For example, name-generator surveys have a bias towards collecting data on already established ties when constructing ego-nets – the people who are named by ego tend to be those they have known for a significant period of time. In some cases, however, it is the newly forming ties – or the breaking away from established ties – that reveals most to us about the interactive processes shaping change in the network (Monsted 1995). These interactive processes of tie-formation lend themselves to investigation using network stories (Coviello 2005). Sources such as letters and diaries for example are dated and give us a way to see how relationships form and change (Edwards and Crossley 2009; McLean 1998). Narrative sources such as biographies can be useful in this respect too. Crossley (2015) draws upon biographical narratives to analyse how the networks of the early punk scene formed, enabling him to establish time lines around the links shown on sociograms (see Figure 5.1).

'On Saturday 2 August 1975 Mick Jones and Tony James went there to check out a new group [...] crashing into future Clash manager Bernie Rhodes' (Gilbert, 2005).

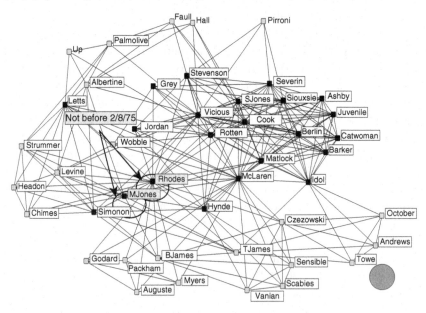

Figure 5.1   Using narratives in the analysis of tie formation
Source: Based on data from Crossley (2015)

Using narratives, the data we input into matrices can be dated, enabling us to produce snapshots of networks at different points in time and, importantly, to consider in analysis 'the mechanisms through which these relationships are reproduced or reconfigured over time' (Emirbayer and Goodwin 1994: 1447). Qualitative data are particularly adept at helping to identify the 'mechanisms' at play in forming, sustaining and breaking network ties. Referring back to Figure 5.1, Crossley (2015) uses biographical narratives to identify the mechanisms by which early punk networks formed. These included 'transitivity' (meeting through friends of friends) and 'foci' (meeting through a certain context of activity and then embarking upon further joint activities together) (Feld 1981). The network stories told in published biographies help to unpack these mechanisms in more detail by focusing on some of the cultural processes underlying the formation of ties and how, once established, networks come to share common cultural characteristics which exert a certain amount of pressure on network members to act in particular ways. For example, biographical narratives revealed the emergence of a 'punk look' through the exertion of interpersonal pressure:

> Bernie nearly threw a party when Mick got his hair cut [...] it was a struggle. Mick, Mick, Mick [...] everyone was saying it. Get your fucking hair cut. You had to drag him along. I don't think he ever liked it. (Gilbert 2005: 147)

Network stories can also reveal the way in which the definitions and categorisations of social relationships (that we discussed earlier in terms of tie-types) can change over time. Actors relate to one another in ways that are multiplex: they invoke different relationship models at the same time (for example, friends who are also colleagues). Network stories can tell us which relationship models are in play in which context, and how actors switch between them. Returning to the suffragette example (Edwards 2014), the ego-net of the suffragette Mary Blathwayt revealed multiplex ties because her activist network contained a high number of people whom she already related to as family and friends. In the course of her activism, the relationship model of 'comradeship' was invoked, and had attached to it a mutual expectation that her family, friends and fellow activists would support and participate in militant protests together. Personal diary accounts show that over time, however, Mary Blathwayt dissociated herself from the militant protests and resigned her suffragette membership. The result of this is not what we might expect, however: she does not break off her ties to other activists, but instead redefines them. She swaps the relationship model of 'comradeship' with that of 'friendship' instead (reverting back to expectations of mutual support but breaking from expectations of co-participation in protest). This is important in terms of thinking about what qualitative data add to the formal analysis of ego-nets: while the sociograms do not appear to change over time we know from the stories told in her daily diaries that she was relating to others in her network in very different ways at different times. Over time, these different ways of relating to others invoked different sets of obligations and expectations (Edwards 2014).

Narratives – like those contained within biographies and personal diaries – therefore enable a multi-layered interpretation of the content, role and meaning of ties and how they are formed and re-formed over time. The initiation and the evolution of social ties is captured in stories of the network where people narrate how and when their ties to others form and to what effect. In this sense, network stories enable us to appreciate how social networks are practices of 'networking' that change over time. They should not be thought of as static webs, but as the processes of social interaction through which these webs are woven.

Networks as Narratives

So far we have thought of 'network stories' as being important to the analysis of ego-nets because they reveal the meaning, formation and evolution of social ties. Here, we consider a further point: that social ties and identities (the building blocks of social networks) are themselves 'narratives'. By this we mean that social ties and identities are constructed in the first place through practices of narrative story-telling. Through spoken and written narratives, actors actively construct the sense of who they are and how they are related to others (McLean 1998; White 2008; Yeung 2005). Narrative descriptions of ties (relationship stories) are not just revealing of ties therefore, they are constitutive of them (Mische 2003; White 2008). This has important implications for ego-net analysis.

Harrison White (2008) has been a prominent exponent of the idea that networks can themselves be approached as narratives. He argues that social networks consist of relationship 'stories' – narratives about how we are connected that are specific to domains (work, family and so on) – and it is through these narratives that identities are constructed in networks (White, 2008). Networks, in this sense, can be thought of as *discursive* formations and thus readily open to narrative forms of analysis. In her study of Brazilian youth activist networks, Mische (2008) shows how actors form ties with one another through ongoing processes of interaction, which involve narratively constructing identities and connections out of the cultural material available in the network. Mische concludes that networks are 'culturally constituted processes of communicative interaction' (Mische 2003: 258). What we can say on the basis of this view is that the achievement or formation of a tie depends upon these narrative (story-telling) processes, such that the way in which relationship stories are told commands our analytic attention when trying to understand ego-networks.

We have seen already that interviews, letters, speeches, diaries and biographies involve actors in 'talking their ties' with others (Edwards and Crossley 2009: 48) and provide insight into how people come to be related. More than this, however, they allow us to actually analyse the discursive methods through which people try to forge connections with others in the first place. In the example below, drawn from a study of suffragette letter-writing networks (Edwards and Crossley 2009), a tie is being constructed through letter writing by appealing to 'transitivity' (being friends of friends and therefore part of the same social circle), and belonging to a common identity category, which commands solidarity (clergyman's daughter). Both these reasons are presented as grounds for the formation of a tie. The appeal being conveyed in the letter through the narrative of connection is that this 'stranger' should be redefined as 'friend':

> I feel I must write and congratulate you on the bravery of your daughter Helen. I met her with Miss Commins first at the house of my friend Miss Ross. I do hope that you will forgive me writing to you like this when I am a stranger. My excuse is that I too am a clergyman's daughter, also I know the two sisters of Mrs Wallis of Nottingham (Miss Kate and Miss Rosa Wallis)… so there are several ties between us. (Letter written by Millicent McClateline to Suffragette Helen Watts' mother, dated 26 February 1909, Nottingham Archive Office)

Suffragette letter writing also reveals the way in which narratives are employed to re-work and repair identities and relationships. Relationships have to be redefined and repaired through discursive work when identities suddenly change, for example when an actor 'comes out' as a militant activist (Edwards and Crossley 2009: 46). The narration of social ties is therefore part of the process through which ties are symbolically maintained and repaired over time.

McLean's (1998) study of the way in which Renaissance Florentines sought favours through letter writing in the fourteenth and fifteenth centuries shows how telling 'relationship stories' is essential to forging ties that matter strategically to the achievement of personal goals (like an improved social or financial position) and therefore to changing your network position (McLean 1998). The narratives employed by Florentines when constructing social ties and presenting themselves through letter writing draw upon culturally available 'frames' of meaning within Renaissance Florence. The network has a 'cultural structure' in this respect – a stock of shared meanings, understandings, symbols, scripts, cues, frames and so on – that network members selectively employ in discursive interaction. McLean explores the frames used through a discourse analysis of 869 private letters (written between 1380 and 1460) in which Florentines sought favours and friendships from influential patrons (McLean 1998: 57). He suggests that:

> the letters effectively tell brief stories about how to construe the relationship between individuals and about individuals' commitment to social groups, using practically and normatively sanctioned framings to accomplish this goal. (McLean 1998: 86)

McLean connects the cultural frames employed in this story-telling to network structure and position through multi-dimensional scaling. He suggests that structural position in the network affects which cultural frames are strategically employed when presenting the self and trying to build social ties, for example whether appeals for favours are made on the basis of friendships or loyalty, or honour. There is a connection between the discursive styles employed by actors when attempting to form social ties and their structural position in the network. Furthermore, successful attempts to forge ties can change network position for the better. Narratives represent social relationships therefore, but they also construct them (McLean 1998: 86), and exploring them can reveal important cultural mechanisms by which relationships are formed.

Connecting Culture and Structure in Mixed Methods Ego-Net Analysis

Approaching social networks as processes of communicative interaction in which actors must draw upon culturally available 'frames' of meaning is useful in focusing attention on networks as 'cultural formations'. The culture of a network can be thought of as 'a system of meanings generated by the social ties of actors' (Yeung 2005: 392). Rather than to the subjective meanings of actors, network culture points to the *intersubjective* level of meaning within a network, where meaning is collectively constructed through shared discourses (Bottero 2010). Networks give rise to shared understandings, frames of interpretation, symbols, scripts and so forth, from which actors must draw in constructing identities and relationships. These frames, symbols and scripts can be identified in narrative analysis. Together, they form an intersubjective layer to ego-nets, which has been referred to as the 'meaning structure of the network' (Fuhse and Mutzel 2011: 1076). Fuhse (2009: 67) defines the meaning structure of the network as interpersonal expectations relating to relationships and identities, plus network culture (consisting of shared symbols, scripts and schemas of interpretation) and suggests that the main purpose of qualitative network analysis is to investigate this structure.

The 'meaning structure' of ego-networks has been analysed qualitatively using interview narratives with ego and their alters. Heath et al. (2009) for example, analysed the ego-nets of 17 young people in order to explore their educational decision-making regarding whether or not to go to university. While ego-net studies often rely upon ego for information about alters, Heath et al. went on to interview the alters independently of ego, generating an interview sample of 107 alters from the initial 17 egos. This allowed for an analysis of the shared discourses, expectations and meanings circulating within the ego-network. They were able to highlight through this analysis that the individual decision made by a young person about whether or not to go to university is influenced by the shared world-view and normative expectations of their network – in short, their network culture.

The main challenge for the researcher when analysing network culture, however, is in making the connection between network culture and network structure (Emirbayer and Goodwin 1994). How do network cultures shape the structure of social networks and how are they shaped by them? Mixed methods approaches to analysis that combine qualitative analysis and formal SNA are particularly adept at addressing this question. Returning to the example of the suffragettes, Edwards (2014) addresses the question of how ego-net structure shapes network culture. Using contrasting cases in which different decisions are made, she analyses the 'meaning structure' (Fuhse 2009) of the ego-networks, and assesses its impact on the decision taken by ego about whether or not to participate in suffragette militancy. Discourse analysis of suffragette letters, diaries and speeches looks to identify the components of the meaning structure (or network culture): the shared discourses, scripts, symbols and schemas, from which individual women had to draw in making their decision. Differing network cultures help to explain why some women did, or did not, have the resources available to construct identities as 'high-risk' activists. Using formal SNA and narrative accounts, Edwards (2014) shows how different network structures were related to these different network cultures. In compositional terms, heterogeneous ego-networks, for example, created more debate on the legitimacy of militancy, while, on the other hand, homogeneous ego-networks enabled the construction of a shared point of view about the legitimacy of militancy.

By also returning to Bellotti's (2008a) study of friendship networks, we can see conversely how a mixed methods approach to analysis can reveal how meaning structures (or network culture) affect ego-net structure. As we discussed earlier in the chapter, there are different ways in which people construct the meaning of friendship and relate to others as friends. Bellotti argues that these differences are reflected in different ego-net structures. By constructing and reflecting upon several ego-net cases she is able to identify general 'types' of network structure that are produced by the different strategies of friendship that participants adopt. The four-fold typology of friendship networks is shown in Figure 5.2 (Bellotti, 2008a: 328).

The clique

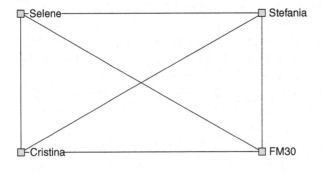

Size: 4
Density: 1
Components (without ego): 1

The company

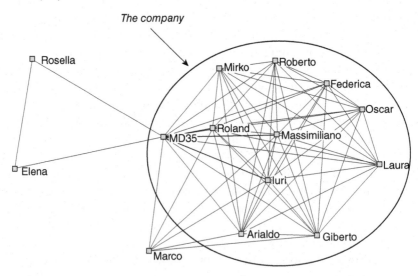

Size: 13
Density: 0.65
Components (without ego): 2

Figure 5.2   Creating typologies: the friendship networks of singletons in Milan

Source: Bellotti (2014)

The core–periphery structure

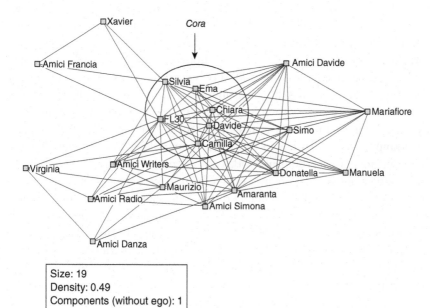

Size: 19
Density: 0.49
Components (without ego): 1

The contextualised components

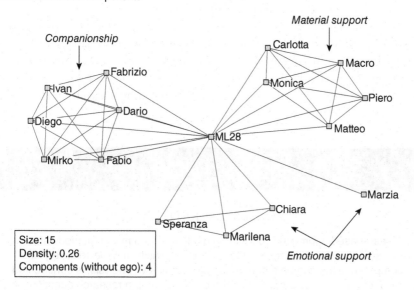

Size: 15
Density: 0.26
Components (without ego): 4

The typologies in Figure 5.2 represent the similarities and differences across individual cases in a way that is useful for producing more general theories about the ways in which friendship operates in the lives of young singletons. The first friendship network type found in the data is labelled the 'clique', which forms when the actor's strategy is one of choosing a 'best' friend who can supply exclusive support, and becomes a kind of 'surrogate for a partner'. The second friendship network type is the 'company', which forms when strategies involve amassing a larger group of friends. High density means that group culture readily forms (for example, rituals which are shared among the members), and friendship communities feel in this respect more like a 'surrogate family'. The third and fourth friendship network types identified are the 'core–periphery' and 'contextualised components', which form when people adopt the strategy of using different friends for different things: long-standing friends for multiplex support and periphery friends to satisfy specialised needs and interests, or different sub-groups of friends for different kinds of support (material, emotional and so on). Across these typologies, subjective meanings of friendship (what you perceive friends to be for) become reflected in strategies for forging and reproducing friendship ties, and these are then revealed in different types of ego-net structure. Qualitative interview data also connects these ego-net structures back to the quality, strength and transience of friendship ties. 'Group' structures, for example, provide dense and cohesive contexts for friendship ties, which mean that people are more likely to stay connected despite tensions or interpersonal distance when compared to ties that are less embedded in a cohesive structure (like ties between periphery and core, for example).

Importantly, therefore, what mixed methods approaches to ego-net analysis can produce are not just detailed 'insider' accounts relating to specific cases, but by comparing and contrasting across cases, analysis can construct typologies of networks that aid more general theorisation. Why a case-based approach to ego-net analysis can be valuable, and how exactly it is carried out, is discussed in Box 5.1.

BOX 5.1

Using Cases in Ego-Net Analysis

A case-based approach is popular in qualitative and mixed methods studies of ego-networks. A sample of case studies, which may be relatively small compared to the numbers demanded by quantitative analysis, is constructed around particular actors with the aim of following up a research question (of analytic interest) in a way that looks closely at the context and content of ties. Usually, a range of available data is drawn upon to explore ties and the particular context (from interviews to historical archives to demographic data), and the ego-network is often drawn out (Emmel and Clark 2009; Heath 2009), or visualised using SNA software (Bellotti 2008a, Crossley 2015, Edwards 2014, Edwards and Crossley 2009). Each of the case studies is analysed in its own right, using tools such as thematic and narrative analysis. The cases are also compared and contrasted with one another in order to generate insights into the mechanisms at play, and to build more general theory in relation to the research questions posed.

The ESRC *Connected Lives* Project (Emmel et al. 2005–09) provides an example of, and reflection on, the case study approach (see Emmel and Clark 2009). The researchers used mixed methods to explore the social networks of people living in inner-city neighbourhoods, and how their networks affected their sense of community, and their health and well-being. The research questions asked about how people perceived their ties to others within their local neighbourhood, and how these ties were formed, maintained and changed over time and across space. There were 24 cases in the sample. Data were collected through participatory mapping interviews, walking interviews around the area, and interaction diaries.

The aim was to analyse these data to capture the 'lived experience' of people's networks in the inner city. The analysis treated each participant (ego) in the research and the data that relates to them and their context as a discrete 'case', and investigated 'how community ties are maintained' in each case (Emmel and Clark 2009: 21). This case-based approach was seen as a useful way to organise the wealth of qualitative data generated in fieldwork, and also offered a method of analysis that could produce both 'particular' and 'generalisable' findings (Emmel and Clark 2009: 23). In terms of the former, the case approach is adept at bringing 'context' to the centre of network analysis. In the *Connected Lives* project, for example, the way in which networks were embedded in, and shaped by, place, could be put at the heart of analysis by exploring individual cases that contained detailed information about the local area and how it affected interactions. In terms of more general findings, researchers also looked across cases to identify the various mechanisms through which ties were maintained. Three main mechanisms for maintaining community ties were identified across the cases: mobility (the ways in which people move around the local area like walking, driving, public transport); maintaining contact (the ways in which people have contact with others in the community, through events, phone calls, texts and social media, and interactions in the street), and avoiding dissembling networks (the ways in which people keep ties going, like face-to-face contact).

Identifying mechanisms helped the researchers to theorise within cases, but it was also useful for comparing and contrasting across cases (Emmel and Clark 2009: 22). The particular and the general findings from the case approach are, furthermore, connected: thinking about how cases are similar and how they differ (and why) often refers the analyst back to the different contexts that shape the networks (Emmel and Clark 2009: 22). The case-based analysis in the *Connected Lives* project led to important findings about the enduring significance of locality for providing a sense of belonging, and the importance of face-to-face interaction over technologically mediated communication. These findings were pertinent because they held across all cases, even the students who were transitory in the area and were adept at using social media (Emmel and Clark 2009: 23).

Measuring Meaning Structures

Ego-networks have more to them than structures of social relations: they have an intersubjective dimension best thought of in Fuhse's terms as the 'meaning structure' of the network (see also Yeung 2005). Qualitative data is valuable because it allows us to explore not only the subjective components of networks, but the intersubjective (cultural) components as well, and to connect them to network structure in formal SNA. Fuhse and Mutzel put it succinctly when they state that:

> while it is useful to model the structure of relationships with formal network analysis, and the embeddedness of actors and connections in statistical analyses of personal networks, qualitative research is indispensable for an 'understanding' of the meaning inextricably intertwined with any structure of social networks. (Fuhse and Mutzel 2011: 1068)

This does not have to suggest, however, that 'meaning structures' can only be investigated using qualitative methods. Formal techniques can also be employed to map and measure meaning structures and to specify their consequences for network structure. King-To Yeung (2005) provides a cogent illustration of how meaning structures can be investigated using Galois lattice theory (sometimes called Formal Concept Analysis) (see also Mische and Pattison 2000).

Yeung (2005) argues that the meaning of social ties is often marginalised in network research because of the tendency to use closed-ended survey questionnaires to gather network data, giving the researcher little room to record qualitative details. The meaning of social relationships is nevertheless a key question, not least because the qualities we attach to relationships and to persons shapes the way in which we form connections with others (a key argument of this chapter so far). We should therefore expect the subjective meanings accorded to relationships to have an effect on network structure. This point about the importance of subjective meaning in forming ties has been part of our earlier discussion when we saw that the meaning of relationship categories, like friendship for example, is neither readily apparent to the researcher, nor fixed. As Yeung (2005: 391) argues, 'friendship' can take on various meanings for different members of a network, but it can also vary across networks. Different social groups, in this respect, have different 'meaning structures' or 'network cultures'. In his study, Yeung takes social networks with different meaning structures in order to contemplate how meaning differentially affects network structure. Specifically, he looks at urban communes in the United States using ego-network data collected by Zablocki (1980).

In studying the data on the communes, Yeung observed quite the opposite to what we may expect to find: the communes with the highest proportion of (subjectively defined) loving relationships (60%+) had around half the lifespan of the communes with a low proportion of loving relationships (less than 20%). Yeung suggests an explanation of this finding that hangs on the different 'meaning structures' of the groups in question. He argues that the communes with high- and low-density loving relationships had different ways of constructing the meaning of 'love', which affected the nature of dyadic relationships and group solidarity. Let us consider his methodology and arguments in more detail.

The Zablocki (1980) data were collected from 49 urban communes set up to live outside of the standard nuclear family. Each actor was asked to select the characteristics of, and their relationship to, other actors in the community from a defined list. There were ten personality characteristics such as 'supportive', 'decisive', 'loving' and dominant', and there were 15 relational qualities, such as 'exciting', 'awkward', 'loving', 'hateful' and so on. For each of the communes, Yeung constructed a 10x9 two-mode binary matrix. The rows represented the personality characteristics, and the columns represented nine of the relational qualities. The entries were dichotomised correlations drawn from each of the respondents in each commune. On this basis, the communes were divided into warm loving communes, which had a relatively high density of loving relationships (60%+), and 'cold communes', which had a low density of loving relationships (less than 20%) (those that fell in the middle were excluded). Aggregated matrices for these two groups were then analysed using Galois lattice theory.

Using this technique, the matrices are represented as a particular type of network called a 'lattice'. The nodes have two sets of labels, in this case 'personal characteristics' and 'relational qualities'. These labels are sets, not individual characteristics or qualities. They are collections – or more technically *subsets* – of the row and column labels. Suppose in our data we had 'supportive' was associated with 'exciting', 'awkward' and 'loving', and that 'decisive' was associated with 'exciting', 'hateful' and 'awkward', then the node labelled 'supportive decisive' would also be labelled 'exciting awkward'. The nodes are arranged in levels and the lines only connect nodes in different levels. There are single nodes at the top and bottom level – one representing all personality characteristics (say the top node), and one all the relational qualities (the bottom node). The lines represent set inclusion so that if the node we just described was connected to a node above it then this node must contain 'supportive' and 'decisive' and any connections below must contain 'exciting' and 'awkward'.

The general structure of the lattice and the paths it contains can be analysed to reveal details in the data. Yeung shows, using these techniques, that in the 'cold communes' positive relationships were closely associated with positive characteristics and that 'loving' had an important structural position. He concluded that being in a loving dyadic relationship was seen as important. In contrast in the 'warm communes' no such relationship existed and the 'loving' relationship was actually sidelined at the dyadic level. Its important position had been replaced instead by a charismatic relationship to the group's leader, but this was associated with both positive and negative characteristics. Essentially, in the warm communes, 'love' had become a generalised notion that operated at group level, but meant little for particular dyads within the group. The meaning structure of the 'warm communes' was therefore ambiguous and lacked clarity, making it more difficult for members to attach subjective meaning to particular dyadic relationships and thus consolidate attachments. In the 'cold communes', however, loving relationships were defined less often because love *meant more* (it was associated with numerous positive qualities and thus harder to achieve), but at the dyadic level when it was achieved it had the effect of creating interpersonal intimacy and thus contributed to network stability.

Yeung's (2005) study shows therefore how Galois lattice theory can be employed to map and measure the 'meaning structure' of social networks. Rather than assuming that individuals or social groups mean the same thing by 'friendship' or 'love' we can explore the differences using formal techniques to establish different network cultures. Taking the meaning of social ties seriously, Yeung (2005) shows that rather than assuming from the outset that 'loving relationships' are always positive for group integration and stability, we need to first establish what 'love' means to the social group in question before we can understand the nature of social connections and the effect on network structure.

Summary

We have said throughout the book that we share a focus on mixed methods in the analysis of ego-nets. While mixing methods is a growing trend, we believe that ego-net analysis, and SNA more generally, provides a particular opportunity to mix quantitative and qualitative methods, both in the collection of ego-net data (Chapter Three), and in the analysis of that data, as discussed here.

This chapter has shown that because ego-networks are both 'structure' (a pattern of ties that we can map out) and process (practices of social interaction that create, maintain and break ties) it is valuable to draw upon qualitative data about ties in our analysis. Indeed, qualitative data in the form of 'network narratives' from the actor's point of view, become crucial if we are to explore, interpret and comprehend certain subjective and intersubjective features of ego-networks, and, importantly, how they relate to the structural properties that we measure and observe.

This point was demonstrated by considering mixed methods approaches to ego-net analysis, which link elements of network culture (like meaning structures, and the subjective categorisation of ties) to the structural properties of ego-networks. These studies show how network culture is shaped by network structure and vice versa. Qualitative data thus inform the complex task of explaining how the outside (form) and inside (content) of ego-networks mutually inform each other. In order to do this we have seen how qualitative analysis often involves looking at a (relatively small) set of ego-net cases in detail. By striving to understand the content and context of particular cases, and how they compare and contrast with one another, qualitative and mixed methods ego-net analysis can help us to:

- identify the mechanisms generating observed patterns;
- construct network typologies; and
- develop more general theorisations.

On a final note, this chapter has also raised an interesting point about networks and narratives by suggesting that identities and social ties (the building blocks of network structure) can themselves be thought of as the products and achievements of 'relationship stories': the stories we tell about who we are and how we are connected. Narratives, then, provide descriptions of relationships that can be used in our analysis of relationships – but more than this – they are the discursive processes through which relationships are formed and maintained in the first place.

Note

1. Blockmodelling was briefly discussed in Chapter One. It is very unusual in ego-net analysis because ego-nets are generally too small to merit blockmodelling, but ego-nets may sometimes be big enough to merit its use (e.g. Edwards and Crossley 2009). In essence the technique compares the pattern of connection of every node in the network, clustering them into 'blocks' of nodes characterised by the (more or less) equivalent position that their members enjoy within the network. It then explores the relationship between blocks (by looking at the relationships between members of those blocks). Edwards and Crossley (2009) found that this technique was a useful way of distinguishing different social circles in the ego-net of suffragette, Helen Watts.

6

MULTILEVEL MODELS FOR CROSS-SECTIONAL EGO-NETS

Learning Outcomes

By the end of this chapter you will:

1. Know how to use a multilevel model to investigate variations in the values of the ties between egos and alters at a single point in time.

2. Know how to use a multilevel model to investigate how similar an outcome variable is for individuals in the same ego-net, compared with individuals in different ego-nets.

3. Know how to use a multilevel model to compare variation in individual outcome variables across different ego-nets with variations for other groupings of the population, such as schools or local areas.

4. Learn about some approaches for modelling alter-alter ties in cross-sectional ego-net data.

Introduction

Having considered qualitative approaches to ego–net analysis in the last chapter, we turn to more statistical approaches in this chapter and in Chapter Seven. Here, we consider ways in which multilevel models can be used to analyse cross-sectional ego-net data. We base much of our discussion on several recent applications of multilevel models to cross-sectional ego-net data in the literature, focusing on two situations in detail. We begin by considering the situation where the values of the ties between ego and alter are the dependent variables in the analysis for cases where the alters of one ego have minimal or no overlap with the alters of other ego-nets. We look at two examples from the literature: firstly, on the use of cocaine in Rotterdam; and secondly, an example based on ego-net data for the support networks of recent immigrants to Spain. In these examples we are interested in the characteristics of ego and alter that are associated with the presence, or the value, of a tie between them, and the extent to which these tie values vary within and between ego-nets.

Later in this chapter we change the focus of the analysis of ego-nets from the *ties* to social network *dependencies* for responses for each of the nodes of the network. For example, the response could be a person's self-assessed health and we are interested in how this is associated with their friendship network. When looking at network dependencies in cross-sectional ego-net data with a multilevel model, we treat the network as being exogenous to a response variable for each node (e.g. person) in the social network, and we are interested in the extent to which the response varies between and within ego-nets. We may take this further and concurrently estimate variation in the individual response between and within the ego-nets and other groups, such as schools or areas. When we look at network dependencies, we will focus on an example in which the dependent variable is educational achievement, and we want to assess how much of the variation in exam performance can be associated with the individual, how much can be associated with the ego-net of the individual, and how much of the variation can be associated with the school or the area in which the individual is based.

Most of the discussion in the chapter focuses upon ego-alter ties only. We only briefly discuss models that include alter-alter ties at the end of the chapter. A more detailed discussion of statistical models that include alter-alter ties can be found in Chapter Seven.

Multilevel models, also called *random-effects* models or *mixed* models in the literature, became widely used in the 1980s when developments in both methodology and computing made such models applicable to substantive studies, avoiding the need to only focus on the individual level, or to aggregate to the group level and lose information about variation in individual level responses within groups. Multilevel modelling also avoids problems of cross-level inference where the analysis is carried out at one level and inferences are made at another – most notably, the problem of the ecological fallacy. The ecological fallacy occurs when group-level data are analysed, for example school means or percentages, and inferences are then made at the pupil level. An example of this would be correlating the percentage of examination passes in a school and relating that to the percentage of pupils on free school meals, then making an inference directly from this correlation about how an individual pupil on free school meals might do in their examinations. Thus, the analysis is carried out at the school level but inferences are made at pupil level. Such analyses are generally biased because they ignore the fact that pupils are clustered in schools; often the absolute value of the correlation at school level will be stronger than that at the pupil level. Multilevel models take individual and group levels into account simultaneously in the analysis and allow the nature and extent of individual and group variations in a dependent variable, and its association with a set of explanatory variables, to be fully explored. Multilevel modelling can thus be used to take clustering into account when it is not of substantive interest but we regard it as a nuisance. However, more often in multilevel modelling the clustering is itself of substantive interest. This is usually true in the context of multilevel models for social network analysis: one of the targets of inference in the analysis of a social network with a multilevel model might be the extent of variation in an individual response between and within ego-nets, as reflected in the estimates of the between and within ego-net variance components. The relative share of these two variance components gives us a measure of the clustering of responses in ego-nets.

Multilevel models were originally used in educational research to assess school effects when looking at variations in examination performance of pupils (level 1) in schools (level 2), and also in studies of the value that a school adds to a child's educational achievement. Other applications have included their use: in human geography – when investigating variations in responses, such as unemployment or health, for individuals in certain areas; in longitudinal studies to predict trajectories of 'growth' – where growth could be a physical measure or could be in terms of a response, such as reading progress; in the analysis of multivariate responses – where several correlated dependent variables may be analysed together; and for combining survey and administrative data such as Census and survey data.

Recent developments in the methods and software to implement such estimation methods, such as Monte Carlo Markov Chain (MCMC) estimation, have allowed multilevel models to also be used for non-hierarchical population structures (Browne 2009). One such model is a cross-classified model where overlapping groups are considered: two school pupils living in the same street may each go to different schools, whereas two people in the same school may live in different parts of a town. Thus area and school are cross-classified for the pupils, and both may have important associations with educational performance. Another important kind of non-hierarchical model is the Multiple Membership (MM) model (Hill and Goldstein 1998).

An MM model could be used for situations where people may 'belong' to more than one area – for example, the area in which they live and the area in which they work – and variations in health are of interest. MM models are valuable in the context of ego-net data because the alters of one ego-net are sometimes also alters of other ego-nets, thus alters are multiple members of ego-nets. Also, social networks often cross other boundaries, such as geographical areas, making model frameworks that allow for cross-classifications a valuable substantive tool. Multilevel models may be fitted in specialist software such as MLwiN (Rasbash et al. 2009) or HLM (Raudenbush 2004), within more general software such as STATA (Rabe-Hesketh and Skrondal 2008), R (Bates 2010) or SAS (Singer 1998). Some of the simpler multilevel models can also be fitted in SPSS (see, for example, Peugh and Enders 2005). An excellent place to read more about multilevel analysis in general is Snijders and Bosker (2012).

Multilevel Analysis of the Ties between Ego and Alter

We begin by considering the multilevel analysis of ego-net data when we are interested in the ties between alter and ego, and where there is little or no overlap between the alters of one ego and the next.

Because of the substantive setting, the method of data collection, or both, it may be that the overlap of the alters of one ego and the others is minimal, or in fact does not occur at all in the available data. A possible substantive setting where this may be true is where clients (alters) may each only use one drug dealer (ego), in which case there is no overlap from one ego-net (drug dealer) to the next. An example where minimal overlap of ego-nets might be a consequence of data collection is when a low sampling fraction (percentage of the population sampled) is used to collect ego-net data over a wide geographical area, so that, by design, minimal overlap will occur for the alters of one ego and the next.

In cases where there is no overlap of ego-nets, a simple multilevel model may be specified and fitted. In other situations, it may be reasonable to ignore very minimal overlap when formulating and fitting a multilevel model for ego-nets. One reason for ignoring minimal overlap is that the modelling framework for non-overlapping ego-nets is relatively straightforward. Furthermore, the impact of a few overlapping networks on the estimated multilevel model parameters will be extremely small.

In situations where there is no overlap of ego-nets, or where it is so minimal that the overlap can reasonably be ignored, it is possible to represent ego-nets in a multilevel model as a two-level structure, with alters at level 1 and egos at level 2, as Figure 6.1 shows. In such cases, we have a fairly simple multilevel structure. In fact, such a structure is the simplest form of a multilevel model, although it has considerable substantive value. As such, the two-level model has been used extensively in the literature. For example: for pupils (level 1) in schools (level 2) when educational performance is an example of a response variable, and where the aim to estimate the extent to which exam scores vary between pupils and schools; or for individuals (level 1) in areas (level 2) where health, voting behaviour or employment status are just a few examples of possible response variables, and the aim of the analysis is to assess the way in which health, voting behaviour, or other individual responses vary between people and between places. Multilevel models may also be used to take the sampling design into account when analysing relationships between the variables collected in the sample. This is sometimes referred to as a 'model based' approach because the sample design for data collection, for example a two-stage sample, is reflected in the model specification. By taking into account the clustering by schools and areas in a population of individuals, the standard errors of regression parameters are estimated correctly; these are usually under-estimated if the clustering is ignored. For example, the standard errors would typically be under-estimated when ordinary least squares regression is used to ana- lyse data from a multi-stage sample, leading to a greater chance of finding regression coefficients significant, and confidence intervals for estimated parameters being too narrow. When we fit a multilevel model to, say, educa- tional data, we may ask realistically complex substantive research questions, because we are allowing for the population structure in the model. For example, using this approach with educational data, we could answer ques- tions such as this: What is the overall relationship between exam score and gender, taking into account the year in which the school was built and the percentage of pupils on free school meals? The multilevel model may be further extended to allow a different relationship between the response and explanatory variables in each group. For example, it is possible to assess whether the relationship between exam score and gender is stronger in some schools than others. (See Snijders and Bosker 2012 and the references therein for further examples.)

Although the formulation for a two-level model for ego-nets is identical to that used for pupils in schools, or individuals in areas, the substantive interpre- tation is different. For the case of ego-nets, the *ties* between alter and ego are the units of analysis, and these may be interval valued, such as the frequency of drug purchasing from dealer (ego, level 2) by client (alter, level 1), or may be binary (0 or 1), such as whether the tie between alter and ego is to a person with a particular characteristic, or not. An example of this is whether a sup- port tie between a recent immigrant (ego) is to another recent immigrant (=0) or to a long-term resident of the country to which the immigrant has moved (=1). As we shall see, the multilevel model framework may also be used to assess the extent to which the *homophily* (similarity) or *heterophily* (difference) of alter and ego is associated with the value of the tie between alter and ego. For example, are certain tie values more likely if alter and ego are of similar age, or where ego is male and alter is female? We can also assess the variation of the values of these ties within and between egos. More variation in the values of ties between egos implies less variation in tie values within ego-nets. Substantively, if this happens it might mean that egos are very different in terms of the ties with their alters. For example, some drug dealers may only be associated with high-frequency drug addicts, whilst others may only be associated with alters who are low-frequency recreational drug users. In this case, the share of variation at the ego level will be greater than that at the alter level. Conversely, if each drug dealer caters for a mixture of addicts and low-frequency recreational drug users, then there will be variation within ego-nets in terms of the value of the ties and the between-ego variation, and thus the relative share of variation at the ego level may be smaller than that at the alter level. We can assess the between and within ego variation prior to adding explanatory variables to the model in a 'null' model and then assess the impact on the variation of adding alter and ego level explanatory variables, as is often done when multilevel models are used in other contexts.

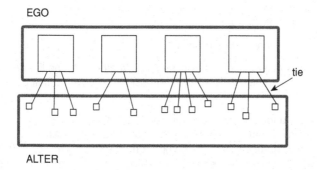

Figure 6.1   Ego-nets with minimal/no overlap as a multilevel structure

When fitting a standard multilevel model to the values of the ties between egos and alters, it is important to keep in mind the assumptions implicit in this approach. Firstly, an alter chosen by ego must be considered exogenous and *independent* of the value of the tie (conditional on unobserved characteristics captured by random effects). Secondly, the values of the ties are considered independent across alters, given characteristics of ego (including random effects). For example, consider an ego's average propensity to have ties to alters who are long-term residents of a particular country. The fact that one alter is a long-term resident of a particular country does not affect the probability that another alter is also a long-term resident of that country. Finally, related to the first point, the size of ego-nets may differ substantially in the ego–net data, but we assume that the number of alters is not related to the values of their ties to ego. We do not address modelling the size of ego-nets in this chapter. This will be addressed in Chapter Seven in a temporal context.

Model Formulation for Minimal/Non-Overlapping Ego-Nets

When we have interval valued (continuous) ties, we may fit a multilevel linear model of this form:

$$y_{ij} = \beta_0 + \beta_1 x_{1ij} + \beta_2 x_{2j} + U_{0j} + e_{0ij} \qquad (6.1)$$

Where:

- i is an index for alter within ego and j is an index for ego
- y_{ij} is the interval value of the tie between ego j and alter i
- x_{1ij} is a characteristic of the alter i in ego net j. For example, a categorical variable such as whether or not the alter is female, or an interval variable, such as the alter's age.
- β_1 is a fixed regression coefficient relating the values of x_{1ij} to y_{ij}
- x_{2j} is a characteristic of the ego, such as whether the ego is female or the age of the ego, and β_2 is a fixed regression coefficient relating the values of x_{2j} to y_{ij}
- U_{0j} is an unobserved ego-level (level 2) residual (error) term which we assume is normally distributed with mean zero and variance, σ^2_{u0}. Hence, σ^2_{u0} is the ego-level variance component, measuring the extent to which the average values of the ties in one ego-net vary from one another
- e_{0ij} is an alter-level residual term component, which we assume is normally distributed with mean zero and variance, σ^2_{e0}. Hence σ^2_{e0} is the alter-level variance component, measuring the extent to which the values of the ties within ego-nets vary from one another
- In this model framework, we assume that U_{0j} and e_{0ij} are uncorrelated so that the total marginal variation in the tie values, $\mathrm{var}(y_{ij})$ is $\sigma^2 = \sigma^2_{u0} + \sigma^2_{e0}$ and hence we can define the variance partition coefficient as $\rho = \sigma^2_{u0} / \sigma^2$. For interval valued ties this is also equivalent to the intra-class correlation, ρ. If $\rho = 0$ then all the variation in the values of ties is between alters within

the ego-net and there is no variation in tie values between ego-nets. If $\rho = 1$ then all the variation in the values of ties is between ego-nets, implying that the ties would all take the same values within ego-nets. In practice, ρ is usually found to lie somewhere between 0 and 1, rather than taking these limiting values. We can assess the share of variation at the ego and alter levels prior to adding explanatory variables and then add explanatory variables to see whether these explain some of the variation at the two levels, and, if so, what the nature of the relationship is between the response variables and explanatory variables in this model framework. Tie-values are assumed independent conditional on U_{0j}.

EGO

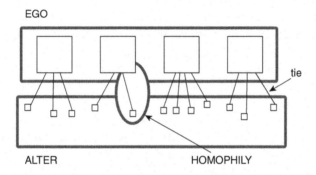

ALTER   HOMOPHILY

Figure 6.2 A framework for homophily

Having assumed this multilevel modelling framework, we can make several extensions, which have considerable substantive value. One extension is the possibility of making the coefficients relating alter characteristics to the tie vary from ego to ego by allowing β_1 to have a random coefficient, such that $\beta_{1j} = \beta_1 + U_{1j}$. Substantively, we could, for example, find that the association of gender on the tie values varies from ego–net to ego–net; gender effects may be stronger in some ego–nets than others. Another model extension allows us to investigate homophily, as Figure 6.2 indicates. Once we specify a model with an ego and an alter level we can include explanatory variables at either the alter or ego levels in the model. Moreover, we can construct indicator variables for the similarity of characteristics (attributes) of alter and ego, to indicate if these are the same or different. Thus we can explore the association of homophily or heterophily (difference) of characteristics of alter and ego on the value of the tie between them – for example, are particular tie values more likely if both alter and ego are female? This is achieved by introducing a term for the interaction of alter and ego characteristics into the model as follows:

$$y_{ij} = \beta_0 + \beta_1 x_{1ij} + \beta_2 x_{2j} + \beta_3 x_{1ij} x_{2j} + U_{0j} + e_{0ij} \qquad (6.2)$$

Suppose x_{1j} and x_{2j} respectively represent the gender of the alter and the ego. Model (6.1) would allow us to assess whether greater or smaller values of the ties are associated with the gender of the alter and the gender of the ego. Model (6.2) would allow us to take a further step and assess the association of homophily of alter and ego characteristics through the addition of the cross-level interaction term: $\beta_3 x_{1ij} x_{2j}$. In Model (6.2) suppose the two explanatory variables x_{1ij} and x_{2j} gender are coded female = 1, male = 0. Then for Model (6.2) the estimated coefficient $\hat{\beta}_0$ would give an estimate of the average tie value when both alter and ego are male; $\hat{\beta}_1$ would tell us how that average tie value changes for cases where the ego is male and the alter is female. $\hat{\beta}_2$ would then tell us how the average tie value changes from the male ego, male alter mean tie value for cases where the alter is male and the ego is female. Finally, $\hat{\beta}_3$ would indicate whether cases where both alter and ego are female differ from the other cases. For each of these estimated coefficients, it is possible to assess their significance, using t-ratios, as is done more generally for regression model coefficient estimates. Likelihood ratio tests can be used to assess the significance of the estimated variance components. Model (6.2) could be extended to include other cross-level interactions between alter and ego level variables, and could also include other levels, for example areas or schools.

Data Structure for Minimal/Non-Overlapping Ego-Nets

Taking the example of drug dealers and their clients, and assuming a valued measure of drug use and binary explanatory variables for the gender of alter and ego, the data structure would be as shown in Table 6.1, for three ego-nets. The final column of the table shows the value of the cross-level interaction of the alter and ego explanatory variable for gender, taking the value 1 only if both alter and ego are female. Recall that unequal numbers of alters per ego are permitted in this model framework. In practice there would be more ego-nets than the three shown in Table 6.1. Ideally the analysis would be based on 30 ego-nets or more, although the models described above could be applied to data for as few as ten ego-nets. In general, each ego-net should include a minimum of two alters to allow an assessment of within ego variation of tie values. Ideally, there would be some ego-nets with more than two alters in the available cross-sectional ego-net data.

Table 6.1 Multilevel data structure for minimal/non-overlapping ego-net data, based on three ego-nets

Ego = j	Alter = i	Drug use frequency y_{ij}	Ego female = $x2j$	Alter female = $x1ij$	Female Homophily $x2j.x1ij$
1	1	10	1	1	1
1	2	1	1	0	0
1	3	15	1	1	1
2	1	19	0	1	0
2	2	2	0	0	0
2	3	7	0	1	0
2	4	10	0	0	0
3	1	11	1	0	0
3	2	12	1	0	0
3	3	9	1	1	1
3	4	13	1	0	0

Binary Valued Ties

In some situations the tie value will be binary rather than interval, for example where the value 1 indicates a tie from ego to an alter with a characteristic, and 0 indicates a different characteristic. When the tie is binary valued we can use multilevel logistic regression to model the ego–net data in a similar way to that described above for valued ties. In this case each tie in the data is coded 0 or 1, and we predict the probability of this being 1, to indicate a tie from ego to an alter with a particular characteristic. For example, is a support tie between an ego who is a recent immigrant to Spain to an immigrant alter, ($y_{ij} = 0$), or to a long-term Spanish resident, ($y_{ij} = 1$)? In this case Model (6.2) above would be modified to model binary ties as follows.

Taking the framework of Model (6.2) in terms of the explanatory variables, we can write down a multilevel logistic regression model – Model (6.3) – as follows, where p_{ij} is the probability that the tie is valued 1, given the explanatory information for that alter and ego. This is written as:

$$p_{ij} = P(y_{ij} = 1 \mid x_{1ij}, x_{2j})$$

We now use logistic regression to model the log-odds, or logit of p_{ij} in a multilevel framework. $\text{Logit}(p_{ij}) = \log(p_{ij}/(1 - p_{ij}))$:

$$\log\text{it}(p_{ij}) = \beta_0 + \beta_1 x_{1ij} + \beta_2 x_{2j} + \beta_3 x_{1ij} x_{2j} + U_{0j} \qquad (6.3)$$

U_{0j} is an ego-level (level 2) residual (error) term, which we assume is normally distributed with mean zero and variance, σ^2_{U0}. Hence, σ^2_{U0} is the ego-level variance component, measuring the extent to which the average values of the (log-odds of the) tie-values in one ego-net vary from one another. The alter-level random components e_{0ij} of the models for valued ties are not defined here because we are modelling probabilities.

The data structure for this case would be very similar to that of Table 6.1, with only the valued column for y_{ij} being replaced with a column containing 0 or 1 to represent the binary ties.

Multilevel Analysis of the Ties between Ego and Alter in the Literature

Snijders et al. (1995) explain how multilevel models can be used to analyse ego-net data, illustrating this approach with an analysis of ego-nets of cocaine users. Specifically, they focus on the significance of cocaine amongst cocaine users and their personal relations with other cocaine users. In their paper they assume that the available ego-net data have been sampled in a sufficiently large social environment so that the overlap between different respondents' social networks is negligible. The authors point out that the multilevel model may be used for the analysis of ego-net data if the following conditions apply: 1) when the dependent (response) variable is at the alter level (level 1); 2) when the data contain no overlap or minimal overlap of ego-nets for different egos; and 3) when the data obtained from different egos can be assumed to be mutually independent. They further point out that the explanatory variable in these models can be from the alter level as well as the ego level, as we have discussed above. Moreover, the authors highlight the substantive value of being able to allow alter-level explanatory variables to have different relationships with the dependent variable for different egos.

Snijders et al. (1995) base their analyses on data from a research project on cocaine use in Rotterdam. Snowball sampling was used to obtain the data since cocaine users are a hidden population, for which the sampling frame is missing. The respondents were asked to mention up to 50 other cocaine users. The respondents were then asked to assign these users to different drug-use categories: entertainment, work, home, private parties, sport or hobbies and the hard drugs scene. Egos could mention up to ten people per category. In total there were 60 respondents (egos) and 269 relations between ego and alter.

Multilevel models were then used to explore which factors contribute to the significance of cocaine in relationships for the respondents. The response variable – the tie between ego and alter – takes the following values and this seven-point scale was treated as an interval tie value in the analyses.

---

1. The contact between respondent *j* and nominee *i* never takes place in the context of cocaine use.

2. The contact between respondent *j* and nominee *i* sometimes takes place in a context of cocaine use. There has not been any relation between respondent *j* and nominee *i* with respect to the procurement of cocaine in the last six months.

3. The contact between respondent *j* and nominee *i* usually takes place in a context of cocaine use.

4. The contact between respondent *j* and nominee *i* sometimes takes place in the context of cocaine use. Respondent and nominee take turns to obtain cocaine, or they buy it jointly from a third person.

5. The contact between respondent *j* and nominee *i* sometimes takes place in the context of cocaine use. Respondent and nominee take turns to obtain cocaine, or they buy it jointly from a third person.

6. The contact between respondent *j* and nominee *i* usually takes place in the context of cocaine use. Respondent and nominee take turns to obtain cocaine, or they buy it jointly from a third person.

7. The contact between respondent *j* and nominee *i* usually takes place in the context of cocaine use. Either the respondent or the nominee usually procures cocaine for the other.

Using multilevel linear models as specified above, Snijders et al. (1995) found that the respondents of Rotterdam's hard drugs circuit assigned a higher importance to cocaine than was the case for other respondents, whereas respondents using cocaine mainly at home or at private parties put a lower significance on cocaine with respect to relationships with other users.

De Miguel and Tranmer (2010) looked at the personal support networks of immigrants to Spain via a multilevel analysis of ego–net data. In each case the ego is a recent immigrant to Spain, and is asked to name the most important people in their support network. In general, these support networks comprised six alters, each of whom could either be another recent immigrant to Spain or a person who has lived in Spain all their lives (for convenience, referred to as a 'Spaniard' in the discussion). As discussed above, in a multilevel analysis of cross-sectional ego–net data, the unit of analysis is the tie between ego and alter. In this case the focus was on whether the tie from ego (always a recent immigrant) is to another recent immigrant (tie value = 0) or to a Spaniard (tie value = 1). Hence the focus is to predict the probability of a support tie being to a Spaniard as opposed to another recent immigrant, given the characteristics of ego, alter, homophily of ego–alter, the nature of the support, and information about the geographical area of immigration. The authors are interested in how these characteristics are associated with variations of the chances of ties to recent immigrants or Spaniards in the ego–net data they collected.

The support information comprises four types: help in finding a job, help with accommodation, general information about the local area, and material help. The geographical information includes the province of Spain to which the immigrant moved, and the percentage of people from the same country of origin of the immigrant in the area; the idea behind the latter variable is that the presence or absence of other recent immigrants in a support network may be associated with the extent to which other people originating from the same country as the immigrant also live in that area. Inclusion of such an explanatory variable thus allows the *contact hypothesis* to be explored, where it is hypothesised that where there are higher percentages of other people in the local area from the same country of origin as the recent immigrant (ego), this may then result in a greater number of recent immigrants from that country in their network, as opposed to Spaniards. The following two research questions are of particular interest to de Miguel and Tranmer (2010).

1. Which characteristics of the alter, the ego, the homophily of alter-ego, the support role, and the local area to which the immigrant has moved, are most strongly associated with a tie between an immigrant and a Spaniard, as opposed to a tie between an immigrant and another recent immigrant?

2. What kind of support is exchanged between immigrants and Spaniards, and how does this differ from the support exchanged between immigrant egos and alters?

Because the tie value between ego and alter is a binary response – either a tie to a Spaniard or to another recent immigrant – multilevel logistic regression was used here, where ego is at level 2, and the alters in the support network at level 1. The sampling strategy uses a low sampling fraction over a wide geographical area, so that there is minimal overlap between alters of one ego and the next. Hence, a simple two-level model is reasonable here, as shown in Model (6.3) above.

Here, the dependent variable is whether the support tie between ego (a recent immigrant) and an alter in their network is to a Spaniard as opposed to a non-Spaniard. Explanatory variables in the model may be characteristics of the ego, the alter, homophily of ego-alter, type of support exchanged, or characteristics of the local area of Spain to which the immigrant has moved. If there were many areas in the dataset, area could have been included as another level in the multilevel model – area would be included at level 3, ego at level 2 and alters at level 1. However, dummy (indicator) variables for the local areas were used in the explanatory part of the model here, rather than extending the model to a third level for 'area', since there are only five areas in total in this ego-net dataset.

De Miguel and Tranmer (2010) first modelled the ego-net character-istics only in the multilevel framework and found older egos tend to have lower probabilities of ties to Spaniard alters. Females are more likely to have ties to Spaniard alters. If the immigrant is not a *pioneer* and has no previous contact with Spain it is less likely that their support ties are to Spaniards. The country of birth of the ego was also associated with differential ties to Spaniard alters. For example, fewer Spaniards were found in the networks of immigrants from North Africa. Portuguese immigrants were more likely to have ties to Spaniards. This is not surprising, given the geographical proxim-ity of the two countries. Portuguese immigrants also tended to have smaller ego-nets than immigrants from other countries of birth. Again, the geo-graphical proximity of Portugal and Spain may be the reason that smaller support ego-nets are found for Portuguese immigrants.

Once the characteristics of alter are also added to the model, it is also possible to add indicator variables for the similarity or difference of char-acteristics of alter and ego as discussed above – to allow for homophily or heterophily. The inclusion of these terms improved the predicative power of the model. Many of the homophily (or heterophily) of alter and ego terms are significant, suggesting homophily and heterophily effects. For example, when compared with the case where ego is of average age among the immi-grants in the sample and alter is of similar age, if the alter is younger than the ego, the alter is less likely to be a Spaniard, and, if older, more likely to be a Spaniard. This effect was found to change for egos of above-average and below-average age.

The authors also found some gender homophily effects. Compared with male egos with female alters, if alter and ego are both male, the alter is signifi-cantly less likely to be a Spaniard. There is a greater chance that alter is a Spaniard if both ego and alter are female compared with male egos with female alters.

Moreover if alter and ego both work in the employment sector of 'Domestic help', the alter is less likely to be a Spaniard. This may reflect the fact that, for this employment sector, the type of occupation a Spaniard alter has may be very different from that of the immigrant ego. Other employment sectors, such as 'Agriculture' were also associated with differential chances of ego-alter ties to Spaniards and other recent immigrants.

In terms of the nature of support, help in finding a job was found to be equally exchanged with either a Spaniard or non-Spaniard alter. Help with accommodation and providing information about the local area to which the immigrant has moved are much more likely to be exchanged with another recent immigrant alter. Material support was found to be more likely to be exchanged with Spaniard alters.

When the local area characteristics were included in the model, the predictive power of the model improved slightly. When an immigrant moved to a municipality with a higher percentage of other co-nationals, the chance of ties to Spaniard alters in that area was lower, supporting the contact hypothesis: if there are higher percentages of people already living in an area with the same cultural and ethnic background as the immigrant, the chances of exchanging support with these immigrants will increase.

The authors concluded that the different types of support exchanged between immigrants and Spaniards and immigrants and non-Spaniards suggest current shortfalls in the way help and support is currently exchanged between Spaniards and immigrants. The authors also show where this support is successfully being exchanged. The results of these multilevel analyses of ego-net data thus provide a focus for further study, including qualitative or mixed methods approaches. Finally, the authors suggested that a detailed longitudinal study of the composition and role of immigrant support networks over time is also likely to have considerable research value. Lubbers et al. (2010) considered such an analysis for Argentinian migrants to Spain.

Multilevel Analysis of Ego-Net Dependencies

Models for overlapping ego-nets where the tie is the unit of analysis, are more complex than those shown above. In the models shown above, each alter is a member of exactly one ego-net because they do not overlap, or we can reasonably ignore the minimal overlap that might occur in the ego-net data. Identifying cases where alters are multiple members of ego-nets may be different for some ego-net samples, as this requires sensitive information (such as the names of the alters) which may have been suppressed prior to the release of the sampled ego-net data to ensure anonymity of respondents. In the following discussion, we consider instead extracting ego-nets from completely observed networks, where overlap (and hence cases where alters are multiple members of ego-nets) may be identified. When overlap is considerable and hence alters are members of more than one ego-net, a type of multilevel model called a 'multiple membership model' can be used. Here, alters are members of multiple ego-nets, and associated membership weights are required, to indicate the extent of ego-net membership for each alter. We do not describe such a case in this chapter for directly modelling *ties*, but the multiple membership model framework is described below for a different situation: in a multilevel analysis of ego–net network dependencies for responses for each person in a social network.

Multilevel Models for Network Dependency in Ego-Net Data

Network auto-correlation models are often used to assess network dependencies in social network analysis. This model framework was developed from spatial auto-correlation models, where weights derived from a proximity or contiguity matrix in the geographical case were replaced by weights derived from the adjacency matrix in the case for social networks. For a review see Leenders (2002). Such models can be fitted in R using packages for social network analysis (Butts, 2010) or geographical analysis (Bivand, 2006). An alternative method, which is especially useful when there is a desire to assess variation in network dependencies, is to fit a Multiple Membership (MM) model, as Tranmer, Steel and Browne (2014) have shown. The MM model formulation is as shown in Model (6.4) below. Such a model framework allows for overlapping ego-nets because alters can be multiple members of several ego–nets.

The Multiple Membership (MM) Model for Ego-Net Dependencies

$$y_{ij} = \beta_0 + \beta_1 x_{1ij} + \sum_{j=1}^{m} w_{ij} u_{oj} + e_{0ij} \qquad (6.4)$$

Where:

---

y_{ij} is a response variable for alter i of ego j.

β_0 is a constant term.

β_1 here relates an alter-level explanatory variable to the response variable. The model could be extended to include more explanatory variables.

$\sum_{j=1}^{m} w_{ij} u_{oj}$ is a sum of m random effects, where m is the total number of egos in the dataset. These are weighted for each alter i in j's ego net by w_{ij}.

e_{0ij} is an alter-level error term.

Furthermore, we assume that the u_{oj} and e_{oij} are both normally distributed with zero mean and with variances σ_u and σ_e respectively. We assume that the random effects u_{oj} and e_{oij} are uncorrelated, and thus the total variance in y_{ij} is the $\sigma_u + \sigma_e$. Given these assumptions, we can estimate the variation in the response between and within egos, and because we are using a multiple membership model we take into account overlapping ego-nets because alters can be multiple members of several ego-nets.

Several extensions are possible to Model 6.4. Firstly, we can estimate variations for other ways of grouping the individuals in the ego-nets (such as the schools and areas to which they belong) by introducing additional random effects into the model, to make it a Multiple Membership Multiple Classification (MMMC) model. Tranmer et al. (2014) used such a model to investigate variations in academic achievement by ego-net and by school and area, as described below. We could also include random coefficients at the ego level so that characteristics of the alters have different associations with the response variable in different ego-nets by allowing explanatory variables to have random coefficients. Moreover, this framework could be used to add time as a level, or to take into account multiplex or multilevel networks (for an example of the latter see Tranmer and Lazega 2013).

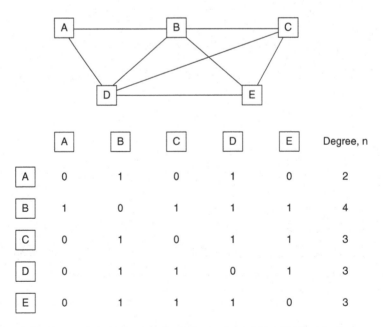

Figure 6.3   An undirected network of five individuals, with their adjacency matrix and the degree (number of connections, *n*) of each individual in the network

Data structure

Table 6.2   Example data structure for the overlapping ego-nets depicted in Figure 6.3

Alter = i	Ego-net membership weights: (1/n)					Y_i
	W_{iA}	W_{iB}	W_{iC}	W_{iD}	W_{iE}	
A	0	.5	0	.5	0	66
B	.25	0	.25	.25	.25	55
C	0	.33	0	.33	.33	43
D	0	.33	.33	0	.33	52
E	.0	.33	.33	.33	0	45

In Table 6.2 we see an example of the data structure that would be used to model ego-net data. The first stage of obtaining these data is to extract the ego–nets for each individual in the network by taking their respective row of the adjacency matrix, as shown in Figure 6.3. We then get the total degree (number of connections to other individuals in the network) for that individual, n. This then allows us to assign ego-net membership weights for each individual. At first glance it does not look like multilevel data for ego-nets. However, the ego-net membership of egos A–E by alters A–E is reflected through the ego-net membership weights: $W_{iA}, W_{iB}, W_{iC}, W_{iD}, W_{iE}$. For each ego the most obvious way to calculate ego-net member-ship weights is to equally allocate each individual to the ego-nets to which they belong with a weight of $1/n$, though other weighting schemes could also be used (see Tranmer et al. (2014) for a fuller discussion). In Table 6.2 the responses for some variable for each alter are denoted by Y_i, as shown in the final column. We may wish to use a Multiple Membership (MM) model to assess the variation of Y_i between and within ego-nets. In this example we have extracted the ego-nets from a complete network in order to model variation between and within the ego-nets, taking into account the overlap. Here, each individual takes a turn being an ego, and can also be an alter in the ego-nets of other individuals. A similar approach could be used to model variation between other sub-groupings of the network, as Tranmer et al. (2014) showed for cliques. In other situations it is possible that egos and alters could be completely separate people; this could happen, for example, if sampled egos only name non-sampled alters. Because the same non-sampled alters may be named by two or more of the sampled egos, we could also use the MM approach to take into account this overlap if it was considerable. If overlap was minimal or non-existent, a simple two-level model for alters in egos could be used to model the ego-net dependencies.

The data structure shown in Table 6.2 could be extended to include other ways of grouping the population, such as schools and areas. These classifications could be modelled alongside the ego-net data by extending the model to a Multiple Membership Multiple Classification (MMMC) model (Browne et al. 2001). The MMMC framework could then be used to model the relative share of variation in a response variable for individuals (alter), egos, and other classifications such as schools or areas.

Multilevel Models for Ego-Net Dependencies in the Literature

Tranmer, Steel and Browne (2014) used an MMMC model with data from the US Adolescent Health ('Add Health') survey (Harris et al. 2009) for one state in the US. Friendship networks are available for the individuals in the Add Health data, where each respondent is allowed to name up to five male and up to five female friends. Having extracted the networks from the Add Health data, these authors used this empirical analysis to illustrate a way of assessing the nature and extent of social network dependencies in an individual-level response variable, in this case academic achievement, in the context of other group dependencies such as the school or the area to which an individual belongs.

The MMMC model allows two important substantive results to be obtained for this example. Firstly, the overall individual-level relationship between academic achievement and characteristics of the individuals, such as ethnic group and gender, across all schools, areas and networks, and secondly estimated measures of variation in academic achievement at the individual (alter), ego, school, and area levels.

The ideas for Tranmer et al. (2014) are based on the development and application of the 'Multiple Membership' model (Hill and Goldstein 1998) for social network data, such as ego-nets. The multiple membership model has previously been used in other contexts. For example, students can go to more than one school in the course of their education and are sometimes therefore multiple members of different schools. In disease mapping we can treat the areas surrounding a focal area for which we wish to estimate the extent of an illness as multiple neighbours of the focal area in the multiple membership model (Lawson et al. 2003).

Tranmer, Steel and Browne developed and applied these ideas to social networks by treating the individuals in a network – in this case pupils in schools – as 'members' of ego-nets where each individual may 'belong' to more than one of these ego-nets and where weights reflect ego-net membership, as we have illustrated in Figure 6.3 and Table 6.2.

Having modelled the data using the MMMC approach, Tranmer, Steel and Browne (2014) found that some of the variation in academic performance is associated with the friendship ego-network of the school pupil, even when other classifications of the population structure such as school and areas are accounted for. The authors explain how the average ego-net membership weight can be used to scale the ego-net variance component estimate for comparison with other group-level variance components. The MMMC approach could be applied to other situations given data availability. For example we could consider individuals, households, social networks and geographical groups, though it might be hard to find secondary data with all these features in practice because of confidentiality restrictions. Further extensions could be made to the MMMC model to allow for different time points – for example, with several waves of data we could include time as a level in the MMMC model framework. We could also include random coefficients at the ego-net level to allow explanatory variables to have different associations with the responses of the individuals in the network in different ego-nets.

Analysing Alter-Alter Relations

Up to this point the chapter has offered a gentle introduction to what we may term standard statistical approaches to ego-net analysis. However, we have not yet considered statistical approaches to the modelling of alter-alter ties, a key topic of earlier chapters. To do this requires that we consider more specialised statistical techniques. Many of these techniques are considered in the next chapter. To foreshadow this, however, in this final section of the current chapter we will give a very brief overview of statistical approaches for *binary* alter-alter ties.

For these purposes we assume that for each of n egos we have collected information both on alters and on ties between those alters. The variables we collect are thus the binary variables X_{ijk} that indicate whether ego i reported that alter j has a tie to alter k. We can think of this as n networks described by the adjacency matrices $X_i = \{X_{ijk} : 1 \le j, k \le m_i\}$, where m_i is the number of alters nominated by i, for $i = 1, 2 \dots, n$.

Whole Network Approaches

In each of the networks X_i ego is tied to everyone else. For some purposes, however, ego might be thought of not as a member of the network but rather as its setting or boundary condition and may therefore be removed, generating 'ego-depleted networks', each of which may then be considered a whole network in its own right. In effect we are using ego to select and delimit our node set (including only those nodes whom ego nominates as alters) as we might use a school or a workplace in whole network analysis (including only those nodes who are pupils at the school or workers at the workplace). In contrast to most whole network analyses, however, doing this gives us multiple whole networks to analyse (one per ego) and we want to analyse them simultaneously, as a set.

Two main approaches may be taken to analysing all of the networks at once: (a) fit the same model to all the ego-nets $X_1, ..., X_n$; or (b) fit the same model to all networks but allow the parameters or processes associated with structures to vary across egos. The conceptual trick for (a) is to group all the ego-nets into one big (block-diagonal) matrix:

$$X = \begin{pmatrix} X_1 & 0 & \cdots & 0 \\ 0 & X_2 & & 0 \\ \vdots & & \ddots & \vdots \\ 0 & 0 & \cdots & X_n \end{pmatrix}$$

where the (ego-depleted) ego-nets are on the diagonal and all other entries are zero, thus indicating that we force the ties between ego-nets to be absent. The implicit assumption, therefore, is that there is no overlap between ego–nets.

There are several statistical approaches for analysing binary adjacency matrices. These models and techniques typically aim to identify tendencies towards particular types of structure in the networks, e.g. clustering (which we might measure via the prevalence of triangles in the networks). That is, they seek to ascertain the likelihood that such tendencies might arise by chance in a network so as to determine whether their presence in the observed networks might tell us something. If clustering, to continue that example, is highly likely to arise by chance in networks with the same properties as our ego-depleted networks, then we must assume that any tendency towards clustering in our observed, ego-depleted networks has arisen by chance and is not of analytic interest in itself (it may still be a condition which we must consider in explaining something else, which is of interest). If, however, a structural tendency such as clustering is unlikely to arise by chance, at least to the extent that we find it in our observed, ego-depleted networks, then we may surmise that processes are at work in our networks which generate such tendencies and this clearly might be of analytic interest. In other words, we test to see whether our network structures depart from what might be expected by chance to a statistically significant extent.

There are a variety of ways in which we might do this. The Quadratic Assignment Procedure (QAP) is an intuitive and straightforward procedure, whereby the 'significance' of a structure is assessed via a comparison with a permutation distribution; that is, rows and columns of our observed matrix are permuted multiple times and the resulting structures compared against the original (Borgatti et al. 2013). Alternatively we may compare our observed networks against multiple random networks and the null distributions for particular network properties which they allow us to generate, controlling for other properties such as network size and density. For example, we might simulate 1,000 random networks of the same size and density as our observed network, measure clustering in each case, and then compare the clustering we find in our observed networks against the distribution of clustering scores derived from our random networks. If our observed networks figure at one of the extremes of the distribution then they are very unlikely to have arisen by chance. Something is at work within our networks, we might conclude, which is generating clustering – and we may then proceed to find out what that is. Moreover, we may consider applying a sequence of further tests that are increasingly more restrictive in order to single out which structural patterns explain other structural patterns (see, for example, Pattison et al. 2000).

Another more direct approach for assessing structure is to model it, rather than rejecting the absence of structure by reference to null-distributions. One such framework for this is the Exponential Random Graph Model (ERGM). The aim of the ERGM is to assess 'how strong' or 'important' different structural features are to the overall structure of the network. In practice this amounts to fitting a log-linear model to the network where parameters associated with different sub-graph configurations are estimated. If the parameter associated with triangles (i.e. clustering) is distinctly different from zero, this means that there is a tendency towards clustering in the network, given all the other effects in the model. For an introduction to ERGMs see Lusher et al. (2013).

All of the methods for complete networks mentioned above may be applied to the combined matrix X, with the proviso that the estimation or randomisation procedure respects the restriction that there are no ties between ego-nets. For example, when generating random Bernoulli graphs, only ties in the ego-nets are randomised – the rest are constrained to be zero. ERGMs may also be defined for constrained graphs – most constraints of which are implemented through the algorithm used to simulate graphs (Snijders and van Duijn, 2002). For the particular case of restricting some tie-variables to be zero, that is to say, conditioning inference on graphs that are block-diagonal in the same way as X, the ERGM is specified as for the unrestricted case but the null-ties between ego-nets are taken as exogenous and given. In MPNet this is done by specifying a 'structural zeros' file and in the ERGM R package the fixed null-ties are defined through manipulating the 'blockdiag' argument to constraints.

Multiple and Multilevel Network Approaches

Fitting the same model (approach a) to all ego-nets entails making the rather strong assumption that alter-alter ties do not depend on ego. We may relax that assumption by allowing the processes to vary across egos by adopting a multilevel scheme. Instead of generating a null-distribution for X that is calibrated, say, to match the overall density of the non-null blocks of X (a block-diagonal Bernoulli model), we may generate a null distribution where the diagonal blocks are constrained to have the same densities as the observed ego-nets. This is as a kind of a priori stochastic block-model where the probability of between-ego-net ties is set to zero.

This approach is borrowed from Lubbbers and Snijders (2007), who present a joint analysis for 102 separate networks collected across different contexts. They propose to fit an ERGM separately to each of the networks and then combine the results using meta-analysis. This requires that the same *model-specification* is used for each of the networks but parameters are allowed to vary across networks. The same approach may be applied directly to ego-nets. The practical complications of applying this technique to ego-nets are that each individual network might be small and have considerably less information than the typical networks (schools) that Lubbers and Snijders' (2007) approach was designed for. A solution would be to model multiple observed ego-nets simultaneously as a multilevel analysis of ERGMs. The hierarchical ERGM of Schweinberger and Handcock (2009) (where networks are clustered according to latent groups rather than egos) could be used in this case.

There have been few studies specifically addressing how to model (statistically) alter-alter ties in ego-nets. A notable exception is the work by Smith (2012). While the focus of that approach, like the two related articles by Morris et al. (2009) and Krivitsky et al. (2011), is on using ego-net data to make inferences about the population, it also provides estimates for the population-level ERGM. This means that you have the tacit understanding of the ego-nets as being sampled from one and the same large network and in this sense this approach is to be classified as a version of (a).

There is a vast and growing literature on various latent space and latent variable approaches to modelling tie-variables (see Salter-Townsend et al. 2012). Most of these models are well suited for applications to joint analysis of multiple ego-nets, particularly those that capture tie-dependencies with latent classes.

Ego-nets as Sampled Networks

As ego-nets (with alter-alter ties) may be considered two-wave snowball samples where the ties of the first wave are restricted to be connected to other nodes in wave one, it is natural to consider analysis of ego-nets as analysis of network samples. These network samples now include the ego-alter ties (i.e. are not ego-depleted) and ties of alters to nodes not in wave one, missing by design. The seminal work of Thompson and Frank (2000) provides the conditions under which it is possible to fit models to snowball-sampled data. Building on this work Handcock and Gile (2010) provide an approach for estimating ERGMs from snowball-sampled data. In fact, provided that we know which nodes ego *has not mentioned*, we can fit an ERGM using only the nominations by egos – the alter-alter ties add information but are not necessary for fitting the model. Ego-alter ties only will typically not provide enough information for a standard ERGM, however – (triangles may only be constructed by the overlaps created by egos choosing each other) and alter-alter ties are necessary. In order to apply this approach we need to know the total number of nodes in the network that the ego-nets were sampled from as well as attributes that are relevant to our analysis for all nodes (Koskinen et al. 2013 demonstrate how missing attributes may be handled in a Bayesian framework). All likelihood-based approaches for fitting ERGMs to ego-nets will involve some form of imputation of non-sampled ties, something that becomes computationally burdensome for large populations.

If it is reasonable to assume that ego-nets are sampled from the 'same' network and that the size of the network is known, it is appropriate to fit an ERGM to the sampled data. If ego-nets are sampled across a wide variety of different contexts, for example based on egos in different cities, this assumption may be less plausible. The larger the population network the more difficult fitting an ERGM will be and the less likely it will be that the same processes are at work in the different ego-nets. If all ties of alters are measured, and you have a full two-wave snowball sample including nodes that are not directly tied to ego, then the conditional ERGM analysis of Pattison et al. (2013) may be used in the way proposed by Stivala et al. (2014).

Summary

In this chapter, we have explained how the multilevel modelling framework may be used to investigate variations in the values of binary or continuous ties between alters and egos given a set of cross-sectional ego-net data. We can take into account characteristics of the egos and alters, and their similarity, in modelling these variations. We have explained that when there is little or no overlap of the alters of one ego and the next, a relatively simple multilevel model can be used to investigate variations in the ties; a linear multilevel model for continuous ties and a logistic multilevel model for binary ties. We have illustrated this approach with examples from the literature.

We then considered a more complex multilevel model for overlapping ego-nets – the Multiple Membership (MM) model – and looked at its application for modelling ego-net dependencies in responses for the alters in an ego-net, where in some cases all the individuals in a social network can be considered both egos and alters when ego-nets are extracted from a complete network. We further explained how the Multiple Membership Multiple Classification (MMMC) model could be used to concurrently model variations in individual responses, variations between ego-nets, and between other groups such as areas and schools. We have illustrated this approach with an example from the literature based on educational data from the US.

For both cases we have provided schematic diagrams to explain the underlying data structures and given details of software that may be used for the multilevel modelling of cross-sectional ego-net data.

We have provided a brief discussion on how to model binary alter-alter ties, and reflected on the various challenges by reference to available approaches. There are not many empirical applications to date that use statistical models tailored to ego-nets. The next chapter on longitudinal analysis will illustrate further the fundamental issue that while we know who is in ego's ego-net we do not know who is not in it.

7

STATISTICAL ANALYSIS OF NETWORK DYNAMICS

Learning Outcomes

By the end of this chapter you will:

1. Have a good understanding of the added issues in temporal analysis of ego-nets.

2. Have a basic knowledge of how standard longitudinal techniques apply to analysis of ego-network size.

3. Have a basic grasp of different approaches to dynamic analysis of alter addition and alter-alter ties.

Introduction

In this final chapter we turn our attention to statistical methods for analysing ego–nets over time. These methods are not well developed. Consequently there is not much experience to draw on for understanding the dynamics of ego–nets. There are studies of egos over time where alter nominations have been collected through, for example, name generators (Valente and Saba 1998; Valente and Vlahov 2001). While many standard approaches may be applied if aggregate features of the alters are considered properties of ego, explicitly considering the nominations as network ties poses a number of challenges as we shall see in this chapter. In the first part of this chapter we will focus on some of these methodologically important issues. In particular, the first section introduces the notation necessary to define ego–nets with the added element of time. We then move on to discussing how network-level measures, such as those defined in Chapter Four, may be analysed over time using statistical techniques. This includes analysing the change over time in the number of alters that ego selects and the density, or clustering, of the ego-nets over time. We then turn to the more complicated issues of analysing the details of the ego-nets, such as defining statistical models for (a) what alters are added and dropped over time, and (b) what processes determine the creation and deletion of ties amongst the alters. This chapter's structure implies that we start with trying to understand basic, 'macro-level' features, and then build up towards more complexity by considering the networks in more detail. The increasing complexity means that the later parts of this chapter are likely to appeal more to the advanced network analyst or methodologist. Throughout we will assume that data consist of observations over time for multiple egos as this makes most statistical sense.

As we have seen in previous chapters, going beyond only analysing the number of alters an ego nominates by also incorporating alter-alter ties may offer us a lot of insight into the local social environment of ego. Additionally, ego-nets may differ radically across egos with the same number of alters, as has been illustrated in Chapter Four. At first glance it may seem straightforward to extend the previously presented approaches for cross-sectional ego-nets to ego-nets observed across time. As we shall see in this chapter, however, adding a temporal dimension poses considerable conceptual difficulties. To date there are very few examples of longitudinal analysis of ego-nets with alter-alter ties. Some notable exceptions are the studies of Cornwell and Laumann (2015), Keim et al. (2013) (for subset of alters), and Waite et al. (2010). The most elaborate and comprehensive treatment of ego-nets over time is provided by Lubbers et al. (2010), where a number of different aspects of longitudinal networks are investigated.

Because of the relative lack of previous research on dynamic ego-nets, this chapter will start by making some conceptual clarifications. In order to define the basic properties of the typical data structure we will introduce some new notation. A further consequence of the lack of precedence is that we will have to develop some concepts from first principles, with the added result that the section on birth and death processes and parts of the section on approaches derived from complete network analysis in this chapter requires a little more experience of statistics in order to fully delve into the details. These sections may nonetheless give you a flavour of their purpose and main inferential targets and direct you to alternative sources of information.

A basic premise throughout this chapter is that we have observed ego-nets over time for *multiple* egos independently. Analysing only one ego-net over time gives very limited statistical information. Furthermore, the focus is on explaining the ties of the ego-nets and we do not consider valued ties in any detail.

When analysing ego-nets over time we may choose to adapt methods for completely observed or whole networks. Here we outline the additional formatting of data and additional considerations that need to be made. We may also choose to develop methods that cater especially to the problems and issues of longitudinal analysis of ego-nets.

Notational Preliminaries and Definitions

Adding a temporal dimension to the study of ego-nets introduces a number of complications compared to cross-sectional analysis. The fact that the set of alters of an ego may change over time means that the set of potential ties between alters varies over time and we have to take into consideration that

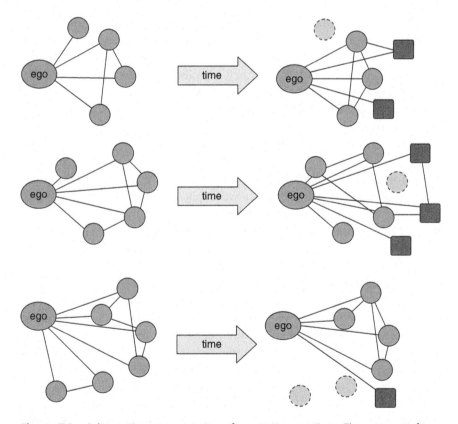

Figure 7.1 Schematic representation of ego-nets over time: The ego-nets for three egos observed at one time-point (left), and the same ego-nets observed at a later point in time (right). A greyed-out node on the right is a node that was an alter at the first time-point but was not nominated at the second time-point. A square, dark node, is a node that was nominated by ego for the first time at the second time-point.

a tie between two alters may disappear as a result of one of the alters being dropped by ego. To accommodate some of this added complexity and to add some analytical clarity we need to introduce some additional notation. Furthermore, in this chapter we shall deal exclusively with analysing the ties of the ego-nets and not the potential effects of these ties on attributes of the nodes. All examples are produced using the software programme R.

We assume the typical data illustrated in Figure 7.1, where a number of egos (here three) have nominated their alters on at least two occasions. We generally take it that for each snapshot the tie between ego and alter is superfluous – either an alter is nominated by ego or the individual is not an alter. The longitudinal set-up if anything illustrates the fact that the node-set of the ego-net is *generated by ego*. For cross-sectional ego-nets, defining the node-set is unambiguous but for repeated observations there are nodes that may represent alters that have not been re-nominated by ego (pale grey, round nodes in Figure 7.1); and there are nodes that were first nominated as alters at, say, the second observation point (dark grey, square nodes in Figure 7.1). These simple considerations raise a host of questions: Why were these alters dropped? Why were they mentioned in the first place? Why were they not mentioned in the first place? Why were they added? Are there other actors that have been added and removed in between observations? Were the new/old alters connected to any of the visible alters? Can we match the identities of the alters? etc.

We denote the collection of egos by $J = \{1,...,n\}$ and assume that they give information on their alters for time-windows $\Delta_i \subset \mathbf{R}^+$. That the time-windows depend on i means that we explicitly allow for the n egos to have their ego-nets observed at different points in time. We let attributes of ego i that do not depend on alters be denoted $v_i(t)$, which we allow to depend on time $t \in \Delta_i$. An example of an attribute that (typically) does not change is sex, for which we may then write $v_i(t) = v_i$, setting it equal to 0 or 1, according to whether ego i is male or female. An outcome like, say, a depression score, however, is likely to change over time. Naturally, we may in principle tag on any relevant information for the egos, such as affiliations or contexts that may link them to other egos.

For any point in time t we let the set of actors nominated by ego i be denoted by $A_{i,t}$. For example, if i=Martin at time t nominated as his alters Nick and Gemma, and at time $t+1$ nominated Nick and Mark, $A_{i,t} = \{\text{Nick,Gemma}\}$ and $A_{i,t+1} = \{\text{Nick,Mark}\}$. Across all time points $t \in \Delta_i$ we may conceive of a 'total' set of all alters ever nominated by ego i, $\mathbf{A}_i$. Note that this not a completely unambiguously defined set – it may be unambiguous if we observe all the nominations made by ego in a certain interval but if we only make observations in discrete time, there may be alters that have been nominated and de-nominated between observations. For practical purposes we define $A_i = \cup_t A_{i,t}$. For the example of Martin, we thus have $A_i = \{$Nick,Gemma,Mark$\}$. (We refrain here from allowing this set to change over time, something which it may well do if, say, ego moves cities, changes school, or in any other way alters its context.)

The time-changing set of alters of an actor i is illustrated in Figure 7.2. At time-point t_1 ego i has nominated the alters $A_{i,t_1} = \{h,k,j,l\}$ and at time-point t_2 ego i has nominated the alters $A_{i,t_2} = \{h,j,l,u,v\}$. Actors in the intersection $A_{i,t_1} \cap A_{i,t_2} = \{h,j,l\}$ are those that have been observed at both time-points; k belongs to A_{i,t_1} only; and u and v belong to A_{i,t_2} only. For this particular example we may define the total set of alters $A_i = \{h,k,j,l,u,v\}$. If we are only interested in the dynamics of properties of the alters, seen as a property of ego, we shall see that there is an important distinction to be made between an analysis that requires us to explicitly take A_i into account and an analysis that allows us to consider $A_{i,t}$ separately.

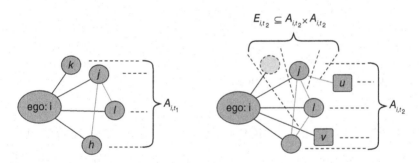

Figure 7.2 The time-dependent alter set of an ego and the time-dependent alter-alter set

Considering that two ego-nets with an identical number of alters still may differ in many other important aspects that depend on the configuration of ties between alters (e.g. structural holes, see Burt 1992), we would like to allow for alter-alter ties in our analysis. For each ego i and time-point t, we may consider the set of ties $E_{i,t} \subseteq \binom{A_{i,t}}{2}$ between alters, that is, a subset of all the possible ties between the alters that have been nominated at time t.

In Figure 7.2 the edge-set at t_1 is $E_{i,t_1} = \{\{h,j\},\{j,l\}\}$ and the edge-set at t_2 is $E_{i,t_2} = \{\{h,j\},\{h,l\},\{j,l\},\{j,u\}\}$. Note that the way we define $E_{i,t}$ means that the fact that $k \notin A_{i,t_2}$ implies that we do not have any information on whether there are any ties between k and any of the nodes in A_{i,t_2}.

Arguably, if k has not been nominated by i at t_2, i has not reported on any ties that k may have. Not making this distinction would imply that we would have to account for ties of an arbitrary set of potential alters.

BOX 7.1

Alter Set and Alter-Alter Ties for Longitudinal Ego-Nets

- The alter set and hence ego-net size varies over time.
- Based only on snapshots of the ego-net in time we cannot know if an alter that is reported for the first time may have been tied to other alters previously.

In UCINET, you may calculate descriptives of the ego-nets $X_{i,t}$ induced by $A_i \cup \{i\}$, where $X_{i,t}$ is a square adjacency matrix defined such that the ij-element of ego i at time t has $X_{ijk,t} = 1$ if $(j,k) \in E_{i,t}$ (0 otherwise). Thus, ties for alters that are not in $A_{i,t}$ are automatically set to absent, even if these are in effect unobserved. UCINET furthermore assumes that ego is included in each adjacency matrix time-slice.

Analysing the Evolution of Global Network Measures

If we have repeated observations on a collection of ego-networks we may consider any of the descriptives of Chapter Four and how these change over time. As these are summary measures of the ego-networks we may use standard longitudinal and panel data time-series techniques. However, it is worthwhile considering classifying descriptives into four categories, namely descriptives that:

(a) for all $t \in \Delta_i$ only depend on $A_{i,t}$
(b) for all $t \in \Delta_i$ only depend on $A_{i,t}$ and A_i
(c) for all $t \in \Delta_i$ only depend on $A_{i,t}$ and $E_{i,t}$
(d) for all $t \in \Delta_i$ depend on $A_{i,t}$, $E_{i,t}$, and A_i

For (a) we do not need to match nodes of $A_{i,s}$ and $A_{i,s}$, for $t \neq s$. This is a strong assumption meaning that it does not matter if we replace all the actors in $A_{i,s}$ with identical alters (with respect to relevant covariates). Things that we may investigate that correspond to (a) include summaries that only depend on the collection of alters at any given point in time such as the Blau heterogeneity and E-I index (as defined in Chapter Four). The simplest such summary measure would be the number of alters $m_i(t) = |A_{i,t}|$. If Martin nominated Nick and Gemma at time t, and nominated Nick and Mark at time $t+1$, his ego-net has the same size $m_i(t) = m_i(t) + 1 = 2$ at both time-points. The number of males is 2 and 1, for t and $t+1$ respectively. Calculating the number of males at $t+1$ does not require any knowledge of the network at time t.

Measures of category (b) in addition require that we match nodes of $A_{i,t}$ and $A_{i,s}$, for $t \neq s$. We may be interested in knowing the stability of the alter set, knowing for example how many alters are added, removed and kept. A measure of this, pair-wise for different time-points, is the Jaccard (1900) index

$$\frac{N_{11}}{N_{++}}$$

where $N_{11} = |A_{i,t} \cap A_{i,s}|$ is the number of alters reported at both time-points, and $N_{++} = |A_{i,t} \cup A_{i,s}|$ is the number of alters that were mentioned at either time-point (note that this may be interpreted in an identical fashion to how it is used in Snijders et al., 2010, if you let $N_{hk} = \sum_{j \in A_i} I\{x_{ij}(t) = h, x_{ij}(s) = k\}$, using $x_{ij}(t)$ as an indicator for whether $j \in A_{i,t}$ or not). While for $A_{i,t} = \{\text{Nick,Gemma}\}$ and $A_{i,t+1} = \{\text{Nick,Mark}\}$, and $A_{i,t}^* = \{\text{Nick,Gemma}\}$ and $A_{i,t+1}^* = \{\text{Mark, Joe}\}$, the number of males increases from 1 to 2, $A_{i,t+1}$ has one alter in common with $A_{i,t}$, but $A_{i,t+1}^*$ has no alter in common with $A_{i,t}^*$.

Summary measures of category (c) deal explicitly with the alter-alter ties. Examples include the number of ties in the ego-net, $s_i(t) = |E_{i,t}|$, and the clustering (or density) $c_i(t) = s_i(t) / (m_i(t)(m_i(t) - 1))$. Similarly, 'effective size' only depends on knowledge of the number of alters and the ties between them at any one point in time.

When you compare something like $c_i(t)$ across time, you are comparing densities of networks with different numbers of nodes, something that confounds the varying sizes of the ego-nets with how clustered they are. An alternative is to only consider average degree. Another alternative is to normalise the density by a common factor across networks. For example, dividing the number of ties at time t by $|A_i|(|A_i| - 1)$ yields a measure of category (d), requiring knowledge of the total alter set. This is in contrast to the corresponding clustering measure of type (c) that does not require knowledge of the overall aggregate alter set.

We will now proceed to illustrate some standard longitudinal models you could apply in some of the cases (a) through (d). In these examples, and the examples to follow, we shall be using 21 egos, each chosen from one of 21 schools in a Dutch study of schools in the Netherlands over four waves. (Networks in 21 school classes from the study by Andrea knecht (2008); see also Knecht et al. (2010)).

Throughout we will only treat the case of discrete time with observations at $t = 0,1,...,T$, $(T > 1)$ for all actors. A potentially promising alternative that we do not pursue here would be to apply event history techniques to retrospective designs.

Modelling the Dynamics of the Size of Alter Set

We will now give an example of how you may analyse a measure of category (a). We will consider the sequence $\{m_{it}\}$ $(m_{it} = m_i(t))$ of alter set cardinalities as repeated measures for ego in time.

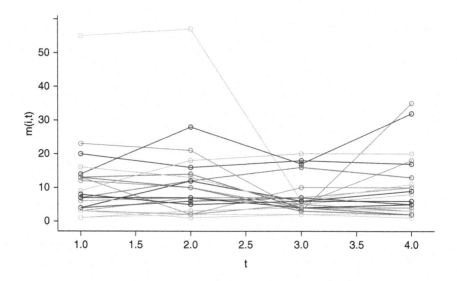

Figure 7.3 The evolution of the sizes of alter sets for 21 egos in Dutch schools observed at four points in time

Figure 7.3 gives m_{it} for the $n = 21$ egos in the Dutch school data set. We shall use the covariates sex, $v_{i1}(t) = v_{i1}$ (Male: 1), and a five-point scale of delinquency $v_{i2,t} = v_{i2}(t)$ that varies across the four waves.

It is customary to take into account the fact that we have repeated observations for individuals, recognising that it is implausible to assume that observations are independent within an individual. Here the 'individual' is the ego, which unit will be considered level two, and the measurement occasions will be considered level one (for more details on the use of multilevel models for repeated observations see Snijders and Bosker, 2012). Our first model is a so-called compound symmetry model:

$$m_{it} = \alpha + \beta t + \gamma_1 v_{i1} + \gamma_2 v_{i2t} + \gamma_3 v_{i2t} t + \epsilon_{it},$$

where $V(\epsilon_{it}) = \sigma^2 + \tau^2$ and $Cov(\epsilon_{it}, \epsilon_{is}) = \tau^2$. This is of the form of a time-series regression where the correlation between repeated measures is captured by the covariance of the error terms. This means that the variation in network size across time has one component that is due to the ego – egos differ in the overall level of their network sizes – and one component that reflects variation from occasion to occasion. We have formulated it here in terms of the marginal model rather than in terms of a multilevel model with explicit random effects on ego-level (for details see Chapter 15 of Snijders and Bosker, 2012). Note that while we take the nesting of measures in egos into account, the correlation between measures for the same individual does not depend on the distance between these observations in time. The results for the compound symmetry model fitted to the Dutch school data are given in Table 7.1.

Table 7.1 Three models fitted to the change in the size of the alter set for the 21 egos in the Dutch schools example

Coefficient	Compound sym		AR1		Cond. Poisson	
	Est	s.e.	Est	s.e.	Est	s.e.
α	8.88	2.63	9.15	2.41	1.67	0.21
β	0.60	2.71	−0.98	2.79	−0.08	0.78
γ_1	0.72	1.94	−0.06	1.71	0.03	0.10
γ_2	0.54	1.27	0.85	1.11	0.18	0.08
γ_3	−1.05	1.61	0.29	1.55		
δ					0.01	0.005
σ^2	62.09		109.03			
τ^2	44.31				0.47	0.68
ϕ			0.57			

Judging by the results in Table 7.1, there is no significant change in the size of the alter sets as a function of time (β) and in fact none of the effects is significant. The amount of variation between individuals as measured by τ^2 is, however, large in comparison to the overall variation.

The fact that the correlations in the compound symmetry model do not take the order of the observations into account might seem unrealistic. It is assumed that an observation at time $t = 3$ is just as highly correlated with the observation at $t = 1$ as the observation at $t = 2$. We may improve on this by fitting the same model but with an alternative correlation structure, for example of the first order auto-regressive form: $\epsilon_{it} = \phi \epsilon_{i,t-1} + \xi_{it}$, $\xi_{it} \sim N(0,(1-\phi^2)\sigma^2)$. The results, presented in Table 7.1, do not differ substantively from those of the compound symmetry model. Here the strong dependence between consecutive observations for an individual is reflected in the relatively large ϕ.

As the number of alters is a count and not a continuous measure with infinite range, it may be more appropriate to use a count model. For example, we may assert a sequential Poisson model, assuming m_{it} is conditionally Poisson with mean

$$\left(m_{it}\,|\,t,m_{i,t-1},v_{i1},v_{i2,t},u_i\right) = \exp\left\{\alpha + \beta t + \gamma_1 v_{i1} + \gamma_2 v_{i2,t} + \delta m_{i,t-1} + u_i\right\},$$

where $u_i \sim N(0,\tau^2)$ is a random effect capturing between-individual variance; the covariates enter in the linear predictor in the same way as in the linear model; and, δ captures the dependence between successive observations. Note that we are conditioning on the first observation m_{i0}, losing an observation. As seen from Table 7.1, this model does pick up a significant effect (γ_2) of delinquency, stating that people with higher delinquency scores tend to select more alters, everything else being equal.

Modelling the Dynamics of the Ego-Net Clustering

As a simple example of a descriptive of type (b) we may consider the clustering sequence $\{c_i(t)\}$ as a stochastic process. Note that this, taken as a measure of clustering over time, has to be interpreted in relation to the ego-network size and if there is a large variation in size across egos a bivariate model for $\{c_i(t),m_i(t)\}$ might be helpful.

Figure 7.4 give the trajectories for the ego-net clustering for 21 egos from Knecht's study over four waves. For a few egos and waves, the clustering is undefined when they only nominated one alter. These egos have subsequently been removed in the analysis.

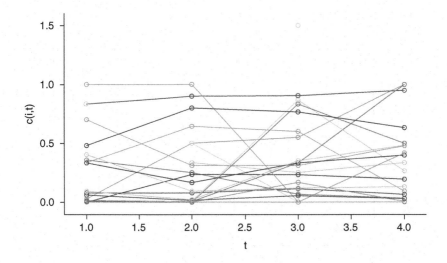

Figure 7.4   The evolution of the clustering of ego-nets for 21 egos in Dutch schools observed at four points in time

Similar to the case of modelling of the size of alter sets in (a), we may try as our first model a compound symmetry model:

$$c_{it} = \alpha + \beta t + \gamma_1 v_{i1} + \gamma_2 v_{i2t} + \gamma_3 v_{i2t}t + \epsilon_{it},$$

where, as before, $V(\epsilon_{it}) = \sigma^2 + \tau^2$ and $Cov(\epsilon_{it}, \epsilon_{is}) = \tau^2$. We may compare these results with those from a model that is auto-regressive through the error terms (AR1 in Table 7.2) as in the previous example. The results for these two models are given in Table 7.2. The results for the two models are similar and give the same substantive interpretations. The clustering does for example increase over time (β) but clustering for individuals that have high delinquency scores tends to decrease over time (γ_2).

We may consider a model that allows for correlation in the error terms according to a compound symmetry but that in addition accounts explicitly for dependence between the outcomes for successive observations. The latter may be achieved by including an auto-regressive term for the outcome variable (similar to *analysis of covariance*) according to the equation

$$c_{it} = \phi c_{it-1} + \beta t + \gamma_1 v_{i1} + \gamma_2 v_{i2t} + \gamma_3 v_{i2t}t + \epsilon_{it},$$

in which we assume for the error terms that $V(\epsilon_{it}) = \sigma^2 + \tau^2$ and $Cov(\epsilon_{it}, \epsilon_{is}) = \tau^2$ but also that a fraction (ϕ) of the clustering at time t is due to the clustering

Table 7.2 Results for four different modelling approaches to ego-net clustering applied to ego-nets extracted from Knecht's Dutch schools

Coefficient	Compound sym		ARI		Comp. sym and lag		Fixed effects	
	Est	s.e.	Est	s.e.	Est	s.e.	Est	s.e.
α	0.24	0.11	0.26	0.11				
β	0.27	0.09	0.21	0.09	0.31	0.12	0.066	0.038
γ_1	0.07	0.11	0.08	0.12	0.13	0.08		
γ_2	0.04	0.05	0.02	0.04	0.07	0.04	−0.021	0.044
γ_3	−0.14	0.06	−0.10	0.05	−0.18	0.06		
δ								
σ^2	0.066		0.108		0.064			
τ^2	0.041				0.012			
ϕ			0.567		0.47	0.12		

at time $t - 1$. The results for this model (Comp. sym and lag in Table 7.2) are not notably different compared to the previous two models with the exception of the coefficient for sex increasing relative to its standard error. The dependence between observations captured by ϕ accounts for some of the within-ego variation that the error-term previously had to take care of, the latter being reduced to about a fourth (0.012) of what it was in the previous two models.

If the main interest is to look at the effect of change in one variable on the change in the clustering, we may try to infer the causal effect using a fixed effects model. For example, we may infer the causal effect of, for example delinquency, on clustering with the fixed effects model:

$$\ddot{c}_{it} = \beta \ddot{t} + \gamma_2 \ddot{v}_{i2t} + \ddot{\epsilon}_{it},$$

where $\ddot{c}_{it} = c_{it} - \sum_{t=0}^{T} c_{it} / (T+1)$ and $\ddot{v}_{it} = v_{it} - \sum_{t=0}^{T} v_{it} / (T+1)$ are the time-demeaned values. The sign of the coefficient for delinquency (model 'Fixed effects' in Table 7.2) is now negative as the interpretation of the coefficient is closer to that for γ_3 in the previous models – an increase in delinquency leads to a decrease in clustering.

Modelling Properties Depending on A_i

Incorporating information on the total alter set A_i of ego allows us to investigate turn-over in alters and look at clustering measures that are scaled to reflect potential actors. In addition, measurements are made comparable across time-points. Interpretation is, however, complicated by the fact that we are using the future to predict the past. For example, an alter j may be included in calculating c_{it} if $j \in \cup_{s>t} A_{i,s}$ even if $j \notin A_i$. This would mean that $(j,k) \notin E_{i,t}$ even if this tie did exist.

These standard longitudinal approaches are straightforward to apply also to attribute-based descriptives such as the EI index. It is worthwhile keeping in mind the assumptions that are implicit in the different ways of formatting data and calculating measures.

Hierarchical and Mixed-Membership Growth-Curve Models

If the focus of interest is on analysing properties of the ego–alter ties over time or analysing (functions) of alter–alter ties over time, the statistical approaches of Chapter Six are straightforwardly extended to take time into account. For example treating the emotional strength Y_{ijt}, of a tie (i,j), as the outcome variable we may apply multilevel techniques to accommodate the dependence on time. In particular, the occasion t is level 1, alter j is level 2 and ego i is level 1. If $j \notin A_i$ but there are occasions $\{t : j \notin A_{i,t}\}$, then Y_{ijt} is coded as missing value for $\{t : j \notin A_{i,t}\}$. Great care has to be taken to consider the implications of the different data structures (a), (b) and (c).

A particular property of ego–alter ties that may be of interest is their persistence – whether alters mentioned at one time-point are nominated again at a later time-point. This involves only analysing a subset of the alters mentioned across time. Lubbers et al. (2010) demonstrated that both the structural position of alters as well as a variety of attributes were important in explaining the persistence of ego–alter ties.

If we are interested in properties of the alter–alter ties, $Y_{i(j,k)t}$ may be the value of the tie from j to k, where we let the variable be cross-classified by alters $j,k \in A_{i,t}$. An approach for dealing with this type of cross-classification is given in Koskinen and Stenberg (2012).

Birth and Death Processes for Evolution of Alter Set

Only analysing summary measures of the ego-nets ignores all the information provided by the identities of the individuals. We may be interested in directly modelling the appearance (birth) and disappearance (death) of alters in ego's alter set. Here, we will define a process for continuously observed alter additions and deletions so that the model can be fitted directly to time-stamped data (collected from retrospective samples or collected, say, electronically in real time). In analogy with how the continuous-time stochastic actor-oriented models (Snijders, 2001) are fitted to panel data however, the birth and death model may be fitted to observations in discrete time. We give here a brief, compact and rather technical description of how this model may be construed. This is for the interested reader and you may skip ahead to the 'Illustrative Example' to get a flavour for the types of inferences the birth and death model may provide.

Conditional on the current state of the ego-network $\{A_{i,t}, E_{i,t}\}$ and a global alter set $\mathfrak{A}_i$ from which ego i can add alters, we assume that two types of events may occur: the ego removes an alter or the ego adds an alter.

Borrowing the notation from Butts (2008) we let $e = (i, j, b, t)$ represent the event that i adds (deletes) j to (from) $A_{i,t}$ when $b = +$ ($b = -$). We adopt the notational convention of using the elements of e as functions such that $j(e)$ returns the alter of the event e, $\tau(e)$ the time of the event e, and $b(e)$ returns $+$ or $-$ according to whether $j(e)$ is added to or deleted from $A_{i,\tau(e)}$, respectively. It is convenient to denote the collection of past events at time t by $\mathcal{E}_t = \{e_a : \tau(e_a) \le t\}$, ordered such that $\mathcal{E}_{t-1} \cap \mathcal{E}_t = e_t$ and the collection of events that *could* occur at time t by $\mathbb{E}(t)$.

Marcum and Butts (2012) proposed an extension to Butts (2008) relational event model to handle ego–net data. Similar to the case considered here, the main challenge of this extension is to take into account the fact that the alter-set is unknown. The assumptions made about what events are modelled and what events are considered exogenous may be elaborated and worked out in great technical detail. We focus here on a simplified model where departures from the framework of Marcum and Butts (2012) are dictated by the fact that we use a relational event framework to model ties, i.e. states are modelled through treating the onset and deletion as events. As we shall see further on, this opens up possibilities for rephrasing the process in terms of stochastic actor-oriented models (according to the framework of Greenan, 2014). Nevertheless, the contributed R-package `informR` (Marcum and Butts, 2012) may in principle be adapted to the case considered here.

Model Formulation

At time t, given $\mathbb{E}(t)$, we assume that the time until e occurs is exponential with rate $\lambda_{b(e)}(e; \mathcal{E}_t, \theta)$, independently for all $e \in \mathbb{E}(t)$. Consequently the time until any event is exponential with rate $\sum_{e \in \mathbb{E}(t)} \lambda_{b(e)}(e; \mathcal{E}_t, \theta)$, and the probability that the event e is the first to happen after e_{t-1} is

$$\frac{\lambda_{b(e)}(e;\varepsilon_{t-1},\theta)}{\sum_{a\in\mathbb{E}(t)}\lambda_{b(a)}(a;\varepsilon_{t-1},\theta)}.$$

We can thus write up the probability distribution function (pdf) for any sequence $\cup_a \varepsilon_{t_a}$ of adding alters to and deleting alters from $\{A_{i,t}: t\in\Delta_i\}$ as

$$p\left(\{e_a\}\mid\theta,i\right)=\prod_{e_a\in\cup_a\varepsilon_{t_a}}\lambda_{b(e_a)}\left(e_a;\varepsilon_{\tau(e_{a-1})},\theta\right)$$

$$\times\exp\left\{-(\tau\left(e_a\right)-\tau\left(e_{a-1}\right))\sum_{s\in\mathbb{E}(\tau(e_a))}\lambda_{b(s)}\left(s;\varepsilon_{\tau(e_{a-1})},\theta\right)\right\}$$

$$\times(1-e^{-(T-\tau(e_{a*}))\sum_{s\in\mathbb{E}(T)}\lambda_{b(s)}(s;\varepsilon_{\tau(e_{a*})},\theta)})$$

This is the pdf of a sequence of conditionally independent exponential distributions where the last factor stems from censoring. An alternative characterisation is as a marked point-process, $\{Y_i(t): t\in\Delta_i\}$, where $Y_i(t)$ is a binary vector with elements $\{Y_{ij}(t)=1_{(j)}\{A_{i,t}\}: j\in\mathfrak{A}_i\}$.

The rate functions may incorporate any function of ε_t, which may include attributes of egos $v_{i,<t}=\{v_i(s): s\leq t\}$, alters $w_{ij,<t}=\{w_{ij}(s): s\leq t, j\in\mathfrak{A}_i\}$ and ties $E_{i,<t}=\{E_{is}: s\leq t\}$ if treated as exogenous. As the rates are non-negative it is convenient to model them using a log-link $\lambda_{b(e)}(e;\varepsilon_t,\theta)=\exp\{f(e;\varepsilon_t,\theta)\}$ for some additive function f that may be a weighted sum of statistics. We may model the tendency to add alters as a function of the current number of alters, by including a count $\sum_{j\in\mathfrak{A}_i}\gamma_{ij}(t)$, or the effect of some attribute $v_i(t)$ or its interaction with network size $v_i(t)\sum_{j\in\mathfrak{A}_i}\gamma_{ij}(t)$. To capture a tendency for ego to recruit alters k through other alters j, whom j is tied to we may include a statistic for $\sum_{j\in\mathfrak{A}_i}\gamma_{ij}(t)1_{(j,k)}\{E_{i,t}\}$, such that if the corresponding parameter is positive in $\lambda_+((i,k,+,t);\varepsilon_t,\theta)$ alters k that are tied to j already in $A_{i,t}$ tend to be nominated by ego at a faster rate than unconnected alters. As a consequence of the assumed observation process however, that $k\notin A_{i,t}$ implies that $(j,k)\notin E_{i,t}$ for any j and a tie will have to be assumed, for example by imposing the rule that if the set $\{s>t: (j,k)\in E_{i,s}\}$ is non-empty then there must have been a tie (j,k) at some $s\leq. t$

If data are time-stamped and $\mathfrak{A}_i$ known, the model is fully identified and may be fitted with any available likelihood-based technique. For time-stamped data and $\mathfrak{A}_i$ unknown, properties of j are only known for j dropping out of the alter set. Consequently only λ_- may be fully specified and only provided that the rate at time t only depends on $A_{i,t}$ and the rate for anyone joining the alter set is well defined. The issues with unknown $\mathfrak{A}_i$ is an expression of the fundamental technical challenge of modelling ego-networks – we know whom the ego has nominated but we do not know whom they have not nominated. In $p\big(\{e_a\}\,|\,\theta,i\big)$ the risks are competing with each other and the rates $\lambda_+(e;\varepsilon_t,\theta)$ for all $j(e)\in\mathfrak{A}_i\setminus A_{i,t}$ enter in the sum over $\mathbb{E}(t)$.

If in addition the data are not time-stamped, the number of events and event times are unobserved. As mentioned above, this is a standard premise in estimation of SAOMs, and the issue may be dealt with in an analogous manner. An added complication here is that an unknown number of alters may have been nominated and then dropped by ego so that there is always the risk of non-observed alters.

Illustrative Example

To illustrate the model, we fit a simple specification to the 21 egos of the Dutch schools data set. The parameters have been estimated using Bayesian methods and a Markov chain Monte Carlo algorithm. Here we treat all students (recall that the ego-nets were extracted from complete school class data) as $\mathfrak{A}_i$. We include covariate effects for alter and ego-alter similarity. To capture the growth of the network as depending on current size we include $|A_t|$ as a covariate in both the rate at which ego adds alters and the rate at which ego removes alters. To assess the effect of a potential alter being indirectly tied to ego, we include the statistic $(\mathbf{1}_{(j,k)}\{E_{i,t}\}+\mathbf{1}_{(j,k)}\{E_{i,t}\})$ in both rates. We make the simplifying assumption that only changes that are recorded between waves may have occurred. In other words, we disallow alters entering and leaving the alter set unseen in between observation points. Had this assumption not been made, we would have to account for the possibility that any number of alters could have entered the alter set and then left it unseen.

The results for a simple model are given in Table 7.3. They take into account: the current size of the alter set; the sex and delinquency score of a potential alter; the similarity (homophily) between ego and alter with respect to delinquency; and the effect of alter being connected to alter already in the alter set of ego. Recall that the model has been fitted in a Bayesian framework. Hence we deal with posterior means and standard deviations rather than, say, maximum likelihood estimates and standard errors. For the birth process it appears that the only parameters whose posterior lends support to the parameter being non-zero is the effect of alter being connected to alters already in the alter set. The posterior lends support to the parameter being positive, suggesting that egos add alters that are at distance two at a quicker rate than alters at greater distances. There is not enough support for interpreting the effect of alter being delinquent or being delinquent at a level similar to that of ego. The former parameter is positive and the latter negative but there is a lot of uncertainty in these estimates. For the death process, it appears that ego tends to drop alters at a quicker rate the larger their alter set. There is no conclusive evidence for the covariate-related effects but the transitivity parameter is clearly negative, suggesting that egos tend to drop alters that are embedded in their ego-nets at a slower rate.

Table 7.3   The posterior distributions for the parameters in a birth and death process for the alters in 21 Dutch schools

	Posterior adding		Posterior removing	
	Mean	Sd.	Mean	Sd.
Intercept	−0.452	0.415	0.004	0.273
Size alter set	−0.228	0.190	0.618	0.205
Alter sex	−0.203	0.404	0.229	0.360
Alter delinquent	0.515	0.364	−0.307	0.311
Ego*alter del.	−0.449	0.299	−0.024	0.275
transitivity	1.247	0.316	−1.435	0.345

Further Considerations

The effect on results of different assumptions regarding the alter set are likely to be dependent on the nature of data and the specifics of the model formulation. Robustness of the results to these assumptions may have to be evaluated though a comparison under different assumptions for $\mathfrak{A}_i$, such as comparing $\mathfrak{A}_i = A_i$ with a completely unknown alter risk set, where the latter may have to be represented by fictitious alters. You may want to circumvent some of these issues by only evaluating $\lambda_+(.)$ if k is in the primary setting. It may make sense to assume that the rate $\lambda_+(.)$ is constant for $j \in \mathfrak{A}_i \setminus A_i$.

Furthermore, as event-times are unknown we may want to generalise the model beyond conditioning on parsimonious paths, for example using the augmentation technique of Koskinen and Snijders (2007). This could be phrased in terms of missing data generating mechanisms which would help shed light on what types of assumptions make the model amenable to inference. In particular, most models with unrestricted alter set would imply that unobserved events are missing not at random (MNAR), especially when something other than functions of $\{(y_{ij}(t), w_{ij}(t)) : t \in \Delta_{i,j}, \in A_j\}$ are used.

BOX 7.2

Modelling the Addition of Alters

- Before an alter is reported and after an alter has been removed from the alter set, we have no data on this individual.

- Any attempt at studying the likelihood of adding alters of a certain characteristic must 'benchmark' this against the alters that could have been added from among some pre-specified pool of alters (we may call it the alter risk set).

Complete Network Methods for Longitudinal Ego-Nets

As described in Chapter Four, by removing ego from the ego-net, we may apply SNA methods for completely observed networks to ego-nets. Similarly, methods developed for longitudinal analysis of completely observed networks over time (Hanneke et al. 2010; Koskinen and Lomi 2013; Snijders 2001; Snijders and Koskinen 2013; Wasserman 1977, 1980a,b) may be applied to ego-depleted ego-nets. The issues regarding the endogenously defined and time-varying set of alters treated above remains. In the following we will assume that a universal set of known alters $\mathfrak{A}_i$ can be defined. Conveniently this may be defined as $\mathfrak{A}_i = A_i$ or $\mathfrak{A}_i = \cap_t A_{i,t}$. Furthermore, we will assume that we have independently observed egos and that $\cap_i \mathfrak{A}_i = \varnothing$.

We describe only the approach for analysing pairs of observations, $E_{i,0}$ and $E_{i,1}$.

The purpose is to explain ties $E_{i,1}$ using ties $E_{i,0}$ and a collection of dyadic covariates $w_{i,t}^{[jk]}$ for $j,k \in A_i$. The dyadic covariates may be derived from attributes of the alters of i as well as attributes of i.

Permutation-Based Analysis

A convenient technique for analysing complete networks over time is to regress networks on networks at prior time-points. A common way of accounting for the lack of independence of ties when doing this is to calculate standard errors of regression coefficients using a permutation-based procedure – the quadratic permutation procedure (QAP). Typically this is done for pairs of observations in time, but for multiple waves of observations in time the analysis may be made pair-wise, giving a sequence of inferences. The QAP approach is also straightforwardly extended to analysing the ego-nets at time t regressed on properties of ego-nets for multiple observations t-1, t-2, …, 0. In the following we provide a formal explanation of the approach. Essentially this amounts to applying the QAP procedure of Borgatti et al.(2013) to the networks of the n egos simultaneously.

Specification of the Regression

For a suitably defined set A_i, create n ego-depleted pairs networks $x_{i,t}$, where the entry $(x_{i,t})_{jk}$ is equal to one or zero according to whether $(j,k) \in E_{i,t}$ or not, respectively, for $t = 0,1$ and $j,k \in A_i$. Let $Y_t = (x_{i,t})_{t=1}^n$ be the collection of ego-nets at time t with an associated vectorisation function $vec(Y_t)$ that returns a vector of (the non-redundant) entries of Y_t. In a similar way we stack the covariates into matrices $w_{i,t}$ the entries of which are $(w_{i,t})_{jk} = w_{i,t}^{[jk]}$, and collect these in $W_t = (w_{i,t})_{t=1}^n$ that permit the same vectorisation operation as Y_t.

In the permutation-based approach we regress $vec(Y_1)$ on some function of Y_0, W_0, and W_1, and then permute the regressors (or the dependent network) and refit the model many times in order to get a distribution of parameters. If we want to investigate the persistence of ties, whether a tie between j and k at time 0 is likely to be associated with a tie between j and k at time 1, we may regress $vec(Y_1)$ on $vec(Y_0)$. To investigate whether a tie at time 0 from k to j is likely to be associated with a tie from j to k at time 1, we regress $vec(Y_1)$ on $vec(Y_0^{rec})$, where $Y_0^{rec} = (x_{i,0}^T)_{t=1}^n$. We may also be interested in whether a tie (j,k) at time 1 closes a two-path $\{(l,k),(l,j)\}$ present at time 0 by using as a predictor $vec(Y_0^{S_2})$, $Y_0^{S_2} = (x_{i,0}x_{i,0}^T)_{t=1}^n$.

A number of potentially important network effects may be investigated through including various transformations of the network at time 0 as a prediction (Borgatti et al. 2013). Additionally, when ties are binary it may be appropriate to employ a logistic link function rather than a linear link function. Here we use the latter for the sake of convenience. This means that the regression coefficients are calculated using ordinary least squares regression and the model may be understood as a so-called 'linear probability model'.

Illustrative Example

We return to the example of the symmetrised ego-nets extracted from Knecht's (2008) Dutch schools. We include three attributes in the model. For each tie-variable $x_{ijk,t}$ the corresponding *main effect* of an attribute is a covariate that is the sum of the attribute values of j and k. The corresponding homophily, or interaction effect, is the product of the attribute values of j and k.

We model persistence for each tie-variable $x_{ijk,t}$ through including a covariate $x_{ijk,t-1}$, in other words, we regress the tie-variable at one point on the tie-variable at a previous point in time. The triadic closure is modelled by including as a covariate to $x_{ijk,t}$ the count $\sum_{h\neq i,j,k} x_{ijh,t-1} x_{ikh,t-1}$ of indirect paths between j and k. This may be interpreted as the extent to which a tie at time t closes a triad that was open at the previous point in time. However, this formulation does not exclude the possibility that the triad was closed already at the previous point in time, nor does it tell us whether the indirect paths are still present at time t.

Results

Table 7.3 reports the results of network regressions of the (ego-depleted) ego-nets at time 1 on the ego-nets at time 0, for two types of models: a homogeneous model that does not take differences between egos into account; and, a fixed effects model where the differences in density among the ego-nets is accounted for by an ego-specific fixed effect (represented here by each ego-net having its own intercept). The results for the homogeneous model under standard assumptions of independent observations and normality (as represented by the t-statistics) indicate that there is a main effect of ethnicity and a homophily effect of sex. Furthermore there is a positive effect of persistence (i.e. ties that were present at time 0 tend to be present at time 1), the model also indicating a tendency towards triadic closure. Taking the network structure into account when assessing uncertainty does however show that none of the effects is significant and, if anything, the transitive closure is less than we would expect by chance (however, this is not statistically significant). Taking differences between egos into account, the significance of the triadic closure effect disappears in the standard regression analysis as does the effect of ethnicity. The QAP-statistics generally increase in absolute value when the fixed effects for egos are included; however, none of the effects is statistically significant.

Note here that each ego-net has been permuted separately in the analysis and, as each network is of a relatively small size, its permutation distribution is likely to be relatively close to the observed network. This may account for the drastic difference between the standard t-statistics and the QAP-statistics. Additionally, we have not here accounted for the difference between network and attribute level effects. A more sophisticated approach would be to use the modifications to QAP regression proposed in Dekker et al. (2007).

Table 7.4   Network regression: regression estimates for regressing time 1 on time 0 networks and attributes for 21 egos extracted from Knecht's (2008) Dutch schools. The homogeneous model has one intercept common to all egos (not reported) and the fixed effects model includes one ego-specific intercept for each ego (not reported). T-statistics are the standard regression (lm()) output based on standard assumptions. QAP-statistics are the pivots based on the permutation distribution with the dependent variable permuted.

	Homogeneous model			Ego fixed effects		
	estimate	t-stat	QAP-stat	estimate	t-stat	QAP-stat
Main sex	−0.105	−1.867	−0.685	−0.026	−0.392	0.191
Main ethnicity	−0.087	−2.083	−0.867	−0.028	−0.593	−1.143
Main delinquent	0	−0.007	0.724	0.025	0.573	0.469
Hom sex	0.227	2.313	0.464	0.316	3.126	−0.308
Hom ethnicity	0.136	1.478	1.377	0.096	1.044	1.666
Hom delinq	−0.045	−1.415	−0.836	−0.057	−1.846	−0.715
Persistence	0.304	6.448	0.795	0.311	6.537	0.911
Triangles	0.038	4.35	−1.125	0.013	0.807	−1.181

Stochastic Actor-Oriented Models for Ego-Nets

The Stochastic Actor-Oriented Model (SAOM) (Snijders 2001; Snijders and van Duijn 1997), assumes that the network changes incrementally over time by individual ties changing one at a time. More specifically, the SAOM assumes a discrete Markov chain in continuous time that may be specified by opportunities to change and mini-steps. The model is called *actor-oriented* as it is assumed that change is driven by the actors' purposeful action. The time until an actor decides to make a change is exponential with rate $\lambda_j(x_i(t), \theta)$. Given the current state x_i, and that an actor j makes a change (or has the opportunity to make a change), the actor changes one of their outgoing ties to an actor $k \in \mathfrak{A}_i \setminus \{j\}$, resulting in a new state of the network, denoted $x_i(j \rightsquigarrow k)$, which is the network that is equal to x_i for all elements apart from (k, j) which is equal to $1 - x_{ijk}$. The probability of j thus toggling the tie to k is

$$p_{ijk}(x_i, \theta) = \frac{\exp\{f_{ij}(x_i(j \rightsquigarrow k), \theta)\}}{\sum_{\ell \in \mathfrak{A}_i \setminus \{j\}} \exp\{f_{ij}(x_i(j \rightsquigarrow \ell), \theta)\}},$$

where $f_{ij}(x,\theta)$ is a function that represents actor j's evaluation of the network x and that depends on statistical parameters θ that are the target of inference. For undirected networks, a change in a tie-variable x_{ijk} may not be unambiguously defined as a change by either of the actors k or j as the tie does not have a direction. In the stochastic actor-oriented framework there are currently four approaches for handling undirected networks (Snijders, 2010): unilateral initiative and reciprocal confirmation; pair-wise disjunctive (forcing) model; pair-wise conjunctive model; and pair-wise compensatory (additive) model. The first option is identical to the directed model with the exception that the 'utility' of the state $x_i(j\ k)$ from the perspective of k is also taken into account. The model is estimated either using method of moments (MoM), maximum likelihood or Bayesian inference.

An alternative to the actor-oriented model may be a longitudinal ERGM (Koskinen and Lomi 2013; Snijders and Koskinen 2013) or discrete-time versions of cross-sectional models (Hanneke et al. 2010; Robins and Pattison 2001).

Adapting Ego-Net Analysis to the Complete Network Paradigm

The SAOM has been developed explicitly for the analysis of single networks and while we could consider each ego-net a network in its own right and analyse the ego-nets separately, we typically have a large number of egos and the target of inference is to say something about patterns across egos. We here present three approaches for simultaneous analysis of multiple networks. These approaches are, as in the previous example, developed under the assumption that the multiple networks are all complete networks. As a consequence we shall have to be careful when interpreting the SAOM from an actor-based perspective. When we assume that an alter considers making a change to their outgoing ties we only allow them to choose from actors in ego's alter set. Consequently, we are making the implicit assumption that any other ties they may form are described by a process that is independent of the changes of ties among the alters of ego.

Multigroup Option

A straightforward approach for analysing multiple networks is to assume that the process is identical for all networks, i.e. each ego-net follows the same SAOM. The SAOM is applied in an identical fashion to how it is done for a single network with the exception that data has to be set up using RSiena's multigroup option.

An obvious drawback is that assuming the model to be the same for each ego is a very strong assumption. The ego-nets are typically of different sizes, have different covariate compositions, and may reflect properties of wildly different contexts. Restricting parameters to be the same across ego-nets also means that we do not know how much the estimates are influenced by any one network.

Meta-Analysis

A compromise between analysing each ego-net separately and assuming that the models are identical across egos is to assume that the form of the model is the same across egos, allowing the parameters to vary freely and then pooling the estimates (see Lubbers et al. 2013). Lubbers et al. (2010) applied the meta-analysis technique proposed by Snijders and Baerveldt (2003) to the case of multiply observed ego-nets. In practice, this means that you estimate the ego-nets separately and pool the results using the meta-analysis routine siena08.

Hierarchical Bayesian Approach

The meta-analysis approach requires that we fit the same model independently to all our n ego-nets. As we are typically not in control of the sizes $m_i(t)$ of the alter sets there is a risk that some ego-nets are small. For a small network there may be little information on things like transitivity. Additionally, in order to perform the meta-analysis, we have to make sure that all of the n estimations have converged and given us valid estimates, something that is likely to be both time-consuming and tedious. The Bayesian hierarchical model allows us to fit all the ego-nets simultaneously without — as in the multigroup option — requiring that parameters are identical across egos.

The Bayesian hierarchical SAOM (Koskinen and Snijders 2015) assumes that the ego-net parameters $(\theta^{[i]})$ are themselves independent draws from a distribution which is Gaussian with expected value μ and covariance matrix Σ. Assuming a prior distribution for μ and Σ, inference is done simultaneously for $(\theta^{[i]})$, μ and Σ, giving posterior distributions over these unknown quantities given the observed data. This estimation procedure is implemented in the routine sienaBayes in the contributed R package RSiena. Details for how data, the model, and estimation are set up are given in the RSiena Manual (Ripley et al. 2014). With multiple egos, and knowledge of additional properties about the egos, it is also likely that we may want to include (ego-)network level properties as predictors of

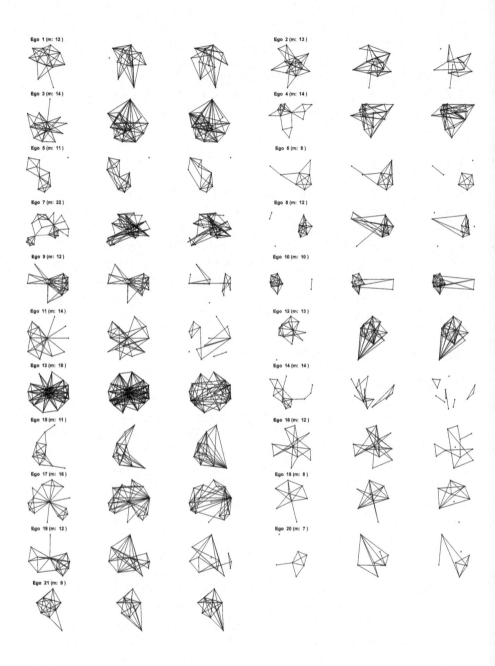

Figure 7.5 Ego-nets for 20 egos extracted from Knecht's (2008) Dutch school data across three time-points

dynamics as well. For example, do extrovert egos tend to have denser networks than introverted egos? In order to include a network-level effect, we need to restrict the corresponding coefficient to be the same across ego-nets. In sienaBayes setting network level effects is done through setting the column random effect to FALSE.

We now proceed to illustrate the hierarchical Bayesian approach for the extracted ego-nets from Knecht's data illustrated in Figure 7.5. This analysis set-up illustrates the issues we encounter in longitudinal analysis of ego-nets well. First of all we need to decide on an alter set. We have chosen as the alter set $A_i = \cup_{t=0}^{3} A_{i,0}$. That means that there may be alters in the first wave $(t = 0)$ that were not nominated by ego until at a later occasion, for example at the second wave $(t = 1)$. Any tie-variable for such an actor is by design missing. In this example we have ignored this principled approach and set unobserved ties to null ties. Like in previous examples we have also symmetrised the networks (here we chose the union rule). We fit a simple model with density, triangles and the main effect of sex (male=1) to 16 out of the 21 ego-nets of Figure 7.5.

Table 7.5 Hierarchical SAOM estimates of population means

	Estimate	Posterior sd
Rate t0-t1	5.345	0.594
Rate t1-t2	4.729	0.447
Degree (density)	−1.179	0.214
Triads	0.449	0.172
Sex	0.196	0.228

The estimates of μ for this simple model are given in Table 7.5. There is no effect suggesting that alters who are boys create and maintain more ties than girls. We may notice that there is evidence for global tendency towards triangles being positive. Note that the transitivity parameter need not be positive for all is – the inference for μ is pooled across all egos. The inference procedure also generates predicted parameter values for all ego-nets. These are provided in Figure 7.6 for the transitivity parameter. All the ego-level parameters are positive in expectation but there is one ego for which posterior gives some support of non-positive values (group one in the sequence of boxes).

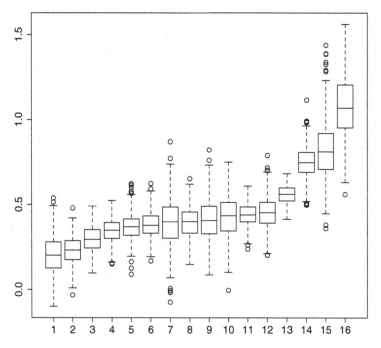

Figure 7.6   The posterior predictive distributions for the transitivity parameter for 16 ego-nets extracted from Knecht's (2008) Dutch schools (ordered according to the posterior predictive mean)

Remarks

This analysis is for illustrative purposes and a more in-depth analysis would require more principled decisions regarding the data set and a more elaborate model. For the former, we may want to treat unobserved as truly missing values. Furthermore, a genuine ego-net would be defined in terms of undirected ties and not be symmetrised as here. The fact that we have included the fourth wave in defining the network means that the networks are slightly larger than if they had only been based on the first three waves. Natural elaborations of the simplistic model would be to include additional covariate effects. As we have observations across different networks, we may also include network level effects in the modelling. For example, we may test whether networks of egos that are boys are more dense than those of female egos. Constraining a parameter to be the same across ego-nets is done through defining `random=TRUE` in the effects structure. In general, the homogeneity of any (non-rate) effect can be assessed and checked in a similar manner.

Further Issues

An obvious limitation of treating ego-nets like repeated observations on completely observed networks is that the alter set is treated as fixed and exogenous when in fact, in most instances, it is endogenous. We have here provided modelling approaches that deal with these different parts separately – one model for the alter set and one model for the ties conditional on the alter set – and it would seem natural to combine the SAOM with the birth and death process. One avenue may be representing the latter by the binary inclusion indicator $\{Y_i(t) : t \in \Delta_i\}$. The inclusion indicator may be treated like the diffusion indicator of Greenan (2014) with the modification that $Y_{ij}(t) = 0$ implies structural zeros for $X_{ijk}(t)$ for all k. The interdependence of ego-net properties and properties of ego need to be further explored – ego is more than just context.

Summary

In this chapter we have presented a number of approaches for studying different aspects of changing ego-nets over time. We have explained that it is of crucial importance to consider whether we are interested in properties of ego, properties of the alters or properties of the ties between alters. We reiterate that as this is a relatively new field of study. There are few readily available analysis procedures. Some approaches, as we have seen, rely on tried and tested methods that have been developed for completely observed network data. In these cases analysing your ego-net only requires you to edit and format your data. For other approaches, more effort is needed in setting up your data.

REFERENCES

Agneessens, F. (2006) *Social Capital in Knowledge Intensive Teams: The Importance of Content, Structure and Resources for Performance of Researchers at University*, Doctoral Dissertation, Ghent University.

Antonucci, T. and Israel, B. (1986) Veridicality of Social Support: A Comparison of Principal Network Members' Responses, *Journal of Consulting and Clinical Psychology* 54, 432–7.

Barabási, A.-L. (2003) *Linked*, New York, Plume.

Barnes, J.A. (1969) Networks and Political Process, in Mitchell, J.C. (ed.) *Social Networks in Urban Situations*, Manchester University Press, Manchester, pp. 51-74.

Barrera, M., Baca, L.M., Christiansen, J. and Stohl, M. (1985) Informant Corroboration of Social Support Network Data, *Connections* 8, 9–13.

Batchelder, E. (2002) Comparing Three Simultaneous Measurements of a Sociocognitive Network, *Social Networks* 24, 261–77.

Bates, D.M. (2010) *lme4: Mixed-Effects Modeling with R*. Available at: http://lme4.r-forge.r-project.org/book.

Bellotti, E. (2008a) What Are Friends For? Elective Communities of Single People, *Social Networks* 30, 318-29.

Bellotti, E. (2008b) *Amicizie. Le Reti Social Dei Giovani Single*, Milano, F. Angeli.

Bellotti, E. (2010) Comment on Nick Crossley/1, *Sociological* 1 Available at www.sociologica.mulino.it/main.

Bellotti, E. (2012) Getting Funded. Multi-level Network of Physicists in Italy, *Social Networks* 34, 215-29.

Bellotti, E. (2014) *Qualitative Networks: Mixed Methods in Sociological Research*, London, Routledge.

Bernard, R. and Killworth, P.D. (1977) Informant Accuracy in Social Network Data II, *Human Communications Research* 4, 3–18.

Bernard, R., Killworth, P.D. and Sailer, L. (1979/80) Informant Accuracy in Social Network Data IV, *Social Networks* 2, 191–218.

Bernard, R., Killworth, P.D. and Sailer, L. (1981) Summary of Research on Informant Accuracy in Network Data, and on the Reverse Small World Problem, *Connections* 4, 11-25.

Bernard, R., Killworth, P.D. and Sailer, L. (1982) Informant Accuracy in Social Network Data V, *Social Science Research* 5, 30–66.

Bernard, R., Killworth, P.D., Kronenfeld, D. and Sailer, L. (1984) The Problem of Informant Accuracy: The Validity of Retrospective Data, *Annual Review of Anthropology* 13, 495–517.

Bernard, R., Killworth, P., McCarty, C., Shelley, G. and Robinson, S. (1990) Comparing Four Different Methods for Measuring Personal Social Networks, *Social Networks* 12, 179–215.

Bernardi, L., Keim, S. and von der Lippe, H. (2007) Social Influences on Fertility: A Comparative Mixed Methods Study in Eastern and Western Germany, *Journal of Mixed Methods Research* 1(1), 23–47.

Bidart, C. and Charbonneau, J. (2011) How to Generate Personal Networks: Issues and Tools for a Sociological Perspective, *Field Methods* 23(3), 266–86.

Bidart, C. and Lavenu, D. (2005) Evolution of Personal Networks and Life Events, *Social Networks* 27, 359–76.

Bivand, R. (2006) Implementing Spatial Data Analysis Software Tools in R. *Geographical Analysis* 38(1), 23–40.

Blumer, H. (1969) Collective Behaviour, in McClung-Lee, A., *Principles of Sociology*, New York, Barnes and Noble, pp. 166–222.

Borgatti, S.P. (2002) *NetDraw: Graph Visualization Software*, Harvard, MA, Analytic Technologies.

Borgatti, S.P. (2006) *E-Net Software for the Analysis of Ego-Network Data*, Needham, Analytic Technologies.

Borgatti, S., Everett, M. and Freeman, L. (2002) *Ucinet 6 for Windows: Software for Social Network Analysis*, Harvard, MA, Analytic Technologies.

Borgatti, S.P., Everett, M.G. and Johnson, J. (2013) *Analysing Social Networks*, London, Sage.

Boswell, D.M. (1969) Personal Crisis and the Mobilization of the Social Network, in Mitchell, J.C. (ed.) *Social Networks in Urban Situations*, Manchester, Manchester University Press, pp. 245–87.

Bottero, W. (2010) Intersubjectivity and Bourdieusian Approaches to Identity, *Cultural Sociology* 4, 3–22.

Bourdieu, P. (1984) *Distinction*, London, Routledge.

Bourdieu, P. (1986) The Forms of Capital in Richardson, J. (ed.) *Handbook of Theory and Research for the Sociology of Education*, New York, Greenwood, pp. 241–58.

Bourdieu, P. (1992) *The Logic of Practice*, Cambridge, Polity.

Bourdieu, P. (1993) Social Space and the Genesis of Classes, in *Language and Symbolic Power*, Cambridge, Polity, pp. 229–51.

Browne, W.J. (2009) *MCMC Estimation in MLwiN (Version 2.10)*, Centre for Multilevel Modelling, University of Bristol.

Browne, W.J., Goldstein, H. and Rasbash, J. (2001) Multiple Membership Multiple Classification (MMMC) Models, *Statistical Modelling* 1(2), 103–24.

Bulmer, M. (1984) *The Chicago School of Sociology*, Chicago, Chicago University Press.

Burt, R. (1984) Network Items and the General Social Survey, *Social Networks* 6, 293–339.

Burt, R. (1987) Social Contagion and Innovation: Cohesion versus Structural Equivalence, *American Journal of Sociology*, 92, 1287–1335.

Burt, R. (1992) *Structural Holes*, Cambridge, MA, Harvard University Press.

Burt, R.S. (1995) *Structural Holes: The Social Structure of Competition.* Cambridge, MA, Harvard University Press.

Burt, R. (2005) *Brokerage and Closure*, Oxford, Oxford University Press.

Butts, C.T. (2008) A Relational Event Framework for Social Action, *Sociological Methodology* 38(1), 155–200.

Butts, C.T. (2010) *sna: Tools for Social Network Analysis*. R package version, 2.

Campbell, K.E. and Lee, B.A. (1991) Name Generators in Surveys of Personal Networks, *Social Networks* 13, 203–21.

Coleman, J. (1988) Free Riders and Zealots: The Role of Social Networks, *Sociological Theory* 6(1), 52-7.

Coleman, J. (1990) *Foundations of Social Theory*, Harvard, Belknap.

Conti, N. and Doreian, P. (2010) Social Network Engineering and Race in a Police Academy: A Longitudinal Analysis, *Social Networks* 32, 30-43.

Cornwell, B. and Laumann, E.O. (2015) The Health Benefits of Network Growth: New Evidence from a National Survey of Older Adults, *Social Science and Medicine* 125, 94–106.

Coviello, N. (2005) Integrating Qualitative and Quantitative Techniques in Network Analysis, *Qualitative Market Research* 8(1), 39-60.

Crossley, N. (2005) The New Social Physics and the Science of Small World Networks, *Sociological Review* 53(2), 351-8.

Crossley, N. (2008a) Small World Networks, Complex Systems and Sociology, *Sociology* 42(2), 261-77.

Crossley, N. (2008b) Networking Out, *British Journal of Sociology* 59(3), 475-500.

Crossley, N. (2008c) Pretty Connected: The Social Network of the Early UK Punk Movement, *Theory, Culture and Society* 25(6), 89-116.

Crossley, N. (2009) The Man Whose Web Expanded: Network Dynamics in Manchester's Post-Punk Music Scene 1976–1980, *Poetics* 37(1), 24-49.

Crossley, N. (2010) The Social World of the Network: Qualitative Aspects of Network Analysis, *Sociologica* 2010 (1). Available at www.sociologica. mulino.it/main.

Crossley, N. (2015) *Networks of Sound, Style and Subversion: The Punk and Post-Punk Musical Worlds of Manchester, London, Liverpool and Sheffield, 1975–1980*, Manchester, Manchester University Press.

Degenne, A. and Forsé, M. (1994) *Introducing Social Networks*, London, Sage.

Dekker, D., Krackhardt, D. and Snijders, T.A.B. (2007) Sensitivity of MRQAP Tests to Collinearity and Auto-Correlation Conditions, *Psychometrika* 72(4), 563–81.

de Miguel, L. and Tranmer, M. (2010) Personal Support Networks of Immigrants to Spain: A Multilevel Analysis, *Social Networks* 32(4), 253-62.

DeWall, C.N. (ed.) (2013) *Oxford Handbook of Social Exclusion*, New York, Oxford University Press.

Dodds, P.S., Muhamad, R. and Watts, D.J. (2003) An Experimental Study of Search in Global Social Networks, *Science* 301 (5634), 827–9.

Dominguez, S. and Watkins, C. (2003) Creating Networks for Survival and Mobility: Social Capital among African-American and Latin-American Low-Income Mothers, *Social Problems* 50(1), 111-35.

Dunbar, R. (1992) Neocortex Size as a Constraint upon Group Size in Primates, *Journal of Human Evolution* 22(6), 469-93.

Durkheim, E. (1952) *Suicide*, London, RKP.

Durkheim, E. (1964) *The Division of Labour*, New York, Free Press.

Edwards, G. (2010) *Mixed Methods Approaches to Social Network Analysis*, National Centre for Research Methods (UK) Review Paper.

Edwards, G. (2014) Infectious Innovations? The Diffusion of Innovation in Social Movement Networks: The Case of Suffragette Militancy, *Social Movement Studies* 13(1), 48-69.

Edwards, G. and Crossley, N. (2009) Measures and Meanings: Exploring the Ego-Net of Helen Kirkpatrick Watts, Militant Suffragette, *Methodological Innovations* 3(2) [online].

Emirbayer, M. and Goodwin, J. (1994) Network Analysis, Culture and the Problem of Agency, *American Journal of Sociology* 99, 1411-54.

Emmel, N. and Clark, A. (2009) *The Methods used in Connected Lives: Investigating Networks, Neighbourhoods and Communities*, National Centre for Research Methods (UK) Review Paper.

Emmel, N., Hodgson, F., Clark, A., Prosser, J. and Birkin, M. (2005-09) *Connected Lives: Understanding Networks, Neighborhoods, and Communities*, research project as part of ESRC National Centre for Research Methods, Real Life Methods, www.reallifemethods.ac.uk/research/connected/.

Epstein, A.L. (1969a) The Network and Urban Social Organization, in Mitchell, J.C. (ed.) *Social Networks in Urban Situations*, Manchester, Manchester University Press, pp. 77–116.

Epstein, A.L. (1969b) Gossip, Norms and Social Networks, in Mitchell, J.C. (ed.) *Social Networks in Urban Situations*, Manchester, Manchester University Press, pp. 117–27.

Everett, M. and Borgatti, S. (2013) The Dual-Projection Approach for Two Mode Networks, *Social Networks* 34(2), 204-10.

Everett, M.G. and Borgatti, S.P. (2014) Networks Containing Negative Ties, *Social Networks* 38, 111–120.

Feld, S. (1981) The Focused Organization of Social Ties, *American Journal of Sociology* 86(5), 1015-35.

Field, J. (2008) *Social Capital*, London, Routledge.

Fine, G.A. and Kleinman, S. (1983) Network and Meaning: An Interactionist Approach to Structure, *Symbolic Interaction* 6(1), 97-110.

Fischer, C. (1975) Towards a Subcultural Theory of Urbanism, *American Journal of Sociology* 80(6), 1319-41.

Fischer, C. (1982a) *To Dwell Amongst Friends*, Chicago, University of Chicago.

Fischer, C. (1982b) What Do We Mean by 'Friend'? *Social Networks* 3, 287–306.

Fischer, C. (1995) The Subcultural Theory of Urbanism: A Twentieth-Year Assessment, *American Journal of Sociology* 101(3), 543–77.

Fitzgerald, M. (1978) *The Content and Structure of Friendship: An Analysis of the Friendships of Urban Cameroonians*, Unpublished doctoral dissertation, Department of Anthropology, University of Toronto.

Freeman, L. (2006) *The Development of Social Network Analysis*, Vancouver, Empirical Press.

Freeman, L.C. and Romney, A.K. (1987) Words, Deeds and Social Structure: A Preliminary Study of the Reliability of Informants, *Human Organization* 46, 330–34.

Freeman, L. and Thompson, C. (1989) Estimating Acquaintanceship Volume, in Kochen, M. (1989) *The Small World,* Norwood, Ablex, pp. 147–58.

Fu, Y.C. (2005) Measuring Personal Networks with Daily Contacts: A Single-Item Survey Question and the Contact Diary, *Social Networks* 27(3), 169–86.

Fu, Y.C. (2007) Contact Diaries: Building Archives of Actual and Comprehensive Personal Networks, *Field Methods* 19(2), 194–217.

Fuhse, J. (2009) The Meaning Structure of Social Networks, *Sociological Theory* 27, 51–73.

Fuhse, J. and Mutzel, S. (2011) Tackling Connections, Structure, and Meaning in Networks: Quantitative and Qualitative Methods in Sociological Network Research, *Quality and Quantity* 45(5), 1067–89.

Gilbert, P. (2005) *Passion is a Fashion*, London, Aurum.

Goffman, E. (1959) *The Presentation of Self in Everyday Life*, Harmondsworth, Penguin.

Goffman, E. (1961) *Asylums*, Harmondsworth, Penguin.

Granovetter, M. (1973) The Strength of Weak Ties, *American Journal of Sociology*, 78, 1360–80.

Granovetter, M. (1974) *Getting a Job*, Chicago, Chicago University Press.

Granovetter, M. (1982) The Strength of Weak Ties: A Network Theory Revisited, in Marsden, P. and Lin, N., *Social Structure and Analysis*, Beverley Hills, Sage, pp. 131–45.

Greenan, C.C. (2014) Diffusion of Innovations in Dynamic Networks, *Journal of the Royal Statistical Society*: Series A (Statistics in Society). DOI: 10.1111/rssa.12054.

Gurevitch, M. (1961) *The Social Structure of Acquaintanceship Networks*, Unpublished PhD dissertation, Department of Economics and Social Science, MIT.

Halgin, D.S. and Borgatti, S.P. (2012) An Introduction to Personal Network Analysis and Tie Churn Statistics Using E-NET, *Connections* 32(1), 37–48.

Halpern, D. (2004) *Social Capital*, Cambridge, Polity.

Handcock, M.S. and Gile, K. (2010) Modeling Networks from Sampled Data, *Annals of Applied Statistics* 4, 5–25.

Hanneke, S., Fu, W. and Xing, E.P. (2010) Discrete Temporal Models of Social Networks, *Electronic Journal of Statistics* 4, 585–605.

Hansen, D., Shneiderman, B. and Smith, M. (2010) *Analyzing Social Media Networks with NodeXL: Insights from a Connected World*, Burlington, MA, Elsevier Morgan Kaufmann.

Harris, K.M. (2009) *The National Longitudinal Study of Adolescent Health (Add Health), Waves I & II, 1994–1996; Wave III, 2001–2002; Wave IV, 2007–2009* [machine-readable data file and documentation], Chapel Hill, NC, Carolina Population Center, University of North Carolina at Chapel Hill.

Heath, S., Fuller, A. and Johnston, B. (2009) Chasing Shadows: Defining Network Boundaries in Qualitative Social Network Analysis, *Qualitative Research* 9(5), 645–61.

Hill, P.W. and Goldstein, H. (1998) Multilevel Modeling of Educational Data with Cross-classification and Missing Identification for Units, *Journal of Educational and Behavioral Statistics* 23(2), 117–28.

Hogan, B., Carrasco, J.A. and Wellman, B. (2007) Visualizing Personal Networks: Working with Participant-Aided Sociograms, *Field Methods* 19, 116–44.

Hollstein, B. (2011) Qualitative Approaches, in Scott, J. and Carrington, P.J. (eds) *The Sage Handbook of Social Network Analysis*, London, Sage, pp. 404–16.

Hollstein B. (2014) Fuzzy Set Analysis of Network Data as Mixed Method: Personal Networks and the Transition from School to Work, in Hollstein, B. and Dominguez, S. (eds) *Mixed Methods Social Networks Research*, New York, Cambridge University Press, pp. 238–68.

Hollstein, B. and Dominguez, S. (eds) (2014), *Mixed Methods Social Networks Research*, New York, Cambridge University Press.

Jaccard, P. (1900) Contributions au problème de l'immigration post-glaciaire de la flore alpine: étude comparative de la flore alpine du massif de Wildhorn, du haut bassin du Trient et de la haute vallée de Bagnes, *Bulletin de la Société Vaudoise des Sciences Naturelles* 36(136), 87–130.

Jack, S. L. (2010) Approaches to Studying Networks: Implications and Outcomes, *Journal of Business Venturing* 25(1), 120–37.

Kahn, R.L. and Antonucci, T.C. (1980) Convoys over the Life Course: Attachment, Roles and Social Support, in Baltes, P.B. and Brim, O.G. (eds) *Life-Span Development and Behavior*, New York: Academic Press, pp. 253–67.

Kapferer, B. (1969) Norms and Manipulation of Relationships in a Work Context, in Mitchell, J.C. (ed.) *Social Networks in Urban Situations*, Manchester, Manchester University Press, pp. 181–239.

Keim, S., Klärner, A. and Bernardi, L. (2013) Tie Strength and Family Formation: Which Personal Relationships are Influential? *Personal Relationships* 20(3), 462–78.

Killworth, P.D. and Bernard, R. (1976) Informant Accuracy in Social Network Data, *Human Organization* 35, 269–96.

Killworth, P. and Bernard, R. (1978/9) The Reversal Small World Experiment, *Social Networks* 1, 159–92.

Killworth, P.D. and Bernard, R. (1979/80) Informant Accuracy in Social Network Data III, *Social Networks* 2, 19–46.

Killworth, P., Bernard, R. and McCarthy, C. (1984) Measuring Patterns of Acquaintanceship, *Current Anthropology* 25, 381–97.

Killworth, P., Johnsen, E., Bernard, R., Shelley, G. and McCarty, C. (1990) Estimating the Size of Personal Networks, *Social Networks* 23, 289–312.

Kirke, D. (2010) Comment on Nick Crossley/2, in *Sociologica*, 1. Available at: www.sociologica.mulino.it/main.

Knecht, A. (2008) *Friendship Selection and Friends' Influence. Dynamics of Networks and Actor Attributes in Early Adolescence*, PhD Dissertation, University of Utrecht.

Knecht, A., Snijders, T.A.B., Baerveldt, C., Steglich, C.E. and Raub, W. (2010) Friendship and Delinquency: Selection and Influence Processes in Early Adolescence, *Social Development* 19(3), 494–514.

Knox, H., Savage, M. and Harvey, P. (2006) Social Networks and the Study of Relations: Networks as Method, Metaphor and Form, *Economy and Society* 35(1), 113–40.

Kochen, M. (ed.) (1989) *The Small World*, Norwood, Ablex.

Koskinen, J. and Lomi, A. (2013) The Local Structure of Globalization – the Network Dynamics of Foreign Direct Investments in the International Electricity Industry, *Journal of Statistical Physics* 151(3), 523–48.

Koskinen, J.H. and Snijders, T.A.B. (2007) Bayesian Inference for Dynamic Social Network Data, *Journal of Statistical Planning and Inference* 137(12), 3930–38.

Koskinen, J. and Stenberg, S.-Å. (2012) Bayesian Analysis of Multilevel Probit Models for Data with Friendship Dependencies, *Journal of Educational and Behavioral Statistics* 37(2), 203–30.

Koskinen, J.H., Robins, G.L., Wang, P. and Pattison, P.E. (2013) Bayesian Analysis for Partially Observed Network Data, Missing Ties, Attributes and Actors, *Social Networks* 35(4), 514–27. DOI: 10.1016/j.socnet.2013.07.003.

Koskinen, J.H. and Snijders, T.A.B. (2015) Multilevel Longitudinal Analysis of Social Networks. In preparation.

Krackhardt, D. (1987) Cognitive Social Structures, *Social Networks* 9, 104–34.

Krackhardt, D. and Stern, R.N. (1988) Informal Networks and Organizational Crises: An Experimental Simulation, *Social Psychology Quarterly* 51(2), 123–40.

Krivitsky, P.N., Handcock, M.S. and Morris, M. (2011) Adjusting for Network Size and Composition Effects in Exponential-Family Random Graph Models, *Statistical Methodology* 8, 319–39.

Labianca, G. and Brass, D. (2006) Exploring the Social Ledger: Negative Relationships and Negative Asymmetry in Social Networks in Organizations, *Academy of Management Review* 31(3), 596–614.

Labianca, G., Brass, D.J. and Gray, B. (1998) Social Networks and Perceptions of Intergroup Conflict: The Role of Negative Relationships and Third Parties, *Academy of Management Journal* 41, 55–67.

Laumann, E.O. (1966) *Prestige and Association in an Urban Community*, Indianapolis, Bobbs Merrill.

Laumann, E.O. (1969) Friends of Urban Men: An Assessment of Accuracy in Reporting Their Socioeconomic Attributes, Mutual Choice, and Attitude Agreement, *Sociometry* 32(1), 54-69.

Laumann, E.O. (1973) *Bonds of Pluralism: The Forms and Substance of Urban Social Networks*, New York, Wiley.

Laumann, E.O., Marsden, P.Y. and Prensky, D. (1983) The Boundary Specification Problem in Network Analysis, in Burt, R.S. and Minor, M.J. (eds) *Applied Network Analysis: A Methodological Introduction*, Beverly Hills, Sage, pp. 18-34.

Lawson, A.B., Browne, W.J. and Rodeiro, C.L.V. (2003) *Disease Mapping with WinBUGS and MLwiN* (Vol. 11), Chichester, Wiley.

Lazarsfeld, P. and Merton, R. (1964) Friendship as Social Process, in Berger, M., Abel, T. and Page, C., *Freedom and Control in Modern Society*, New York, Octagon Books, pp. 18–66.

Leenders, R.T.A. (2002) Modeling Social Influence Through Network Auto-Correlation: Constructing the Weight Matrix, *Social Networks* 24(1), 21–47.

Leffler, A., Krannich, R.S. and Gillespie, D.L. (1986) Contact, Support and Friction: Three Faces of Networks in Community Life, *Sociological Perspective* 29, 337–55.

Lin, N. (1999) Building a Network Theory of Social Capital, *Connections* 22(1), 28–51.

Lin, N. (2002) *Social Capital*, Cambridge, Cambridge University Press.

Lin, N. and Dumin, M. (1986) Access to Occupations Through Social Ties, *Social Networks* 8, 365–85.

Lin, N., Ensel, W. and Vaughn, J. (1981) Social Resources and Strength of Ties: Structural Factors in Occupational Status Attainment, *American Sociological Review* 46, 393–405.

Lin, N., Vaughn, J. and Ensel, W. (1981) Social Resources and Occupational Status Attainment, *Social Forces* 59, 1163–81.

Lonkila, M. (1999) *Social Networks in Post-Soviet Russia: Continuity and Change in the Everyday Life of St. Petersburg Teachers*, Helsinki, Kikimora Publications.

Lubbers, M.J. and Snijders, T.A. (2007) A Comparison of Various Approaches to the Exponential Random Graph Model: A Reanalysis of 102 Student Networks in School Classes, *Social Networks* 29, 489–507.

Lubbers, M.J., Molina, J.L., Lerner, J., Brandes, U., Ávila, J. and McCarty, C. (2010) Longitudinal Analysis of Personal Networks. The Case of Argentinean Migrants in Spain, *Social Networks* 32(1), 91–104.

Lubbers, M., Snijders, T.A.B. and Koskinen, J. (2013) Analysing Ego-networks over time. Paper presented at ASNA, Zurich, 29 August.

Lusher, D., Koskinen, J. and Robins, G. (2013) *Exponential Random Graph Models for Social Networks*, Cambridge, Cambridge University Press.

Marcum, C.S. and Butts, C.T. (2014) Creating Sequence Statistics for Egocentric Relational Events Models Using Informr, *Journal of Statistical Software* (in press).

Marin, A. and Hampton, K.N. (2007) Simplifying the Personal Networks Name Generator: Alternative to Traditional Multiple and Single Name Generators, *Field Methods* 19, 163–93.

Marsden, P.V. (1990) Network Data and Measurement, *Annual Review of Sociology* 16, 435–63.

McCarty, C. (2010) Comment on Nick Crossley/3, in *Sociologica*, 1. Available at: www.sociologica.mulino.it/main.

McLean, P. (1998) A Frame Analysis of Favor Seeking in the Renaissance: Agency, Networks and Political Culture, *American Journal of Sociology* 104(1), 51–91.

McLean, P. (2007) *The Art of the Network*, Durham, Duke University Press.

Mead, G.H. (1967) *Mind, Self and Society*, Chicago, Chicago University Press.

Milgram, S. (1967) The Small World Problem, in Carter, G. (2004) *Empirical Approaches to Sociology*, Boston, Pearson, pp. 111–18.

Mische, A. (2003) Cross-Talk in Movements, in Diani, M. and McAdam, D. (eds) *Social Movements and Networks*, Oxford, Oxford University Press, pp. 258-80.

Mische, A. (2008) *Partisan Public: Communication and Contention Across Brazilian Youth Activist Networks*, Princeton and Oxford, Princeton University Press.

Mische, A. and Pattison, P. (2000) Composing a Civic Arena: Publics, Projects, and Social Settings, *Poetics*, 27: 163-94.

Mitchell, J.C. (1969) *Social Networks in Urban Situations*, Manchester, Manchester University Press.

Mizruchi, M.S. (1996) What Do Interlocks Do? Analysis, Critique, and Assessment of Research on Interlocking Directorates, *Annual Review of Sociology* 22, 271–98.

Molina, J.L. (2010) Comment on Nick Crossley/4, in *Sociologica*, 1. Available at: www.sociologica.mulino.it/main.

Molina, J.L., Maya Jariego, I. and McCarty, C. (2014) Giving Meaning to Social Networks: Methodology for Conducting and Analyzing Interviews based on Personal Network Visualizations, in Hollstein, B. and Dominguez, S. (eds) *Mixed Methods Social Networks Research*, New York, Cambridge University Press, pp. 305-35.

Monsted, M. (1995) Processes and Structures of Networks: Reflections on Methodology, *Entrepreneurship and Regional Development* 7, 193–213.

Morris, M., Kurth, A.E., Hamilton, D.T, Moody, J. and Wakefield, S. (2009) Concurrent Partnerships and HIV Prevalence Disparities by Race: Linking Science and Public Health Practice, *American Journal of Public Health* 99, 1023–31.

Newman, M., Barabási, L. and Watts, D. (2006) *The Structure and Dynamics of Networks*, Princeton, Princeton University Press.

Padgett, J.F. and Ansell, C.K. (1993) Robust Action and the Rise of the Medici, 1400–1434, *American Journal of Sociology*, 98(6), 1259–319.

Pattison, P.E., Wasserman, S., Robins, G.L. and Kanfer, A. (2000) Statistical Evaluation of Algebraic Constraints for Social Networks, *Journal of Mathematical Psychology* 44, 536–68.

Pattison, P.E., Robins, G.L., Snijders, T.A.B. and Wang, P. (2013) Conditional Estimation of Exponential Random Graph Models from Snowball Sampling Designs, *Journal of Mathematical Psychology* 57, 284–96.

Peugh, J.L. and Enders, C.K. (2005) Using the SPSS Mixed Procedure to Fit Cross-Sectional and Longitudinal Multilevel Models, *Educational and Psychological Measurement* 65(5), 717–41.

Podolny, J.M. and Baron, J.N. (1997) Resources and Relationships: Social Networks and Mobility in the Workplace, *American Sociological Review* 62, 673–93.

Putnam, R. (2000) *Bowling Alone*, New York, Touchstone.

Rabe-Hesketh, S. and Skrondal, A. (2008) *Multilevel and Longitudinal Modelling Using Stata*, College Station, TX, STATA Press.

Rasbash, J., Charlton, C., Browne, W.J., Healy, M. and Cameron, B. (2009) *MLwiN Version 2.1*, Centre for Multilevel Modelling, University of Bristol.

Raudenbush, S.W. (ed.) (2004) *HLM 6: Hierarchical Linear and Nonlinear Modeling*, Scientific Software International.

Read, K. (1954) Cultures of the Central Highlands, New Guinea, *Southwestern Journal of Anthropology* 10, 1–43.

Ripley, R.M., Snijders, T.A., Boda, Z., Vörös, A. and Preciado, P. (2014) *Manual for RSIENA*, University of Oxford, Department of Statistics; Nuffield College (RSiena version 4.0, manual version, 26 June).

Robins, G.L. and Pattison, P.E. (2001) Random Graph Models for Temporal Processes in Social Networks, *Journal of Mathematical Sociology* 25, 5–41.

Salter-Townsend, M., White, A., Gollini, I. and Murphy, T.B. (2012) Review of Statistical Network Analysis: Models, Algorithms, and Software, *Statistical Analysis and Data Mining* 5, 243-64.

Saunders, C. (2007) The National and the Local: Relationships Among Environmental Movement Organisations in London, *Environmental Politics* 16(5), 742–64.

Savage, M. and Burrows, R. (2007) The Coming Crisis of Empirical Sociology, *Sociology* 41(5), 881–99.

Schnettler, S. (2009a) A Structured Overview of 50 Years of Small-World Research, *Social Networks* 31(3), 165–78.

Schnettler, S. (2009b) A Small World on Feet of Clay?, *Social Networks* 31(3), 179–89.

Schweinberger, M. and Handcock, M.S. (2009) *Hierarchical Exponential-Family Random Graph Models*, Technical report, Pennsylvania State University [working paper].

Schweizer, T., Schnegg, M. and Berzborn, S. (1998) Personal Networks and Social Support in a Multi-Ethnic Community of Southern California, *Social Networks* 20, 1–21.

Scott, J. (1997) *Corporate Business and Capitalist Classes*, Oxford, Oxford University Press.

Scott, J. (2000) *Social Network Analysis: A Handbook*, London, Sage.

Scott, J. (2011) Social Physics and Social Networks, in Scott, J. and Carrington, P., *The Sage Handbook of Social Network Analysis*, London, Sage, pp. 55 66.

Shelley G.A., Bernard R. H.and Killworth P. D. (1990) Information Flow in Social Networks, *Journal of Quantitative Anthropology* 2, 201–225.

Shulman, N. (1976) Network Analysis: A New Addition to an Old Bag of Tricks, *Acta Sociologica* 19(4), 307–23.

Simmel, G. (1903) Die Grossstädte und das Geistesleben, *Jahrbuch Gehe-Stiftung* 9, 185–206.

Simmel, G. (1955) *Conflict and the Web of Group Affiliations*, New York, Free Press.

Simmel, G. (1971) *On Individuality and Social Forms*, Chicago, Chicago University Press.

Singer, J.D. (1998) Using SAS PROC MIXED to Fit Multilevel Models, Hierarchical Models,and Individual Growth Models, *Journal of Educational and Behavioral Statistics* 23(4), 323–55.

Smith, J. A. (2012) Macrostructure from Microstructure: Generating Whole Systems from Ego Networks, *Sociological Methodology* 42(1), 155-205.

Smith, J., Halgin, D., Kidwell, V., Labianca, G., Brass, D. and Borgatti, S.P. (2014) Power in Politically Charged Networks, *Social Networks* 36, 162–76.

Snijders, T.A.B. (2001) The Statistical Evaluation of Social Network Dynamics, in Sobel, M. E. and Becker, M.P. (eds) *Sociological Methodology*, London, Blackwell, pp. 361–95.

Snijders, T.A.B. (2010) Actor-Based Models for Network Dynamics. Working paper. Available at: www.stats.ox.ac.uk/~snijders/Political Analysis_NetDyn.pdf.

Snijders, T.A.B. and Baerveldt, C. (2003) A Multilevel Network Study of the Effects of Delinquent Behavior on Friendship Evolution, *Journal of Mathematical Sociology* 27(2–3), 123–51.

Snijders, T.A.B. and Bosker, R.J. (2012) *Multilevel Analysis: An Introduction to Basic and Advanced Multilevel Modeling*, 2nd edition, London, Sage.

Snijders, T.A.B. and Koskinen, J. (2013) Longitudinal Models, in Lusher, D., Koskinen, J. and Robins, G. (eds) *Exponential Random Graph Models for Social Networks: Theory, Methods and Applications*, New York, Cambridge University Press, pp. 130–40.

Snijders, T.A.B. and van Duijn, M.A.J. (1997) Simulation for Statistical Inference in Dynamic Network Models, in Conte, R., Hegselmann, R. and Terna, P. (eds) *Simulating Social Phenomena*, Berlin, Springer, pp. 493–512.

Snijders, T. and van Duijn, M. (2002) Conditional Maximum Likelihood Estimation Under Various Specifications of Exponential Random Graph Models, in Hagberg, J. (ed.), *Contributions to Social Network Analysis, Information Theory, and Other Topics in Statistics; A Festschrift in Honour of Ove Frank*, London, Routledge, pp. 117–34.

Snijders, T., Spreen, M. and Zwaagstra, R. (1995) The Use of Multilevel Modeling for Analysing Personal Networks: Networks of Cocaine Users in an Urban Area, *Journal of Quantitative Anthropology* 5(2), 85–105.

Snijders, T.A.B., van de Bunt, G.G. and Steglich, C.E.G. (2010) Introduction to Stochastic Actor-Based Models for Network Dynamics, *Social Networks* 32(1), 44–60.

Spencer, L. and Pahl, R. (2006) *Rethinking Friendship*, Princeton, Princeton University Press.

Stivala, A., Wang, P., Koskinen, J., Robins, G. and Rolls, D. (2014) Many Snowballs Make Light Work: A Technique for Large Networks. Paper presented at the Sunbelt XXXIV, International Sunbelt Social Network Conference, TradeWinds Island Resorts, St Pete Beach, FL, 18–23 February.

Strang, D. and Soule, S. (1998) Diffusion in Organizations and Social Movements: From Hybrid Corn to Poison Pills, *Annual Review of Sociology* 24, 265–90.

Straus, F., Pfeffer, J., and Hollstein, B. (2008) *EgoNe – Manage your Ego-networks*,www.pfeffer.at/egonet/.

Thompson, S.K. and Frank, O. (2000) Model-Based Estimation with Link-Tracing Sampling Designs, *Survey Methodology* 26, 87–98.

Tönnies, F. (2003) *Community and Society*, New York, Dover.

Tranmer, M. and Lazega, E. (2013) Multilevel Models for Multilevel Network Dependencies. Presentation at the XXXIII International Sunbelt Social Networks Conference of the International Network for Social Network Analysis (INSNA), 21–26 May, Hamburg, Germany. [Slides available by request.]

Tranmer, M., Steel, D. and Browne, W.J. (2014) Multiple Membership Multiple Classification Models for Social Network and Group Dependencies, *Journal of the Royal Statistical Society* (Series A) 177(2).

Travers, J. and Milgram, S. (1969) An Experimental Study of the Small World Problem, *Sociometry* 32, 325-43.

Uehara, E.S. (1994) The Influence of the Social Network's Second Order Zone on Social Support Mobilization, *Journal of Social and Personal Relationships* 11, 277–94.

Uzzi, B. (1997) Social Structure and Competition in Interfirm Networks: The Paradox of Embeddedness, *Administrative Science Quarterly* 42, 35–67.

Valente, T.M. and Saba, W.P. (1998) Mass Media and Interpersonal Influence in a Reproductive Health Communication Campaign in Bolivia, *Communication Research* 25(1), 96–124.

Valente, T.M. and Vlahov, D. (2001) Selective Risk Taking Among Needle Exchange Participants: Implications for Supplemental Interventions, *American Journal of Public Health* 91(3), 406–11.

Van der Gaag, M. and Snijders, T.(2003) *Social Capital Quantification with Concrete Items*, Groningen, University of Groningen.

Van der Gaag, M.P.J. and Webber, M. (2008) Measurement of Individual Social Capital: Questions, Instruments, and Measures, in Kawachi, I., Subramanian, S.V. and Kim, D. (eds) *Social Capital and Health*, Springer, New York.

Van Sonderen, E., Armel, J., Brilman, E. and van den Heuvall, C.v.L.(1989) Personal Network Delineation, in Antonucci, T.C. and Knipscheer, C.P.M. (eds), *Social Network Research*, Lisse, the Netherlands, Swets & Zeitlinger, pp. 101-20.

Waite, L.J., Laumann, E.O., Levinson, W., Lindau, S.T. and O'Muircheartaigh, C.A. (2010) National Social Life, Health, and Aging Project (NSHAP). ICPSR20541-v5. Ann Arbor, MI, Inter-university Consortium for Political and Social Research [distributor], 28 July. DOI:10.3886/ICPSR20541.v5.

Wasserman, S. (1977) *Stochastic Models for Directed Graphs*, PhD dissertation, University of Harvard, Department of Statistics.

Wasserman, S. (1980a) Analyzing Social Networks as Stochastic Processes, *Journal of the American Statistical Association* 75(370), 280–94.

Wasserman, S. (1980b) A Stochastic Model for Directed Graphs with Transition Rates Determined by Reciprocity, *Sociological Methodology* 11, 392–412.

Wasserman, S. and Faust, K. (1994) *Social Network Analysis*, Cambridge, Cambridge University Press.

Watts, D. (1999) *Small Worlds*, Princeton, Princeton University Press.

Watts, D. (2004) *Six Degrees*, London, Vintage.

Wellman B. (1968) *Community Ties and Mental Health*, Working Paper, Toronto, Clarke Institute of Psychiatry, August.

Wellman, B.(1969) *Social Identities and Cosmopolitanism Among Urban Adolescents*, unpublished PhD Thesis, Department of Social Relations, Harvard University.

Wellman, B. (1979) The Community Question, *American Journal of Sociology* 84, 1201–31.

Wellman, B.(1981) Applying Network Analysis to the Study of Support, in Gottlieb, B.H. (ed.), *Social Networks and Social Support*, Beverly Hills, Sage.

Wellman, B. (1985) Domestic Work, Paid Work and Net Work, in Duck, S. and Perlman, D. (eds) (1985), *Understanding Personal Relationships*, London, Sage, pp. 61–80.

Wellman, B. (1990) Different Strokes From Different Folks, *American Journal of Sociology* 96(3), 558–88.

Wellman, B.(1993) An Egocentric Network Tale, *Social Networks* 15, 423–36.

Wellman, B. and Whitaker, M. (1974) High-Rise, Low-Rise: The Effects of High-Density Living, Ottawa, *Urban Affairs Canada*, Paper B. 74. 29.

Wellman, B., Ove, F., Espinoza, V., Lundquist, S. and Wilson, C. (1991) Integrating Individual, Relational and Structural Analysis, *Social Networks* 13, 223–50.

Wheeldon, P.D. (1969) The Operation of Voluntary Associations and Personal Networks in the Political Processes of an Inter-Ethnic Community, in Mitchell, J.C. (ed.), *Social Networks in Urban Situations*, Manchester, Manchester University Press, pp. 128-73.

White, H. (2008) *Identity and Control*, Princeton, Princeton University Press.

Whyte, W.F. (1943) *Street Corner Society*, Chicago, Chicago University Press.

Wilcox, S., and Udry, R. (1986) Autism and Accuracy in Adolescent Perceptions of Friends' Sexual Attitudes and Behavior, *Journal of Applied Social Psychology* 16, 361–74.

Yeung, K. (2005) What Does Love Mean? Exploring Network Culture in Two Network Settings, *Social Forces* 84(1), 391–420.

Zablocki, B. (1980) *Alienation and Charisma. A Study of Contemporary American* Communes, New York, Free Press.

Zachary, W. (1977) An Information Flow Model for Conflict and Fission in Small Groups, *Journal of Anthropological Research* 33, 452–73.

INDEX